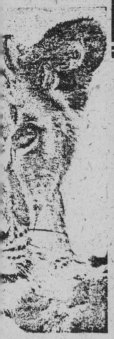

...rist in Utah a real problem.

...Highway

...kes Up
...n Utah

...more, were the next to
...ot the lady lion. She was
...ping along U.S. Highway 91,
...eaking several traffic laws.

"Two cowboys from Levan
...me to the area and tried to
...d her," Stewart said.
"...hey were going to lasso
...r, but couldn't find her."

Tragedy struck about 1:15
...m. today. The lioness had
...urned to the highway about
...miles north of here — possi-
...y seeking her master.

The Californian's auto was
...proaching from the north,
...d a car driven by Raymond
...roves, 167 Gaylen Dr,
...ndy, was coming from the
...uth.

"I didn't know what it was,
...t the headlights seemed to
...it it," Groves said.

The car driven by Cold
...uck the lioness when she
...dded into the southbound
...ne.

She was still alive after-
...ard, but unconscious. A wit-
...ss, thinking she was a
...ountain lion, shot her to
...ath.

The auto's left fender was
...nted by the impact.

Cold drove away, wondering
...w to report the strange colli-
...ion.

...y, eight-month-old Cougar who visited Moses Lake last week, gets
...match with a Labrado retriever. Whiskey's owner, Dick Robinson,
...at a Hollywood movie extract. —Herald photo.

NEVER KICK A BEAR IN YOUR BEDROOM SLIPPERS

NEVER KICK A BEAR IN YOUR BEDROOM SLIPPERS

Dick ROBINSON

OSMOND PUBLISHING COMPANY

Salt Lake City

Published by
OSMOND PUBLISHING COMPANY
1816 Grover Lane
Salt Lake City, Utah 84117

Distributed in Canada
by
Methuen Publishing
a division of
The Carswell Corporation
Canada

Printed and bound in the United States
of America.

Second Printing

Designed by Ronald Crosby

LIBRARY OF CONGRESS CATALOG CARD NO. 80-83051

ISBN 0-89888-010-6

To my Indian guide and friend "Porcupine", who inspired this book. To others who led the way for me and to those who have been behind me: To my wife Karen, and to LaMar McQuaid and his wife, Barbara, who have helped me in my time of need.

Preface

Standing shivering under an umbrella held by a passing tourist, who had been commandeered into doing this duty for the sake of watching a movie being made, I became conscious of my toe throbbing, and throbbing! It was cold and soggy as I leaned against my movie camera waiting for Rick, riding my buffalo, to appear out of the trees coming off the top of the valley through the snow. It was the middle of July, we were at 10,500 feet in the Uinta Mountains where snow still covered the hills everywhere and I, Dick Robinson, who gave you "Brother of the Wind", "Toklat", "Jeremiah Johnson", and "Grizzly Adams", was making a great epic with a man riding a buffalo.

The crew consisted of me as director, cameraman, gaffer and truck driver, and Rick Guinn as actor, buffalo rider and stock handler plus Denise Neilson, Rick's girl friend, nurse, "gofer" and the one who kept us going with her enthusiasm.

We were filming Rick riding across the mountains through the rain and snow, saving this little baby whose parents had been killed by the baddies. My toe throbbed with grim intensity. How could I have got to this state with everything I had going for me? People laughed and joked when I told them that with a crew of two we were making a movie.

The tourist holding the umbrella over my camera became alive....

"Here he comes!...My God!...Look at that!"

It was a strange sight. This man in buckskins, coming down the hillside in the snow, mounted in a saddle on the buffalo.

I was busy filming with the long lens as Rich approached. He was chuffing along through the soft snow with the baby, which was a stuffed, canvas-wrapped doll, banging away in the large bag behind the saddle. Rick was soaked from the rain.

Breaking through into heavy snow the buffalo came to a stop with his belly dragging. Rick, stepped off, took the reins and steered the big critter out of the deep snow and walked him through the trees, dodging the deep puddles from the rain and melting snow.

He brought the buffalo up on the road and jumped it into the back of the stock trailer where he stripped the rigging off, while I thanked the tourist, put the camera away and started warming up the truck. Rick came dashing in along with Denise and we headed down the hill for Kamas, Utah which was 30 miles away.

The rain slowed, it became warmer as we descended the mountain, and finally the sun came out. We stopped at the familiar drugstore in Kamas for grilled cheese sandwiches, then still 35 cents.

My toe got worse. What to do? Denise suggested an aspirin. That was for toothaches. A drink of scotch? Maybe. Why not go to the doctor? No…I'd just have to suffer. I sat musing, while the food was coming, at the life that I'd led to get to this place. All the things that had happened to me, everything that I'd experienced—just to get this damned toe? Crushed by kicking a bear! Someday, I thought, I'll get an X-ray and leave it to my children. It's got to be some X-ray!

Some things that happen to a person in incidents seemingly unrelated, change their lives. My life was changed by a blow on the head. I had always liked to work in the woods and with animals, and, following these interests in Colorado one year, I'd been hit on the head by a moving crane that was used to load logs; and I'd gone to the hospital for brain surgery.

This led me to a couple years of slow recuperation, avoiding heavy work which would put me right back in the hospital. I bought a trailer, built some animal cages on it, and headed down the road with a few animals to trade and to try to make a living.

"No work!" the doctor had told me repeatedly, and said it like he meant it. I headed for Arizona where it was nice and warm and comfortable and set out to loaf. It didn't last long. I got a chimp! That brought a change in my life.

Later on I met Loretta Young, Robert Redford, Marlin Perkins, Bill Burrud and Willie and Whisk and many others who brought changes in my life.

1 / *Cheeta*

Acquiring a chimp was like adding another member to the family, only I did have one advantage, I could leave it locked away for safekeeping instead of having a babysitter, and I could enjoy its company when I wanted to.

Cheeta was three years old when I traded for him from the Phoenix Zoo. He was blind in one eye, though you could hardly notice the defect. He had jumped through a hedge and got a splinter in his right eye and lost its vision. Weighing in at thirty pounds made him just large enough to be a real armful, equipped with a full set of teeth that were just changing to permanent ones, and a personality that was full of holy terror.

The zoo keeper and I removed him from the psycho ward of the ape house (apes also have their problems), put him in a cage I had prepared, and we headed for southern Arizona. I had signed a contract for an animal act at a land development, and now I had a star!

Cheeta had been raised from infancy by a delightful couple whom I subsequently met and they told me his story.

They had purchased him as a small baby, tenderly raised him as any baby would be, changed his diapers, fed him from a bottle and he became a member of the family. For three years he had been the center of their life, a member of the family who had to be taught table manners, how to accept being dressed, learning some speech and everything that any toddler would be exposed to at that age. In short, Cheeta lived the life of a human child. Then one day his life exploded! His "mother" got pregnant! What could she do with a young chimp and a real child? Well, at least with a chimp, she could give it away without any legal restraints but, only with a great deal of agonizing, did they donate it to the zoo which had no way to cope with a chimp like this. He missed his "parents" and became quite unruly to say the least.

Now a chimp is like a child in many ways but it is definitely an animal. You can give it all the tender loving care you want but, by its very nature, it is a creature of the forest and the wild and needs discipline; without it, a chimp can become a monster. Cheeta's discipline needed attunement so I was prepared to give him much T.L.C. and also a good dose of medicine when needed.

We first went to Sierra Vista where I was to do some shows for a real estate development company. The management team and I soon developed an advertising campaign with good ol' Jungle Jim and Cheeta as the drawing cards.

"Folks, come on down and see Jungle Jim's Wild Animal show with Cheeta, the chimp, and get free hot dogs and cake, and, 'Oh! by the way, see our great building sites for a home or a lot for future profit."

They advertised us far and wide on television and radio from Tucson and we soon became regular personalities around those parts.

Cheeta was the star of the act. Whisk, my mountain lion, and Sparky, my little dog, became the other actors beside me. We developed a routine and it worked! We performed on Saturday and Sunday and then took the rest of the week to work on cages, fixing another trailer, trading for more animals and developing our act for the public.

Cheeta was learning fast that discipline was part of his way of life; still smoking was permitted occasionally and even a small sip of wine, when available, was good for the spirits. Chimps like both. In short Cheeta was growing up. When a tooth would get loose, he would show it to me, carefully wiggle it around and I'd remove it tenderly with a pair of pliers when necessary. He was very proud of his teeth, never stopped showing them to me and would use a toothbrush whenever he could get some toothpaste.

Cheeta soon learned that if he would shake a cage for hours it would gradually fall apart, the welds would disintegrate from sheer fatigue, and away he would go strolling through the neighborhood.

We were camped about a half mile from one of the quaintest bars in Arizona, at least with more character. It was like an oasis in the desert on the edge of the Huachuca mountains about eight miles south of the U.S. Army fort and the town. After escaping his cage, Cheeta would terrorize the other animals by his teasing, until he tired of it, and then head for the bar! He simply opened the door and stormed the place. If some person was around, he would try to run Cheeta out, usually to no avail, for the chimp would stay just ahead of him, sampling as he went. Jumping up on the bar, he would take a bottle, screw off the top, take a shot, grimace, put it down, and grab another. When the bartender got too close he would dash for the kitchen where the sampling would continue. Running a finger through a block of butter on the table was just the thing, with a delightful gob on the end of a finger to savor. He could usually make about three or four rounds of the place before I could get there, and I found that the bill generally was forty dollars. How could the bartender total up the drinks that accurately? I never figured it out.

Evenings were dull sometimes so I would take him up to the bar on a chain which would go around his waist and hook on the back. I would put a suit on him with short pants and a T-shirt so he looked presentable, and then take his hand and walk to the bar. He was a kick to watch for he knew he was the center of attention and, as everyone knew, liked to smoke. A cigar was an invitation to a show by itself. He would take a big draw on it, let the smoke curl slowly out of his nostrils, let little clouds out of his mouth to drift up to his eyes, then go into a paroxysm when it touched them. After it cleared he would casually flip the ashes off the butt.

This show kept us in drinks for the evening and helped make up for the $40 tabs for his free-wheeling activities.

Our act was born of what would come naturally to all the animals that were used. Jungle Jim had a safari suit, pointed beard, pistol

(nice shiny 9-shot High Standard with blanks), safari hat with leopard band and shiny boots. To start with I would bring Cheeta in and would have him open a chest, take out an apple, sit on the chest and eat it while I would explain to the audience what would take place; then, on command, Sparky, the dog, would grab him and the two would tussle. Usually Sparky would lose and be dragged about the arena by the hind leg, which brought gales of laughter. Then taking Cheeta by the arm, I would lead him to his tricycle and have him ride it around. Sparky would attack him again and the two would tussle some more and end up with Cheeta throwing the tricycle at Sparky. On command again Cheeta would get on his tricycle, come by me, take my pipe and, puffing it rapidly, would ride around the arena chasing Sparky. Giving my pipe back, he would get off the machine and, on my command, would take my whip (6 ft. long horsewhip), go over to the mountain lion cage, open the door and release the mountain lion. Of course, the cat would come out roaring and snarling and make moves to get him. My story then was that Cheeta was being trained for a movie in which he would have to sneak up on a mountain lion and pinch his tail.

When the cat came out Cheeta would whip it, tease it with the end of the whip and then would start swinging the whip hitting all of us, the dog, me and the lion. Taking the whip away from him, I would tell him to pinch the cat's tail. He would stand in front of me pleading for me to forget it but I would make him do it with much gesturing and hollering. For five minutes he would maneuver around the cat, who was snarling and growling and knew what was going to happen. Cheeta would get the right opening and then make the quick pinch. Everyone loved it; then I would give the whip back and tell him to put the cat back in the cage. A large-scale battle followed but finally, with a flourish, the cat would be driven in and Cheeta would close the door on the lion. It was an act that no one ever forgot!

One of the animal trades that I had brought home was a half llama and half guanaco. It was a long-legged South American animal that people would raise for its hair, use as a pack animal and it could be eaten. It was a strange animal if you hadn't seen one before, the size of a pony. I put it in the pole corral at the bar for it was tame and used to a halter but I found that it liked to roam. It got out of the corral one time and disappeared into the mountains, as I soon found out, so I contacted the radio station, offered a reward and got a little publicity for us in Tucson. Good ol' Jungle Jim had lost his "llama" and was offering a reward to the finder.

I hunted for days looking for it, tracking it around here and there as it wandered higher in the mountains. The hills were full of mountain lion tracks so I didn't think it would last long.

One night while making a visit to the bar something was said about it. Two soldiers started drinking and talking. They said they had met the animal high in the mountains the previous day. It had walked up to them on the trail, begged a sandwich and headed for higher country. They'd been hiking, were returning and wouldn't tell anyone what happened; they thought they'd be laughed at.

Days went by. Announcements on the radio slowed and then one afternoon a woman drove in the front parking lot of the bar. She was well-oiled. She rushed in and told her waiting audience about this crazy animal she'd met. It seems she lived deep in the mountains at a mine, and the road was so bad she'd have a few snorts to fortify herself before the trip to town, which was only a once a month affair. Everybody was laughing and teasing her 'til finally they told her the truth.

I headed off ten miles in the mountains with a bucket of oats and some alfalfa. I could see why the old gal drank. The road was so hairy it even bothered me. I found where the animal had been by its signs. I put out the hay and scattered the oats, beat on the bucket, honked the horn and left. Next morning I got back bright and early and there was the "llama," nibbling. I took the bucket, walked up and put my rope on him while he was eating, jumped him in the panel truck and headed for home. The woman was still at the bar so I gave her the $25 reward which everyone at the bar shared. She certainly had a fine visit.

After a couple of months we moved about 20 miles closer to Tucson to another new development which had 3 or 4 houses on it and we gave more shows. We had some pretty hostesses this time to talk to the people, steer them to the salesmen, pass out goodies to eat and generally entertain them...most were German women who had come with their husbands to Fort Huachuca, attractive, with outgoing personalities, and when things were slow we enjoyed ourselves.

One of them will carry the scars of a shootout with me for life. Just funning around was common and, in a play gunfight, I shot Heidi three times in the abdomen with blanks from my pistol. It was too close; the burning wadding from the blanks went through her clothes and she got some powder burns from the shots and ended up with scars—no hard feelings but I didn't do that anymore.

At that time I had one deer that would stay and live with the mountain lions for they had been brought up together and would tolerate each other...most of the time they had a genuine like for each other. Whisk, my mountain lion, had a cub about a year old, half grown, and still frisky. The arena was put about 50 feet from the trailer where the animals were kept so I would have to go back and forth if I needed to move anything. At that time we were still perfecting the act and once in a while things would go wrong. One Saturday morning when just the hostesses were there and no visitors had shown up yet, I was busy working the animals for the first act at noon—then trouble. First, the mountain lion cub got the dog down and was holding his head in his mouth, (he wouldn't bite too hard for he knew when the dog got loose, he'd be mad and that, if he'd hurt him, the dog would get back with interest.)

I knelt down and pried the cat's mouth open and the instant I did, the dog snapped at the cat and my finger was in the way. It started bleeding heavily and I called for a handkerchief from one of the girls. As I started wrapping it around my finger, I heard a scream from Cheeta. The big cat had chased the chimp 7 or 8 ft. up the side of the arena and was scratching the chimps pants off. She could scratch his bottom with one free paw while holding on with the other.

I grabbed the cat by the tail and yanked her off the side onto the floor where I cuffed her and scolded her. The girls started hollering that the younger mountain lion in the trailer had attacked the deer, so, dropping the first cat, I ran. Opening the door of the arena took time; then, sprinting for the trailer where I jumped up on the platform and got into the cage seemed to take an eternity. The cub, half grown but still good sized compared to the deer, had caught the deer lying down while all the action was taking place in the arena. The young mountain lion had the deer by the scruff of the neck and was holding it. I cuffed the cat and threw it into the next compartment when the girls started screaming again. Looking across at the arena I could see that mama cat had the chimp up the wall again and Sparky the dog, was on the lower end biting the cat's tail.

I raced back to the arena where I broke up the fight and again the girls screamed. They were louder than ever. Dick! Dick! the trailer's on fire! Sure enough...some hot ashes had fallen from my pipe while breaking up that fight, fallen into the straw bedding in the cages and had started to smoulder and burn. I called for the girls to get some water in my watering buckets and I set out for the trailer again at top speed. Opening doors in the trailer brought the cat and deer into conflict again, so, beating on the fire and trying to separate the two 'til the water arrived, was a nightmare. Smoke was everywhere.

The girls were all making a great deal of noise, giving me suggestions, and all the animals were full of noise. When the water arrived, I put the fire out, put the animals back in their separate cages, and I returned to the arena where Cheeta was perched on top of everything chattering and waving at all the action.

The girls thought we should do this four times a day but I was exhausted, bloody, dirty, smoky and completely out of sorts; and besides, my only Jungle Jim suit was a complete mess.

We lay around for awhile building, repairing equipment and cages, and then went to the lake near Showlow, Arizona–the same group of salesmen, only this time it was in the high mountains.

Cheeta and the cat hadn't been worked for several months so I felt it wasn't going to be easy the first time out and my feelings were right. Probably I started in with too much of a negative attitude I guess.

Never Kick A Bear in Your Bedroom Slippers

The act started out as usual only this time the cat came out and had a free-for-all with both the dog and the chimp and I was in the middle trying to break it up. The mountain lion took a swing at me, stuck a claw in my hand between the thumb and forefinger and opened a small artery which pumped blood everywhere. We had a large crowd of about 50 people standing around and one threw me a handkerchief which I wrapped around my hand while I gave the whip to Cheeta and told him to put the cat away.

He did so in great fashion, whipping the cat who was hissing and snarling like any lion in a cage act in the circus. Cheeta was now the big lion trainer and with great flourishes drove the cat back into the cage, shut the cage door and then came over to me to oh and ah over my hand. He had to examine it carefully and then put his mouth down and sample the blood. The crowd thought this was wonderful and gave us a big hand.

Cheeta looked my hand all over again and then took the other one and led me to the door in the arena where he opened it for me very solicitously. Normally I would take him to his cage where I had put an apple in the back, undress him and he'd go in and get the apple, then I could close everything easily. This time he let me undress him and then, slipping between my legs, bolted to freedom. He ran on all fours through the crowd with me right behind trying to catch him. I shouted for him to stop with no results so I pulled my gun and shot him with a blank right on the bare behind. He screamed and, with one hand holding his behind, ran faster. With me hollering for him to stop, we ran thru the sales office and down a road toward the lake.

I would shoot; he would holler and scream. The crowd stared in utter amazement. We ran down the road a couple of hundred yards, and then back. Nine times he got it. No results! No more blanks! Then running along side of him I hit him with the barrel of the pistol as hard as I could on top of the head. More screaming!

This time he stopped, gave me his hand and started to cry. Heading him to his cage, he went in peacefully and ate his apple, still crying. A chimp's got a head like an anvil and later I found that a piece of water pipe was the teaching tool he could understand best.

9

DICK ROBINSON

It seems most good chimp trainers have the same problem. The gun went into the repair shop from over-use.

The next month we moved to Pinetop about 30 miles away where I did a show for a trailer sales company. There were few whites but mostly White Mountain Apache Indians. They figured 6,000 Indians on the reservation and 4,000 came to see the show.

I now had two 30 foot trailers that could carry animals. One had larger cages, a drop-down platform that I could walk on while I lectured about the animals and then be folded up to provide a wall of protection for them, and privacy. The other was used to carry removable cages with animals plus the arena and props for my show. The arena was 18 ft. across and ten feet high when erected, and, while it was a job to set up, I could handle it alone for it came apart in four foot panels which I could just manage. But it was an excellent place to do my shows.

It was hard finding someone to help ferry trucks back and forth between shows and sometimes I would just ride the bus. One truck was a panel that I'd had for years and was made for pulling a trailer and the other was a one-ton International with a roomy van on the back where there was a generator to furnish power, a freezer for animal food, sleeping quarters with plenty of room for all my belongings and which, while in Sierra Vista, had been painted a beautiful green with circus scroll work lettering on the sides for good ol' Jungle Jim. No one could miss me.

I had been dating a woman who had a young son who enjoyed the animals, Clint Rowe. He was about 12 and would stay with me at times, helping to feed and clean. Because I was working that summer at the high lakes while he was out of school, it was a good time for him to stay with me and swim in the lake and roam around.

At Pinetop during one of my shows he became very useful. Along with everything else I would put on a rattlesnake show if I had any snakes and where we had many Indians around, it seemed like a good show idea. I took a big red Ruber (type of rattlesnake) out of the freezer, and carried him into the arena with my snake hook and started showing how we worked snakes. Get them to coil on the floor, put your foot in front of them, sole toward the snake and move it in. If he strikes it will be into the sole which won't hurt anything. Blow up a balloon, tie it to the end of your snake hook and wave it in front of the snake. If he strikes into it, well, there's a big bang, and everyone jumps sky-high and it gives them a thrill.

I would take a snake like this and put it in the freezer for half an hour to cool off so it wouldn't move too much. The red ruber was one rattlesnake that had both kinds of venom, neurotoxic and hemotoxic, meaning it could affect both the nervous and blood systems so it behooved me not to get bit. My emergency snake kit wouldn't handle this. These snakes were big, red colored and slow. Usually they would retreat rather than fight so they went into the act. I had learned about doing rattlesnake shows when I did them at Ross Allen's Reptile Institute in Florida. The climax of my act was to milk a rattlesnake for the crowd. Indians thought this was something really special.

One day a snake wouldn't do anything and then suddenly slithered for the hills. I can just remember the crowd fanning out and a woman with a pair of twins about a year old frantically getting out of the way. Luckily Clint, the boy, was standing outside the arena. He ran and grabbed a pair of snake tongs and caught the snake. Good boy!

Later that day an Indian dressed in Levi's and cowboy shirt came up to the office with a little girl about 3 in a cute but somewhat messy calico dress, and wanted to see the manager. Fritz, the owner, was about 35, young and aggressive, a salesman par excellence but not too much of a public relations expert. He had been upset because so many Indians had shown up and not too many customers. Indians weren't buying trailers. Fritz came out and asked what he wanted. The Indian said,

"That tiger wet all over my little girl." He was very sober about the whole thing. Fritz looked at him a minute; you could see he was trying to think up something to say. Finally he started shouting,

"Well, this is a free country, isn't it? People can do anything they want can't they? What'd you want me to do, talk to the cat and tell him not to? Can you talk 'TIGER'?"

The poor Indian was dumbfounded, turned and walked off into

the crowd without saying another word. Fritz stomped back into his office, mad because he didn't have anything clever to say. The leopard (not a tiger) in the cage was a male and did have a bad habit of spraying and it was necessary to be careful for he had a good 8 ft. range, and it was potent; but most people just laughed about it.

One of the biggest laughs we got was after the show. I would ask Cheeta to make like an Indian. He would get a Navajo blanket out of his chest, come to me, get my pipe and sit on top of the chest with the blanket over his head with just his face showing, puffing the pipe. The Indians seldom laughed in public but this usually brought a storm of laughter from them. He loved it and would take out the pipe and roll his lip down, laugh at them and go back to puffing on the pipe and blowing smoke at the people.

As he grew older Cheeta got tougher to handle. Most trainers baby their chimps with heat at night and a lot of fancy food but I just gave him the Navajo blanket which he couldn't tear apart and fed him monkey chow from Purina. His hair grew several inches long and he stayed in great health even in the cold. Many times we do something for looks so that other people will judge us favorably, not for what is really necessary for animals; and this applies to other things of course.

The cold always reminded me of the night I was crossing the mountains in Northern California from the east going to Eureka. It was really cold and of course it was drafty in the trailer where Cheeta was, so I stopped, let down the side platform and got Cheeta out. Putting him next to me in the warm cab of the truck was my idea of being nice to him. I had a chain around his waist and when I came to the town of Willow Creek, everything was dark as we went through the streets until suddenly we saw a lighted store. By this time it was about midnight and here was an all night grocery! Stopping, I wrapped the chain around the gear shift lever and went inside for some snacks.

Now Willow Creek was the headquarters for most of the "Big Foot" hunts in northern California. That legendary creature had provided more newspaper copy than any other single person or event in the area and was a continuing story in some of the local newspapers. Willow Creek was a lumbering town where I had been many times on my way north to see some of my Yurok Indian friends, for I had participated at one time in an effort to find out more about "Big Foot."

After getting what I wanted, some candybars and cookies, I returned to the truck and noticed that the door was open. Oh no! Not again! Cheeta had unhooked his chain and left. Now what? Having some knowledge by this time of how he would behave I looked around. Cheeta would go to houses 'til he found a door unlocked and go in; and, of course, at night he would look for a lighted house. Number two, find the fridge, open the door and lift a meal.

A block away was a house light. Approaching, it turned out to be a large trailer house. Walking up I found that the door was ajar a few inches. I knocked. No answer. Pushing the door open a little wider I could see Cheeta sitting in the middle of the room with a quart of milk and some bread, busy eating. I asked,

"Anyone home?"

No answer. Again.

"Anyone home?" much louder. Pushing the door wider to look around I could see an old granny in a rocking chair. Must have been 75-80. Her arms were glued onto the arms of the chair, eyes round and straight ahead. She had had been watching TV which was on. Cheeta put up his hand in greeting with a piece of bread in it and said, "hello" in his language. I looked at the woman, her mouth clamped together, and asked,

"Did he take anything else?"

She gurgled, "MMMMMmmmmmmmmmmm!" I replied,

"Well...I'll leave a dollar for the bread and milk...Okay?"

He gave me his hand and we left with Cheeta still carrying the quart of milk and finishing a piece of bread in his mouth. Pulling the door shut behind, we walked quickly through the dark to the truck where I put him back, put the chain on tight, gave him a candy bar and then, really lashing the chain to the gear shift lever, I went back inside the store and asked the lady if she knew who owned the trailer house, pointing it out. She said,

"I do."

"Oh, wellll...ah..." I said, "My friend got loose, opened the door to that house and got a quart of milk and a loaf of bread and I left a dollar to cover it. Sorry about it."

"Well," she said, "he better not have." I quickly got in the truck and headed across the mountains for Eureka. I always did wonder what the old lady thought about the chimp. Big foot?

2 / Whisk, the mountain lion

Whisk was a small body with spots and blue eyes when she first came to me. Saving up $250 from a hard month's work driving a logging truck in the dead of winter bought this little bundle of energy. On the advice of a friend, I drove to Golden, British Columbia where a family had a baby mountain lion. They were hunters of mountain lions and; after bagging a large cat, found the dogs playing with a bundle of fur, examined it and discovered a small baby. They took it home and fed it a bottle. It survived. Turning over the money to them stripped me but I had a good, tame, small lion at last.

Having been injured in a logging accident the previous fall, one that had left me crippled for months, had made it mandatory that I receive treatment regularly, so the animals and I spent the next 3 months in Spokane with me in an out-patient status at the hospital and living on my workman's compensation.

"We" at that time (before Cheeta) were a large black bear, two half-tame cubs (mountain lions) and my small one, plus my dog, Sparky, who was a mutt but would work with anything. "Whiskey", as I named the small lion, thrived. Having nothing but $37 a week left to survive on, we did. It helped finding chicken necks for 3 to 4 cents a pound, which was the best feed for the animals, and made good soup for me.

My body condition got better slowly and that summer I went

back to work in the woods driving a logging truck. Whisk, as I called her, grew rapidly, lost her spots and got new permanent teeth. Later, when traveling south to see what there was in a better line of work, I got a contract for my animals at the Disney Studios. This started me on the road of my real life's work, the movies, and started Whisk and me into the work of acting. She became one of the best working mountain lions there was in animal performing and made me a living for years. Later, when I had to have additional brain surgery, she was close by, the only animal that was left of my once plentiful supply of critters. She had been with me for eight years and was like a child, the best friend there was.

I remember having her bred in Idaho while we were roaming around and all at once she was ready to have kittens. This was something new to me. How would she react? What would happen with the kittens. I spent much time talking to people about how to handle the kittens. Should I leave them on her for a few days? Take them immediately? What?...it was a concern. I didn't know when or where it would happen so we went along as usual. A few days later, when parked at a friend's store, her time came!

She went into labor. There was plenty of nice straw to make her comfortable and she let me stay with her while she was having them. We had three nice kittens! They were all nursing so that night, thinking everything was all right, I went to bed. The next morning only two were left and she was eating one of them. It was hard to understand. Immediately I took the remaining one and got ready to bottle feed it. But first I examined it closely. Its side wall was licked through from the washing Whiskey had given it.

Now I was a father again and spent as much time raising this little one as I had its mother.

Eighteen months later, while doing our shows in the high lake country, was a heart-breaking time for me. Whiskey was not eight, and her one remaining cub was doing fine, now a year and a half old, and working with everyone nicely including the deer that lived with them. Then Whisk had a convulsion in Tucson and the doctor diagnosed it as encephalitis, a disorder of the brain.

I started her on drugs for it immediately, but the fits came back again the next month, then the next week, and finally every day. It was scary when it first happened for she didn't have control of herself and it was hard to help her. Afterward I would clean her up, wiping up all the blood and saliva from her face and body.

Lying on her side she would be exhausted and the deer, who was living with her, would stand over her and wash her. It licked her face and around her ears and body 'til she sparkled and then it would lie down beside her to keep her warm. Whisk would snarl and roar at her but she ignored the noise and kept on washing. I knew that there was no saving Whisk for we had tried new drugs that didn't have any effect. Finally, she had three convulsions in one day and it was too much. I got some alcohol and injected it directly into a vein on a leg. She died quickly. I cried for she was my friend and I deeply loved her. I had delivered her babies and she had always been with me since her infancy. Even the deer was lonesome. After that I would try to make it a point not to get involved with my animals.

3
The Desert Museum, best of its type

When there wasn't any work or shows I would exhibit around Tucson with my "Ding Jar" and take in enough money to live on. There was a place at a friend's house about 12 miles out in the country where we could clean up and rest.

The Desert Museum is a facility in the desert, 14 miles from Tucson, containing a museum, aviary, zoo with natural environment, aquariums and all kinds of plants, flowers and reptiles and, for its type, it is probably the best in the world.

I knew several of the people at the Desert Museum which has a good sized zoo and many small animals which they use in their TV show. So there would be trading that I could get in on and I could help Hal Gras with the show. Hal worked for the Desert Museum as a publicity man and that included a lot of other things.

This meant doing shows with small animals like squirrels, hawks, birds, porcupines, small pigs (javelinas) and owls, dressing some of them up in costumes. All of them had names, such as "Quilly Mays", the porcupine, or "Gregory Peccory", the javelina. Hal did shows for groups of people in the clubs, colleges and schools to educate them about animals. Hal also wrote a column in the paper and produced a weekly half-hour TV show which was very informative. He had a wife "Nottie" who helped take care of the "nursery" they had at home, for this is where they kept all of their actors and any sick or wounded animals that were brought in. Spring brought a deluge of babies, little birds who had fallen out of their nests, or were struck by cars or picked up by the kids.

Hal and Nottie were a delightful couple who enjoyed their work and tried to keep away from the petty politics that beset an institution of this kind. Becoming friendly with most of the staff at that time, I worked on several of their TV shows and traded and swapped with all of them. One performance that was very popular was having my pet mountain lion, the deer and my dog "Sparky" all drinking milk together out of a bowl, in the TV studio, for the cameras. Three of us talked about these animals and what they did in their normal habitat, while the animals put on their own show.

It was great to see them together and the show was popular. I enjoyed working TV shows and did well talking on them. Hal was one of those rare individuals who should have had a chance for big time TV because he was really good. We need more of this kind of program for teaching young people in schools about animals. But we have to tell them the truth, that it is a hard life in the wilds, that animals eat other animals, that animal life is cruel as we see it, but a natural way for them.

Disney seldom has animals living a true story in his films in the wild but this is what has made many stories on 'Wild Kingdom' accepted, because of their authenticity. People know when they're being conned.

One day Hal asked if I would help them out by using some of my animals in a TV show for Wild Kingdom. Sure. I made a deal to furnish some animals for the show for $750—and worked about a week for them in the desert close to the museum. It was a new experience. Having worked in many movies over the past few years, I found this especially enjoyable. They were satisfied with what I had done and I was getting an education in how they made their shows. I had always seen shots of Marlin Perkins standing with a camera in his hand and thought he filmed the shows, but I was wrong. They had cameramen filming supposedly wild animals but instead used people like me, with tame animals, contriving wild-looking scenes. Very interesting.

Never Kick A Bear in Your Bedroom Slippers

They asked me to get a group of animals together and take them to the Philmont Boy Scout Ranch in New Mexico, this time for $1500. The money paid nothing but expenses, for most of the animals had to be bought and it took a good deal to make the trip but at least it was something new. Marlin was supposedly leading a boy scout troop from Alamagordo thru the mountains. We (the animals and I) would do all the animal work and Marlin would do the acting. I didn't see too much of him but had a great deal of respect for his accomplishments after working with him.

The game people from New Mexico were extremely cooperative. They had a warden with a car on the set every day with two-way radio if we needed anything, and the department furnished an airplane to use for filming. One day the second in command was out, helped me throw mountain lions off a cliff for a piece of excitement and helped move the animals around. Very nice people! The show went well and we all broke up, promising to get together on another show.

With nothing in sight in my line of work, and little extra money, I started to travel "looking."

4 / *The Ding Jar*

Slowly we would go for one day's drive and then put the "ding jar" out in a shopping center in a small town or a crossroad where we could find some people and rest for a day.

The animals and I worked our way slowly to Oregon then through the forests to the fogs and ocean, into the ranch country of Northern California, and back to the ocean. Each part was a delicious experience after surviving the rigors of the previous year's hospital treatment. We poked along south, watching the public enjoying the animals, meeting interesting people and talking to them. I never had enough money but enjoyed hospitality from many and saw new things for the first time and explored many places.

I poked through Jungleland which was, as the name implied, 15 acres of animals, rides, animal acts, animal training facilities and jungle acts for the movies. There were hundreds of animals which could be bought and sold and mostly old facilities from the thirties and forties, but a very engaging place. Many of the people associated with Jungleland lived close by since it was in the town of Thousand Oaks, California. Some interesting people and interesting acts to watch!

Some of these people told me about Africa, USA, in Soledad Canyon so we headed there to visit. We skirted through Los Angeles and headed into the mountains, up a windy road for miles through a canyon that was bare of big trees but had lots of small ones on the hillsides and cottonwoods in the creek bed where there was a little stream. There was a rather primitive road into the site and a very steep pitch where it went down through a creek and up the other side. My trailer was so long that it scraped the bottom of it while crossing but it just scared the animals and didn't damage anything. Good thing it was built for the mountains.

This animal compound was owned by Ralph Helfer who had 100-150 animals that were used by movie companies for parts in films. It was a bigger animal business than I'd ever seen before.

It was late evening when I pulled in and things were quiet except for the noises of the animals. They had one office trailer and many cages surrounding the whole area. There were lions, tigers, leopards, mountain lions and all kinds of hoofed stock. A couple of people came by and Ralph, the owner, came over, said hello, looked briefly at my animals, asked me if I would work for them the following day, and after I answered affirmatively, left. It was some job at Universal Studios.

I parked my truck and trailer by the side of a clearing in the parking area by their office, dropped the sides, fed and watered the animals, and heard a voice behind me. I turned and there was the most beautiful young girl watching me. She asked about the animals, climbed up on the platform and we began talking. My mountain lion purred a "Hello" to her and so we went into the cage, knelt down and began petting and talking to her, the lion that is.

The girl had long dark hair, peasant blouse with a beautiful figure and even better, a bright personality that I couldn't resist. We talked for a little while and suddenly a voice rang out from the office trailer,

"Janet, where are you?"

She replied, and then with her eyes sparkling said she'd meet me here tomorrow night.

"Will you be here?"

"Of course," I replied.

She gave me a quick kiss and headed off through the trees and cag

DICK ROBINSON

The next day we left early for the studio. Universal was making a jaguar picture with Robert Mitchum called "Raunchy". There was a huge inside set built of styrofoam which had all kinds of cliffs and caves and ledges, and it was going to be my job to help contain the jaguar they were using. It had been under considerable stress and strain in the film so far and had mauled two handlers so badly they were incapacitated, and maybe I was going to be the third. I could see why. With lighted torches, rifles and sticks, the people were chasing the cat around in a "pursuit" in the film.

It was my job to get in the back of a cave and, when the cat came in with a man chasing it with a torch, to turn him and make him fight the man. I was crouched behind a four foot piece of plywood jammed up in the back of the cave. The thing to do was to keep the cat from going over the plywood to hide. It was so dark he couldn't see much when he came and didn't know I was there the first time. Some job! It went on all morning. We broke for lunch and then did a stunt with a couple of people falling off a cliff, then back to working the cat again with it being chased around the ledges.

They used CO_2 fire extinguishers to chase and/or stop it and the cat would really panic. No wonder the trainers got mauled! It was a tired man who went back to the compound that night and never even got a glimpse of Mitchum.

Everybody was running around at the compound when we returned. A bobcat had been lost that night coming back from a location at the Disney Ranch. People were out looking for it as they had to shoot the next morning at Producers Studio to finish a flick called "Black Zoo", a real cheapie.

After everything quieted down, I'd got all the animals fed and I cleaned up, then Ralph walked by and brought me a check for $15. I couldn't believe it! $15 for that day's work? What a joke! He asked me if I'd work the next day.

"For $15?" I asked. "No."

He had a money-making thing going. I'd heard that day from one of the men working at the studio that he got $50 a day apiece for the men from the studio, but $15 for me...well...no thanks. And he left.

Now I waited for the girl to return...waited...and waited. No show. It got darker and darker. The night light went on and no girl. Well, I guess it was too good to be true anyhow. I went to bed completely disgruntled. No woman! I had living quarters built into the back of the truck so I left the door open, hoping. For an hour I waited, hoping for her to come by. Nothing.

Only a bear in the rear of the trailer had started pacing madly back and forth. The trailer was so long that when it moved at the back it really jiggled the front of the trailer, so consequently, the back of the truck where I bunked really shook. The bear had been nervous since we had crossed the creek and scratched the back end of the trailer. Everything started to build up. Finally my nerves cracked. I got into my pants, put on my old pair of sheep-skin bedroom slippers and went back, hollered at him with no results, then climbed on the platform, went into the cage and booted him one. He bit my leg! I got mad and kicked him again. He bit me again.

Now my frustration took over and it became a battle. One hundred pounds of bear and me. I would kick, he'd bite. It went on and on. Finally I called a draw. My leg was raw, and my toe hurt like hell. Limping up to the front of the trailer I surveyed the situation. Putting a jack under the tongue of the trailer solved the problem, but my foot! I crawled into bed and lay there frustrated. Well, he'd won by default and I'd learned a lesson. At last I got some sleep.

The next morning my foot was so swollen I could hardly walk. Before leaving I asked about the girl from one of the men working.

"Oh, Ralph's girlfriend." Never did find out more about her.

I loaded up and headed for the open road again. It was better working in a shopping center with my donation bottle than $15 a day with all the risks and expenses I had except, maybe, for the girl.

We would stop at a grocery most of the time, go to the manager, explain that we could draw hundreds of people in to see the animals and that for a paltry $25 we would park and let people enjoy the exhibit. Also, I would put out my donation jar for people to deposit a few coins to help defray part of the expenses.

Most of the time it worked. The donation jar would have to be put on the front with a sign saying that we needed their help to keep this exhibit on the road. A giant gallon pickle jar baited with a dollar bill and change, and with the sign behind it, worked and kept us in a steady but modest supply of eating money. Once a man dropped a silver dollar in, the whole bottom dropped out and money flew every which way. He turned to me and said, "It sure isn't used to heavy money, is it?" Everyone laughed, gathered up all the money, added a little more, while we hunted up another pickle jar. Sometimes it was pennies, nickels, and dimes; other times quarters and half dollars.

Once going through the truck border station in Utah, I was stopped. It was then that the patrolman who ran it discovered that my driver's license had run out and my truck licenses were expired. They dragged me four miles to a Justice of the Peace court in a gas station, convicting me of being without a license. Five dollars plus costs ($2.00), and I could only come up with $1.90. The trooper and JP discussed what to do, called the sheriff, who refused to have anything to do with the situation and absolutely ruled out having any dad-burned animals around to feed. They spent half an hour discussing the problem; I knew what the outcome would be. I could take in the money in Brigham City that afternoon and bring the money back to them. They were relieved to come to an understanding and said to go.

I parked in a large center, tried to get someone to sponsor me. No luck! I put out the "ding jar" and BS'd people all afternoon and evening and made about $10 in small change. When I went back and paid the JP in pennies, nickels and dimes, even he felt ashamed at taking it...mumbled something about the cheapness of people... for I did have a good exhibit and beautiful animals. Anything to get away from that part of the state.

I had been through Las Vegas several times, but I had never had the animal trailer full of good exhibit animals. So this time I decided to pick out a shopping center, and give it a good test. First I visited the game department, so that I could find out what the game laws were in case anyone bothered me. Looking through the laws saddened me. Everything was illegal in the way of native animals, even if they were obtained legally. They could be taken from you unless they were being taken through the state in interstate commerce.

Finally I got to the back of the book and found one little paragraph. If you were showing the animals, as in a menagerie, that game law didn't apply. Good!

I pulled into a nice shopping center near the center of town, stopped, and talked to the manager of a large supermarket. He couldn't pay me anything, but would give me some feed and permission to park in the front of the lot. There were big signs on the trailer, so everybody could see it passing by.

Dropping the sides and getting everything arranged so that the animals looked their best with clean straw, putting out the "ding jar", and cleaning up with my safari jacket and jungle hat, I stood back to see what would happen. There was no zoo in Las Vegas and no chance to see wild animals like this, so it should be interesting.

People started to pull in from every direction. Soon that whole end of the parking lot was jammed. People were so packed they couldn't even see the "ding jar", so I pushed through, took it off its hanger, and put it up on the platform. It started to jingle with joy, so, finding another one and making a new card brought even more results. I had one on both ends of the trailer. I stood at the back of the crowd watching to see that nothing untoward happened, and talked to the people. It brought results I couldn't believe. It was tiresome, and at the end of a few hours I folded up and headed for a truck stop to rest—and count the loot. Ninety-eight dollars. Wow! What a place!

The next morning we hit back to the same spot and went to work. The manager came out, thanked me, and got some feed for me. Then he told me a little story. It seems the large center on the other side of town was kicking, for the people were all coming down here and they were jealous. He warned me of funny business and left.

There were all kinds of people around, and everyone enjoyed the exhibit. There were all kinds of police; sheriff's deputies would bring their children by, and the jars kept jingling. This went on for two days.

Then the law from the game department showed up. They were going to give me a ticket for having native animals in my possession. I said they were welcome to look at the receipts of where they had come from. No. He was just going to give me a ticket. I asked, "Well, what do you consider I am? A menagerie?" He said "I guess so." "Well, take a look at your law book then. What does it say?" He thumbed past the game laws until he found the little hidden paragraph and read it. "Well, that's not fair!" he whined. I'll figure a way to get you." I could see that that was exactly what would happen.

The next morning I got a visit. A man in a business suit came up and asked for my license. A license for donations? Yep. He said I had to have a license. I said, "Ok, I'll go and get one then." Folding up, I took the animal trailer down to the truck stop then headed to city hall for the licensing division. I said, "I'd like a license to show some animals." "Ok, that'll be a hundred dollars." I laid the hundred down on the counter, and he started to fill in a receipt book for the money. Now he said, "If you want to stay beyond tomorrow, be sure and come in again tomorrow night."

"What do you mean?"

"Well," he said, "it's a hundred a day, paid in advance."

I grabbed the hundred and said, "Wait a minute. What's the idea?"

"Well," he said, "you're the same as a circus. It doesn't make any difference how big you are. One animal or a hundred."

I left.

I drove out on the strip and stopped at the Desert Inn, where a couple of friends hung out, and looked them up. They introduced me to Wilbur Clark, who asked me what the problem was. Well, he couldn't help me in town, but help myself to the parking lot at the Desert Inn. I did, but it wasn't successful at all. By the time I paid my bills and got feed and gas, I was broke, and headed down the highway for the next town to recoup. It was Searchlight, Nevada. Some place! I met some nice people, parked in front of the town whorehouse, and made enough in a day to get back to Arizona.

Driving down the highway was always dangerous, and I had to practice defensive driving all the time. People would drive by and try to peer in to see what was there, then they'd follow and wait for me to stop, or just hang behind to figure what was going on.

The highway that I was on was a two-lane main highway that led to the northern route to Kingman. We crossed Boulder Dam and were about 30 miles from Kingman when a Porsche pulled up beside the trailer to pass, and then followed alongside the trailer. I tried to slow down to get it to pass, but nothing. I could see a woman pointing to the trailer, when suddenly she veered right into the side of the trailer, knocking it sideways. She put on the brakes, the trailer straightened out, and the Porsche pulled off the road into a bank and stopped. I pulled up into the bar pit.

There was a good sized dent in the underneath running gear on the bottom of the trailer, I noticed as I walked by, and upon reaching the Porsche, found that it had its front end demolished. The woman got out, unhurt, and brought a poodle with her. Oh! She had been pointing out something to the poodle and lost control. Just at that time a patrolman pulled up and got out. He looked the situation over, wrote the woman a ticket for careless driving, we exchanged addresses, and she left me with her insurance company's address. This is one of those cases where it was just luck that nothing more serious happened. I learned to watch all the time for my own good.

An hour later we pulled into the agricultural check station just before Kingman, and parked behind a furniture van. There was some confusion going on, and I casually stepped out and walked up to see what was happening.

There were bodies lying all over. Several people were running around, and I turned quickly back to the truck to get a gun. Sirens were wailing as police and ambulances were fast arriving. It was all over. I had to wait while they picked up bodies. They waved us through, for cars and trucks were clogging up the highway.

They had told me that three men in a car had been hesitant about going through the check point, waiting around for an hour. The man on duty called the sheriff, who walked up to the men, asked what they were doing, and one of them pulled a loaded revolver and fired it. That brought on a gun fight with several of them. The sheriff shot a couple of them, and then they got him. The other one was captured. It seemed like this was going to be an interesting trip.

DICK ROBINSON

Wandering around the western U.S. was just the rest a man in my condition needed. My recovery from my brain operation was really slow and it was easy to overdo. That had been my trouble all along–overdoing.

It was great to go wandering along the sea coast through Oregon and California, looking at the sights, talking to the people and really enjoying some of the interesting ones. Finally we hit Burbank and looked for a store in the want ads that sold wild animals. With plenty of trading stock it could be a way of getting rid of a few.

Close by was a location in Burbank which saved the time of just looking around. I parked behind a service station next door to it and walked into the pet shop. It had possibilities. There were African lion cubs in the front window and many monkeys in the back.

I had a load of mountain lions, deer, leopard, and small animals. Finding the owner, Brian Bender, feeding the monkeys, and a beautiful blonde in casual conversation with him brought memories of the last girl that had been interested in the animals. Extremely well dressed, blonde hair well put up, elegant face and a beautiful figure, and, from their conversation, she was interested in the animals. Telling him what there was in the trailer brought some interest but he said that he'd have to feed first and then come out.

Lana, the woman said her name was, said she wanted to see my animals and we went out to the trailer. Even with her high heels on she climbed up on the side platform and waded through the bedding straw to meet the animals. All she could talk about was animals, especially her horse, and then she told me she was the only woman executive of a large aircraft corporation in Burbank, the senior buyer.

About this time Brian came out and joined us. Many people were standing around from the adjoining businesses, and it soon became apparent that Brian was her boyfriend from the way he talked. It was getting dark and people disappeared so, I folded up everything, and I asked her where there was a laundromat around to do some clothes. She said why not come over to her house a couple of blocks away and do them.

"Well, I don't want to interfere with your boyfriend," I said.

"Don't worry," she said , "his wife expects him tonight."

Never Kick A Bear in Your Bedroom Slippers

I locked everything up—it was 8:30 or 9 by this time—and walked over to the address she gave me. It was a nice little house, aquariums all around and lots of books. After I put my clothes in the washer, we talked. She excused herself and took a shower, made me a sandwich and talked about herself.

At ten o'clock her daughter came in, a nice girl of 12 or so and she went to bed. It was an interesting time for conversation. With her hair wrapped in a towel and a bathrobe on, she sat down close to me on the davenport and looked at me. Obviously she was feeling the same way I was. We experienced that magnetic attraction that happens between two people occasionally.

Later she told me she was going to move out further from the city. When? As soon as possible! The next day was Saturday and staying around the trailer taking in money with my 'ding jar' proved tiresome and I was ready to leave. Suddenly Lana appeared, and said she had found a place for us. Us?

Telling her there was no money in my kitty didn't phase her. She assured me that there would be plenty. We went out to a small half-acre horse ranch in Sylmar. She'd signed a lease for a year and would I move in? Well, you know I can't work and I don't know what I can do but, well...why not? Sunday we started moving her furniture in.

What was I to do? Regular work was too hard for me, the country was unfamiliar to me for showing the animals and I had no license for California. But loafing around and going to the pet stores, animal dealers and movie compounds started bringing in a few dollars. I went back to Arizona and got my other truck, trailer and more animals. Now I had to find a food supply.

Everything in the way of meat eaters got chicken necks. It was cheap and the best feed obtainable and everyone liked them. Luckily, close by was a custom chicken processor that Lana located for me, which relieved me of going too far.

5 / *The Lesser Los Angeles Zoo*

Living in Sylmar was nothing but a series of traumas. We lived in a nice white ranch house with an attached garage and drive way in the front. It was fenced with white boards and looked very homey. The whole neighborhood consisted of olive groves with ranch houses, horses and kids, on half acre parcels. We had a drive that went beside the garage and the neighbor's garage to the back. Once in the back it became a different land: cages full of animals, several miniature horses, a couple of quarter horses, and an arena set up for the lion show I was working on. There were lions and tigers, mountain lions, deer, chimps and monkeys. A forty to fifty head-count was not unusual.

The next door neighbor was a welder and we were always working together on new cages as an animal trader could only do business according to the number of cages he had. I kept my chimp in the garage and my mountain lion who was expecting.

With a half acre full, I was looking for more room but it was hard to find. Everyone was deathly afraid of the LA Animal Control people and permits were practically non-existent for wild animals in most zoning areas. I had a zoo license from the state people who were most cooperative at that time but the city was something else. Zoning? Well, I understood you could keep a couple of horses in our type of zoning but 50 animals? The state understood my problem and suggested I get a license, but how? Apply by mail, they said. I did and waited with baited breath. I needed two things, a business license and a zoo license from the city of Los Angeles. The zoo in Los Angeles was called the Greater Los Angeles Zoo so I called mine the Lesser Los Angeles Zoo. It came through! No questions about zoning. If the Animal Control people ever caught up with me though they'd ask. The problem was to keep away from any complaints. My neighbor to the back, and that was way back through the olive trees, had a swimming pool and then his house. A man about 65, he worked for one of the aircraft companies and was a complainer. There was nothing he couldn't complain about. Fortunately, he would often call the police about a dog chasing his cat or some other silly complaint. The local police at the precinct house knew him well, so when he called, often in the middle of the night, about an African lion roaring in his backyard, the fuzz always got a great laugh and never came around.

Actually the neighbors got used to the wolves and coyotes howling, jackasses braying and the lions roaring. I did have my anxious moments though. One day a man stopped my truck on the street and asked if I was the man who had the monkeys. Very hesitantly I muttered an affirmative answer. He looked rather funny at what I said and then remarked, "Well, I just saw a big monkey hopping his cage down the middle of the street in front of the high school and thought it might be yours."

He was looking at me and shaking his head as he drove down the street. Me? I went into sheer panic! It was the chimp. He now weighed about a hundred lbs. and, in a cage 3 ft. square and 4 ft. high and weighing 75 lbs., it was going to be a hell of job to load. I was sure someone would have called in a complaint by the time he could be loaded. That chimp was so big and strong that he could hop the cage just about anywhere he wanted and now he was three blocks from home and in front of the high school! Oh... Normally the cage was bolted down in the garage but he could work it loose and go out on his own. I headed for the school. No one around. Maybe I could just play it casual in case someone came by? Just helping out the chimp? Taking the chimp for his exercise? I had some lame excuses figured by the time I got there.

There he was in the middle of the street, hanging onto the side of his steel cage; he could jump it any direction he wanted to go. Cars were driving around him, looking and laughing. I drove up, jumped out and went over and said hello. He held out a hand and talked to me. Quickly dragging the cage to the back of the truck, I tried to lift it on. No luck...A city pick-up pulled up and a young long-hair jumped out, gave me a hand, shoved the cage on and I raced for home quickly after thanking him.

Manhandling the cage into the garage and chaining him down again only took a few minutes and I rushed the truck into the back yard closing everything up. A few minutes later while looking out the front window a news car slowly cruised by.

Finally the neighbor built an enormous cage for him. It was made of steel pipe like a jail cell and must have weighed a thousand lbs. He weighed 125 lbs. when full grown and could still shake the cage around. It took three sets of chains and locks to keep the door closed.

When we needed help for the cats' medical problems we turned to one of our neighbors who had been introduced to us a couple of months previously.

"Doc" Engler lived about a mile from us in Sylmar and for many years threaded through my life. "Doc" had an old house set back off the road in a quiet residential area, unpainted with all kinds of bushes hiding the place. You would enter in the drive, get out in the rear and then become aware of a rather sharp pungent odor. If you walked into the house you were knocked down by the aroma, kind of like being struck by a brick, you gasped silently for awhile until you got used to it. Really cleaned out your sinuses. "Doc" would explain that this was where Valerie stayed. Valerie was a large female African lion, chained to a wall and would lunge at you to the end of her chain when you came in the door. Rather scary!

"Doc" was in his late fifties, worked for the city of San Fernando in the light department, was an engineer, and a veterinarian on the side for cats mostly. He had no formal schooling for his veterinary work but did know his cats. He got drugs from a wholesaler in San

Fernando that he'd made friends with and convinced him somehow that he was legitimate. When he worked on an animal he would make you sign a bill of sale on it so it would be legal for him to work on his own animal.

Bill or William was his real name but he told newcomers that people called him "Doc". He liked the feeling of importance that it brought to him for he was always telling people of the research he was doing and of his successful operations.

In the room next to the African lion was a toothless and clawless mountain lion and in cages scattered around were all kinds of other animals. The house was used only for the kitchen where he cooked and the front room where he could sit around and watch TV with the animals. Out in the back was another small building where "Doc" slept and an operating room with more large pens for his cheeta and other animals. "Doc" slept on a cot and had it arranged so that the cheeta could sleep with him.

His main help for me at that time was to operate on cats and remove their claws and fangs when needed and in this he was good. He worked with the Derbys, another animal compound, and helped them with their animal problems and helped here and there on some movies to make a few extra dollars.

As my spreading association with the zoo people and dealers grew it was a time of much activity. Lana had to be pushed out of bed in the morning to be sent off to her job for she disliked the discipline of having to go to work, any work, especially at 8 in the morning. She got a thousand a month and a thousand in kick backs, (cash) so we had enough to keep going. In a couple months there were enough deer and aoudads that had been acquired in trades to haul to Texas. Once there we would sell and trade for the best we could get, for that country had lots of game farms and zoos to work.

Lana got a week's vacation and we headed off. I had scraped up enough to make the down payment on a new three quarter ton Chevrolet stake truck which could haul my large animal trailer on long trips. We made the trip to the YO Ranch near Kerrsville, Texas, in the heart of the hill country, got the load sold, and then started to wander along on the way back, buying and trading for what animals we could find that would sell in California. We stopped to buy most of the animals at the old Abilene Zoo, for it was being torn down for a new zoo and nearly everything was being disposed of. We needed rhesus monkeys for a friend, Bob Constable, and his lab business, and the zoo had a real cageful. At least fifteen. They were all in a huge cage about 7 ft. high and fifteen feet by thirty feet long. They gave us a dirt cheap price because no one could figure how to catch and box them. Monkeys have a pecking order and it's usually a big, large mean male that rules, then on down in males. Several keepers had been mauled and chewed on, for inside the cage they would gang up on them and now none of the keepers would have anything to do with them. Lana had a system and was absolutely unafraid. She asked me for the jack handle. We always carried a handyman jack for the trailer and it had a removable pipe handle two and a half feet long and probably an inch and a quarter in diameter. I gave it to her.

Inside the old building she told the zookeepers, who were all Chicanos, to open the door. Their eyes really rounded out. What! Let that beautiful woman in with those monsters! Never! She finally got mad, opened the door herself and stomped in. I held the door unlocked to go in and help rescue her. The head monkey faced her ready to fight. His mouth opened to a huge set of snarling teeth and crouched ready to jump her. She raised her pipe and then gave it to him right on top of the head, hard! She flattened him. He was out cold. Daintily she picked up one arm and dragged him over to me in the doorway, never taking her eyes off the rest of the monkeys. He must have been 40 lbs. or so. I threw him in a cage and waited for the rest.

At the sight of this all the monkeys panicked. She was the new chief! Two more big males she slammed! The Chicanos all stood and gaped. There must have been 8 or 10 of them waiting for mayhem. They had a fire hose dragged out to use as a rescue tool. The cage was like a rain storm. All the monkeys were hanging from the ceiling and letting go everything inside them.

She began going up to the females and young ones and simply grabbing them. She would take hold of one of their arms, twist it around behind their backs, take the other arm to where she had a two armlock on them and stuff them in a cage. They didn't even offer to bite. I found later she could take a wild monkey and hold it to her chest and cuddle it without a bite. That's self confidence. We loaded the last of them without incident and then started on some bears.

Now Lana might have been great on monkeys but when it came to lions and other animals she had a fault. She put fingers in cages to rub noses, scratch ears or to pet them. She had her left forefinger in a small lion's cage one day. The cub got hold of her finger and wouldn't let go! She hollered, screamed, whacked at it and finally found a stick and jammed it in his mouth. Her finger came back well mauled. When it finally healed she did it again.

We were busy loading a large black bear when the end of the cage broke loose; a welder was brought out. After a half hours welding the crew finally got it fixed to my satisfaction but the bear wasn't happy for it had been in the cage all the time we were working on it and the flames from the torches really made it nervous. Lana was keeping her back toward me while we were loading the truck and it suddenly dawned on me. I grabbed her and pulled her hand loose from her vest. She'd done it again! Well, she said, someone had to keep the bear back from the welding. So he caught her finger! At least she didn't lose it. We headed for the doctor.

We'd been gone now for a week and Lana should have been back to work by this time. She'd called and used the sick routine and now tried again. No! She had to be there on Monday. Tomorrow. Well, get on a plane, I said. No, she really didn't like to work and liked this kind of life better. It was a real argument. She ended up not going back. Now it was up to me to make a living.

Lana and I put on shows occasionally on Sunday mornings for the neighborhood kids in an effort to keep good relations going. At least all the kids knew what was going on and we taught them a few manners around the animals in case we weren't home.

Occasionally we brought in rhesus monkeys to sell for our friend, Bob Constable. One got loose from its shipping cage and kept the neighbors a few blocks away upset for weeks. It would waylay the kids coming home from school. Ice cream cones were its specialty. It would watch from a limb in an olive tree, see what the kids were eating, run down and grab it from them and then scamper back into the top of the trees and holler at them. It was wild but wouldn't bite anyone. The newspapers were out for a neat story. Naturally animal control had a field day chasing it to have something to do, and we stayed hidden. Lana's daughter would bring back the stories and keep us informed.

It was natural that I would have to begin traveling to do more trading of animals as it meant going from one zoo to another, finding out what one had to trade and what another wanted. On one trip north to San Jose's zoo I met Peter Batten, the new director, and we had a long talk about what was surplus. He was building a new zoo for the city and wanted to get rid of the excess bears from the old zoo mainly. Directing me to the head employee of the city park department, in the downtown offices, brought quick results. An arrangement was soon made to get an American Black bear and a brown bear and having the empty cages on the back of my small truck made it easy. As I unhitched my big trailer and backed the truck up an alleyway, we unloaded the two cages. The city park department furnished the men and a cart. Going to the back of one of the exhibit cages that was to be torn down, we loaded the black bear. He was a big one and mean. My cages were 3 ft. wide by 6 ft. long and 4 ft. high and made of ¼ inch wire with 2″ x 6″ openings.

The cage was rolled up to the back door of the pen and the keeper coaxed the bear into it. He was tough! As he was rolled down the alley and parked behind my truck the foreman warned the 4 or 5 men around the cage to keep their fingers out as he was a biting fool.

Everyone was going to put hands under the cage, lift it, and then slide it onto the truck. Fine! It was raised waist high when an older man ran up, wedged in, grabbed the wire of the cage, and said,

"Let me help."

It was just sliding on the truck when we heard him yelp! Sliding it on in, some of the men turned to the man who had started to look at his sore finger. He let out a loud yell...

"He ate my finger!"

Amazement was written all over his face. The bear had snapped the left forefinger off between the 1st and 2nd knuckle and had done it so fast and hard that it had stretched the skin over the end and sealed off the blood. A couple of animal keepers searched the cage but the bear just looked around unconcernedly. Finally the foreman said, "I guess you better go to the doctor or hospital or something."

He walked across the grass lawns to his car, looking at his finger from all directions and then looking back at us. He got in his car and left.

Naturally insurance was a concern so I was rather worried, but the foreman said,

"Don't fret, we'll take care of it."

He indicated it was the city's responsibility to get the bears on the truck, that the man was the night watchman, and had just come to work and was a city employee; also he had no right to help out. I didn't have insurance so anything could break me.

Heading for Salt Lake City with little money meant that there would have to be some time spent working the 'ding jar' some place. In a shopping center at Reno, Nevada I made enough to buy gas and supplies to make it in.

It was a long trip but I went straight to the zoo, parked out in front and met LaMar Farnsworth, the director, in his office. We'd made a deal to trade some aoudads of his that were surplus for a rhea that I'd brought from Sylmar. This was a large bird like an ostrich who had a head that reached up four or five feet. Normally with the outside platform folded up, the head of the rhea would be above it, looking at you. LaMar and I casually walked out to the trailer which was parked at the curb in front of the zoo and suddenly it flashed on me. Nothing! Panic struck me in the bottom of my stomach. Quickly I lowered the side platform only to see the bird stretched out obviously dead on the floor with a rock beside its head. Nice little two incher. Some kid had come along, seen its head, pegged a rock, and that was the end of the bird. Well, that was the luck of animal trading. Sadly, I drove down to the Tracy Aviary and was telling my story to Cal Wilson, the director, who just laughed and said that was life. So true! At least it could be laughed about. He did tell me to catch some Sika deer that evening (so as not to get people upset during the day at seeing them being chased around and being caught).

One of my good friends lived in SLC, LaMar McQuaid, who had a service station and had a few animals I had unloaded on him at various times. After he listened to the story of the bird and after voicing his low opinion of some people, he asked if a friend could have it. Sure, I said and unloaded it. It must have stood five ft. high over all and weighed 50 lbs.

We dragged it into the back of a pickup. Later, I heard it had been taken here and there for some amusing times, pulled the leg of a game warden, and used till it got a little ripe.

That evening, LaMar, Tony, another friend, and I headed for the aviary. I had bought some netting at a surplus store to catch the deer in. I was to get six. They weighed about 60-70 lbs. apiece and, while small, were very fast and slippery when you were trying to catch them and they were running in a chain link pen three hundred feet long at the sides and fifty feet on the ends. They would run along the sides just keeping out of reach so we strung a piece of the netting from a tree about 6 ft. from the side and would crowd the deer along the fence till they would try and run through and get caught in the netting.

We were driving one group down when a lone doe jumped over the net onto LaMar's chest and flattened him. It knocked the wind out of him and we all got a great laugh at his discomfort and he got a great deal of kidding from the rest of us for not keeping his hold on the deer. Later I heard the pain from it continued for a couple weeks till he got an x-ray and discovered that he had several ribs cracked and had to have them taped up. Anyhow, he had his fun with the rhea and capturing the deer and had many stories to tell his friends about that night.

On one trip I had unloaded a llama on LaMar at his service station. Now Louie, the llama, was friendly, mooched from everyone, liked attention but had a fault. He was rather sex oriented and you had to be rather careful about getting in front of him for he would try to climb on you. Everybody around got to know him, the police patrol would come by at night and feed him. He just got to be a neighborhood character. LaMar had a farm boy who worked in the lube room who took it on himself to see that the critters were taken care of.

One night a man came by who had been drinking, seriously drinking and started abusing the animal. He left and then came back. He got more abusive and finally the kid told him to leave. No results! With this the kid grabbed him and worked him over good. The man told the police who had come to the hospital that this llama had assaulted him! They did a report, laying the blame on poor Louie. There was much resulting publicity and poor Louie made the trip to the zoo to a pen with others like him, where he could live a more normal life with girl llamas.

LaMar had a bobcat in a good cage that was wheeled out of the lube room in the morning to be looked at by the passing people. Everyone kept a good eye on it. A local doctor supplied vitamins and it got fat and beautiful but the Humane Society ladies would complain about having it here. They said the fumes would bother it. The battle lasted months until I could use it in a movie and took it.

It was going to take at least three days to return from Salt Lake City to Sylmar after loading, a couple of days traveling and a day's stopping along the way to earn enough for expenses.

The last night coming down the large black bear died. Normally bears don't have any disease problems and this bear had been eating well. What happened I don't know and couldn't figure out. All the animals were unloaded in the back yard behind the house, then we headed for Art Bryant's taxidermy shop in Commerce City where we dragged the black bear out of the cage and Art, with a couple of helpers, skinned it out. It would bring me $50 at least for the hide and help with expenses.

Art Bryant was an engaging man who ran a taxidermy shop extraordinaire. He was located in an older part of the city in a large old building crammed with all kinds of taxidermy molds, stuffed animals, hides and tanning equipment. Art and his wife did a regular business and then a movie business on the side. He furnished all kinds of gorilla suits, chimp suits and stuffed animals of all kinds for pictures. Art was the last resort for me. If an animal couldn't be sold or traded and financially couldn't be maintained any longer, Art would take it for a small price for the hide and we would take all the meat for eating if possible.

We usually had an African lion, fallow deer and bear in the freezer. It would be taken to the butcher, ground for hamburger and cut for roast and steaks. Sometimes the kids would come by and we'd ask them if they'd like an African lionburger. Great! They'd stuff one down and ask for more. They really thought we were kidding but they would wolf them down. Art was a good friend who would help us out for things we needed for our shows and could be called on for a stuffed animal to throw off a cliff or a dead one to lay on the ground.

When I got home, Lana was waiting for me with a very important call. A doctor had been calling me from San Jose. I called. A woman came on the line and identified herself as a doctor for the county and asked me about the nightwatchman's finger.

"Well," I said, "Maybe the finger the bear ate disagreed with him, he just died yesterday."

There was a long silence and then a little voice said,

"How about rabies?"

I faintly realized that it somehow had a ten day period of something or other but was vague. She started to get extremely agitated. What happened to the bear? Who had been around it?

I could see bureaucracy was taking over. She phoned later and said the county health lab for Los Angeles was only a block from the taxidermy shop. Could we take a piece of brain in for a test?

The calls started to burn up the wires. Everyone got into the act. Now getting rabies shots was not an easy thing to suffer through. Five or six shots to start and one every few days thereafter all over your stomach. Some 10 to 15 of them and each shot left a 3 or 4 inch section of inflamed skin and swelling which then would start to itch.

Evidently the man was quickly started on his shots in San Jose but I was licked by the bear on the hand so was instructed to report to the Harbor General Hospital in San Pedro fifty miles to the south. I suffered. Why would a bear licking me be a reason for rabies shots?

No one seemed to know. Art, who had cut a finger while skinning, went somewhere else. The helpers, somewhere else. Where was the brown bear? I hedged. I couldn't really believe it was rabies. More phone calls. The lab pronounced the black bear rabid. Now everything broke loose. At the same time a test was sent to the U.S. government lab in Atlanta.

Everyone started the shots with all kinds of results. One of Art's helpers was off work for a month and Art himself went through a severe time. I hated it. It interfered with my time schedule for work. Having to drive fifty miles to Harbor General Hospital in traffic took time; my welts made it hard for me to work and the medics started me on a program of benadril to control the reaction that I was getting from the rabies shots. Then my teeth started to hurt.

The brown bear was killed. Finally the U.S. Lab after a couple of weeks informed everyone that it was not rabid and that the lab for the county had made a mistake. Well, bureaucracy had its way, kept everyone busy, and we had to accept our losses. That was the way of the life of an animal dealer.

6 / Wild Kingdom Tiger Show in Texas

I wasn't well enough to push work too hard and now, working the zoo and driving around the Los Angeles area selling animals, was getting to be too much. In December, the producers of "Wild Kingdom" contracted me to do a show—bengal tigers. I had to furnish the animals, transportation to Waco, Texas, get fencing, and do the work for the cameraman, all for $1,500. That was cheap!—but it was an education.

Marlin Perkins was to go to India, which was in the throes of a drought, film lions in the Gir Forest, and go to another park to film tigers. As usual, when I saw the finished picture, he climbed onto the howdah of an elephant, took out his binoculars, looked through them, and exclaimed.

"Wow! Look at those baby tigers," and proceeded to get out his faithful Bell & Howell movie camera and start filming.

Warren Garst, the chief photographer for Don Meier Productions, who owned the show at that time, and I worked for a solid month putting up the compound and filming what he saw in his binoculars.

A fellow who had worked for the zoo in Waco, Tim Mitchell, quit his job, and joined us as an animal handler. Working my tiger, "Honey", was a scary proposition, for she had come from Africa, USA's compound in Soledad Canyon as one of my trades, and wasn't exactly a good working animal, which was why Ralph got rid of her.

There were two tiger cubs, twenty other Indian animals, and one big peacock. The two cubs provided the heart of the show, along with two Asian otters, who, with their antics, could keep people laughing all the time. There was a sloth bear having a confrontation with the female tiger. Both are a standoff in the wild and normally leave each other alone, but they did stand and hiss and growl at each other for the cameras. When the sloth bear would get mad, he would stand on his back legs and blow saliva out of his pursed-up lips, while making a growling noise. It was very confusing to the tiger, who snarled and struck at the bear with her claws, but would purposely miss. Good for the film, though.

There was a large puddle that had green grass around it for the otters to play in, for they had to do a scene with the tiger cubs. They were jumping and playing around in our arms as they saw the water, and when we turned them loose they would dive and play as fast as they could. Then the tiger cubs were turned loose. They immediately piled into the water and had a free-for-all with the young otters. There was much noise from all the animals playing and with us yelling things for them to do. We seemed to have the idea that they could understand us. Then it was the peacock's turn.

Now the peacock was completely uninitiated in the way of tiger cubs, and didn't move to leave when the cubs charged him. He lost a few tail feathers before he found out that he could get in trouble. After that, we were chasing him a quarter-mile away and pulling him down out of trees, for he found it was much safer there and, besides that, he learned to fly in a hurry to get out of the reach of the cubs.

One of the cubs was put out with a common cobra, with more than a little trepidation. There was nothing to fear though. Cobras are a common snake in India, and that tiger cub knew all about them and put on quite a show. Just instinct! He moved around and teased the snake but wouldn't get in range, even when the snake spread its cape, hissed, and struck. These little snakes kill 50,000 people a year in India.

Colorado Springs Zoo had a good hyena that was young and half tame that was available for the tiger show. $350. Now hyenas just don't seem to be the type of animal for a pet or a good working film animal to me. They don't have the personality or that genuine fondness that an animal can have for his master besides that of just food. Many of my animals, even hungry for food, would leave it and come to be petted for they needed that personal contact between the two of us more than food which they take for granted. Hyenas, no, not for me. Several of my friends used to tell me about wart hogs in Africa. Terrible looking but what a personality they can have and what friendships they can develop. The main thing is that an animal needs to be given love. Like people, if you don't show or tell about love, how will the other person recognize it?

We used this hyena in the compound with the other animals. Everyone expects to see hyenas in India doing something in the background, like eating old carcasses or sneaking around looking hungry. Most people don't realize that there are two types of hyenas: one from South Africa and one from India, and for this show we actually got a genuine Indian hyena.

We had a dead goat for the tiger. It was supposed to have been the tiger's victim and she was taking a few bites on it while we were busy filming. We turned loose the hyena who was supposed to be hungrily lurking around watching, waiting for the bones or something. Instead it went right over to the tiger and snatched the goat right out from under her nose and waltzed away with it. The tiger was furious. She charged over and grabbed on one end of the goat and both began to pull. Neither would let go, and both were threatening each other with all kinds of growls and noises, only those that they could make with their mouths closed, for if either one turned loose now, the other would have the victory. Gradually the goat disintegrated, and both ended up with part of the prize.

It made good filming, and both ate their share of it. Now hyenas supposedly aren't aggressive, but this one always seemed to be. It reminds me of that joke about the two vultures sitting on the limb of an old tree. One looks at the other and says, "Patience my ass, let's go out and kill something."

It was things like this that made up a good show. Put the animals in a controlled situation and they'll often react excitingly. You never know 'til you try. People will ask how I got that great piece of action, and I tell them, "Well, you put one cage here and another one there with the animals in them, open the doors, and run like hell to the camera."

Sounds easy, and sometimes it is. It depends on the execution most of the time. This hyena would do many things, but had no personality for people to relate to.

We had a porcupine shipped in from a Chicago zoo, which would double for an Eastern Indian porcupine, and immediately we used it. It had long quills that stuck out for protection, but it was so used to a cage that it would only go one direction, and that was round and round to the left. It became prey to the tiger, who parted it from a great many of its quills, and it was sent back to Chicago that afternoon, minus some dignity. The zoo protested vehemently to the Wild Kingdom office in Chicago, who had promised to take good care of it. Our ears were closed to the resulting din.

"Honey", the tiger, would prowl the outside fence perimeter, looking for a way out, so an electric hot wire was placed about two feet off the ground to discourage this. She would then walk down the fence, sniff the wire, get a shock, jump away and then walk a little further. The next time around, she would avoid that place by walking way around, and would then go back to the fence.

The reason Texas was picked was that there was still some green grass at that time of year, and it looked good even without the leaves on the trees. It would also match with India when Warren got there to film.

It was Christmas time, and Warren and his wife had me over for dinner. A diet dinner. All of us had put on weight from the great food a cafeteria close by served at $2 for all you could eat. So now it was time to pay the penalty.

Back in Sylmar, Lana was taking care of the animals and trying to cope with a flood. It had rained for two weeks and everything was running with water. As a result, the back neighbor's pool area and lawn was covered with manure from our zoo, and he was furious.

For the first time, one of his calls took effect. The health department sent out an inspector. When the official appeared at the front door, Lana went to work on him, smothering him with kindness, and then, after finding out he had always wanted an ocelot kitten, she agreed to get him one for half-price.

He cited us for having a pile of manure that should be moved out, and said nothing about the animals, or the fact that we had six horses instead of two, and 50 miscellaneous wild animals. To answer the complaint of the neighbor, he informed him that it was an act of God that the manure was washed next door, and that he should pray for the rain to stop.

What I hadn't known about Lana was that she was married when we started living together, and now, she wanted a divorce from that husband. Money, as usual, was at an absolute low. The drawing account against what was coming from "Wild Kingdom" was gone, and I would have to wait until the show was completed to receive what was left.

Lana telephoned me gleefully at my motel, saying that she had gone to Tijuana with a friend and had got a quickie divorce for only $280, which was the last of the money in the bank. I was furious, and I had to borrow money to get home.

By this time it was apparent that Lana had her good times, but also some really, bad ones. She took about anyone in off the streets that needed help, which was commendable, but it resulted in problems, and losses which I couldn't afford.

It had to stop. She took her lows out on herself and they left her mentally unstable at times, and brought on some great fights. When I got home this time it was sheer desperation to survive.

A few days later Lana informed me that she was pregnant! How could she be? Simple, she had stopped taking her pills. Why? Well don't you think we can get married now? No, it would never work. I could see that clearly.

"Well," she said, "at least I tried."

We agreed to stay together until the baby was born.

7/ New York's finest

Tim Mitchell, who had worked for me in Texas, returned to California with me and was staying at Jungleland where I was now storing some of my animals. He was helping me and taking care of many of the animals and going out on some of the shoots.

Africa USA was booming at this time with the "Daktari" series and needed all kinds of tame animals. I furnished many of them so, when it came time for the annual zoo convention at Milwaukee, Ralph Helfer, who owned the compound with Ivan Torsk, decided to send me to the convention to buy animals and to do some trading. Lana, who had convinced me she was quite a truck driver was going to take my truck and trailer and I would take Ralph's semi-trailer to haul the animals.

They had a new GMC tractor and a large furniture van with zebra stripes all over. You couldn't miss it going down the road. The biggest problem was Lana's navigation. She was the type of person who would do just the opposite of what I did. If I wanted to go one way, she wanted to go another. I think I only saw her a couple times in 1800 miles and, if anything had happened, then what? We made it to Milwaukee with only one wrinkled corner of the big trailer. This was forced on me when I couldn't stop in time while going under a train trestle on a little road.

I found a place to get a tame water buffalo and this was too good to pass up. I loaded it at a small zoo and made it to the convention on the nose. Lana appeared at a reception for everyone later that night dressed to the hilt. She certainly was well endowed and could dress in great taste. It was the first time I had seen her like this since we met. She impressed many of the zoo people and stimulated lots of trades at prices that were more than reasonable.

She found a couple of places where we could get a great many fallow deer (white ones) and aoudads for the YO Ranch in Texas and I bought and traded for several animals for Ralph. We met and enjoyed many people at the convention and then headed for Michigan to pick up the deer.

Lana finally got loaded with 55 head of deer and other critters in the trailer and truck, then headed for Texas. I headed on to Linderman's Game Farm in Catskill, New York to pick up a pair of white bearded gnus.

In Pennsylvania at a truck stop, while casually reading a paper, an article popped out at me on the front page. "LARGEST FREEWAY TIEUP IN THE HISTORY OF OHIO'S TURNPIKE! OVERTURNED TRAILER WITH 30 DEER RUNNING LOOSE!"

Well, guess who? It was a rainy night, going around a bend the trailer got away from her and overturned, luckily not hurting her or the truck. There was nothing I could do but worry about it! I tried calling home and couldn't get anyone and when I did her daughter didn't know anything.

The roads in the east weren't what they are in California or the west so it was much slower going, and after 2 days the game farm finally came in sight. It was really out in what they called the mountains. This game farm was very popular with people with just cause for it had a wonderful children's petting zoo, much food to feed the animals and an extremely good breeding program on African animals that made good exhibits. I met with their vet and we discussed the best way to transport the two gnus that Ralph was going to get. That evening Mr. Linderman took me on a tour of his home and art collection which was one of the finest collections of animal art that I had seen, ever.

He sponsored his own artist who went around the world to study the backgrounds, then do his painting. Linderman's home was built of granite as an old German house would be and had a basement where the art collection was hung. It was great meeting his family and having dinner with them for they were enjoyable people who ate the simple kind of food that I enjoyed.

The next day we built a cage in front of the trailer for the gnus, and everything was covered with burlap so they wouldn't be disturbed. There were no windows in the trailer itself and the burlap would protect them from other animals that we had and some that we would load later. They were caught, slightly sedated and moved in. So far so good. We said goodbyes quickly and I moved on to the highway at a steady pace so they would get used to the truck noises and motion. Our next stop was to be the Worlds Fair in New York. That morning I got in touch with Lana's daughter again and found that she had a telephone number for Lana and that I could make contact with her.

The trailer was thirty feet long that Lana was towing, made of steel bridge trusses on the bottom with cages covered with wire, doors for each of 6 cages and the whole thing was roofed with plywood and had a platform that extended four feet out when dropped down to walk on. When it rolled over, some of the roof was torn off and the deer escaped. The front of the trailer where it hooked on the truck was severely damaged, the room damaged and torn loose, but outside of that not too much. The main problem was the deer running around.

The crew from the Cleveland zoo came quickly with capture guns and ropes and everybody pitched in to help. But, with all the deer milling around and everybody chasing them, it really tied up the freeway, especially in the rain.

Several of the deer were killed but she finally ended up with 45. A man very graciously towed her (trailer) into his back yard, welded up the trailer and then repaired the roof and charged her very little for the job. Knowing Lana, she repaid her benefactor well with the tales she could tell of the life of a woman animal dealer.

After getting off the phone with Lana I called Ralph and found that my next job was to repossess two grown African lions from the South African pavilion at the World's Fair. It didn't sound like too much, so I went along quietly to get the animals used to riding, and sleeping myself in the truck for convenience. At eight in the morning I found myself outside the fair on the freeway, driving up and down, trying to find an entrance to the place that a truck could go into.

At nine in the morning it was still quiet around the fair. Especially on a Sunday morning anyplace seems lazy and quiet. There was little traffic on the freeways and I drifted slowly along looking at the sights. What I needed was to find the trade entrance where all the trucks would be coming and going to service the fair and we could get in and park. The signs along the way indicated that the parking lots were for cars only.

Driving around took twenty miles and no indication of an off ramp so taking an exit for a parking lot seemed the right thing to do even if it said cars only. Maybe I could find some information. Swinging to the right on an off ramp brought me to an underpass under the freeway. After going right it made a left swing under the freeway and here was the rub; it had two lanes going in one direction and, when I got there, I found that the clearance for the trailer was 12 ft. and I was 13½. Now what?

I parked the truck on the grass to the right. There was no way to turn back and go against the traffic that was slowly coming into the parking lot. Now what to do? Finally I decided to call the police. I walked to the top of the overpass, down the freeway a half mile, crawled over the fence to a service station and called. Slowly I walked back to the overpass and stood and waited for the patrol. The traffic got heavier and heavier.

Normally a state highway patrol car would handle this and I knew they'd see what I'd done and really chew me out and probably hand me a ticket.

Finally an old black and white pulled up. Out came a cop that was right out of TV....Whatsa matter? I pointed to the truck at the bottom of the overpass. He looked at the truck, spat like one of the old western sheriffs (as a matter of fact, he looked like one), gun hanging low from a pair of pants that sagged under his stomach, old open shirt with old equipment and badge. He looked at the striped trailer, at me with my beard and plaid shirt and squinted.

"Where you from anyhow?"

I used my best old country twang, "Idahooo."

"What'ya got in there?"

"Wild animals," I said, wishing I had some chewing tobacco to spit. "Gotta repossess a couple African lions from the South African exhibit." I felt more like a bounty hunter just now.

He looked at me, raised his eyebrows, spit, looked at the truck, said, "Let's do something."

Now the freeway was beautifully landscaped with lawn, trees and 10 lanes of traffic. By now it was running full! We walked down to the truck; heavy traffic was now coming off the freeway. I got in and started the truck, wondering what was coming He motioned me to follow him. Blowing his whistle, he stepped out in traffic, raised his hand and stopped the ramp traffic.

He walked across the road with my semi right behind him, casually walking along seemingly oblivious of anything going on around him. We went onto the grass on the other side of the road, around trees, over trees, back up to the freeway on the grass. My eyes bugged out as he casually walked out into 5 lanes of traffic, holding up his arm to stop traffic and blowing his little whistle. I swear, I could hear rubber burning for two miles as cars came to screeching halts. (What that man couldn't have done to a wild cattle stampede a hundred years ago!) With the semi slowly bumping over the curbs and onto the freeway, everybody stared.

I was following right behind as he casually walked to his car, got in, turned on his red light and headed down the freeway.

Now the traffic was building up again. He speeded up now and he had his light and siren going, dodging traffic at 65 mph. It was all the truck could do to follow. Finally we took an exit, roared around a couple of turns and there was the truck gate. He roared up to the guard shack, got out and started talking to the guard gesturing in my direction.

Coming back he pointed to a spot to park and now, as my feet shakily touched the ground, I was going to get the greatest traffic ticket ever. When I thought of all that grass, those nice little trees, wow! Walking around the truck I was just in time to see what I couldn't believe. The cop was roaring off on the horizon, in a cloud of dust and gravel, ready to take on the world again.

My opinion of New York's finest had changed. Meanwhile, the guard smirked as he looked over the truck.

"Going to repossess some lions, eh?"

I knew it was going to be bad and it was. Those people in the African pavilion needed those lions! What would happen if they were taken? They had native drummers and dancers and they needed lions! The wires hummed between Africa, USA and the African exhibit.

After a day and a half it was decided that one African lion was going. I got it in one of my cages, loaded it, and headed for Philadelphia. It was two days of work but I got to see a lot of the fair.

Looking at the map I could see it was by far the easiest to go to the Holland Tunnel and straight to Philly. I wound around the streets of New York finally getting to the tunnel and started in. All hell broke loose! Red lights, sirens, people waving their arms and running after me. I casually stopped, looking around.

"What's the matter?" I said.

"You can't go through our tunnel," a couple of them said. "You're too tall."

"Oh, how am I going to get off this island?"

"Who cares, but not this way," they said.

Again I blocked traffic, turned around in the mouth of the tunnel and out into traffic. I parked on a little side street, and again called the fuzz. Two of them this time in a black and white. Same stuff.

"Ok, how do I get off the island?" I asked

"Well, you can try the Lincoln Tunnel; it's about eight miles up the island," they said.

I tried. Same results, sirens and bells. Finally made it to the George Washington bridge and over. The Philadelphia Zoo had a small hippo for me to pick up by four o'clock. Figuring the time I could make it fine, only I didn't plan on getting lost. Leaving the freeway

1 / John Lily about to rope "Missie" the jaguar for *Wild Kingdom*.

2 / The weather got plenty hot filming in Blanding, Utah.

3 / Marlin Perkins and Jim Fowler at Circle Z Ranch in Nogales.

4 / John Lily and his dogs tree my mountain lion at Circle Z.

5 / After the action commenced. *Wild Kingdom* show in Utah.

6 / "Missie" resting beneath the camera. Ralph Nelson, Marlin, and Don Meier.

7 / Doing a sand painting in a hogan on the Navajo reservation.

8 / Indian Hyena on the *Wild Kingdom* show in Waco, Texas.

somehow I started to wander the beautiful countryside of north Philadelphia which was nice but, when I came in at 5:30, everyone was furious. No one worried about unions in the west and getting rid of animals was always exciting, so everyone hung around, but not here. This whole crew was on overtime and management wasn't happy. Where was the crate to put this hippo in?

"Well, I thought I'd put it behind this partition."

"Are you kidding?" They showed me the baby. A thousand pounds of fury. Calling Ralph, it was agreed that I write a check for a two hundred dollar deposit on a steel lined crate they would furnish, but which had to be returned. After a struggle, they got it loaded. Now hippos are placid looking animals but one is like a train when turned loose, and downright dangerous when mad. Finally, it was loaded with much grumbling. I can see why they stayed around and got it loaded, to be finished with it. Now I headed down the road for the Busch Gardens in Tampa to deliver the African lion.

8 / Augie Busch takes delivery

Traveling through the southern states should have been a vacation for me, leisurely stopping to feed and water the animals. There was a trailer full by this time, in fact double-decked, and to take care of my work I used the truck for sleeping most of the time. The highways were concrete, bumpy for the size of the truck and trailer, and not especially well taken care of.

Stopping at the first weigh station in North Carolina brought a rude surprise. Where is your truck license? Well, I just got in the state. OK, that'll be a $30 fine. You can pay now or, if you want to plead innocent, I'll call the judge and arrange a hearing for you next week. The license will cost you $20 for a one day permit to get through the state. He wrote up a license receipt with all the official stamps on it for $20 and asked what I wanted to do. Of course there was only one answer so I paid. He pulled out a five and dime receipt book and wrote me a receipt for $30. He would use this trick on out-of-state truckers for a little money on the side and maybe split it with the JP. Going through Georgia brought a similar surprise. Got flagged down by a patrolman on a lonely stretch, extorted out of $25 for a fine right on the highway. Some of these cops should be making pretty good money with their own receipt books.

Finally I made it to Busch Gardens in Tampa, tired but happy, for now the lion could go. His roaring didn't do much for the gnus

64

in the trailer.

Busch Gardens was a zoo that was designed to look like an African veldt. There was much grass and the exhibits were built on an island surrounded by concrete moats you couldn't see. The moats were fifteen feet deep and thirty feet across and to get to the island you went down into the moat, opened a door into the island and went up to the top. When I got there the cage was pulled out of the trailer with a lift bucket on the front of a tractor and taken to the edge of the moat.

There it would have to be dropped into the moat and the lion released. Among others, Augie Busch was there and insisted that a gun be brought to him for my safety when I went down and opened the door to release the lion. I was going to stand on top of the cage, open the door and wait for the lion to leave. I was sure he would go straight away, find the door into the island and go there, but I had to be prepared to go up the cable in case he came after me.

Augie had been drinking and gave me a feeling of uncertainty— whether the lion or the gun would get me in case something happened. Releasing the cat was as expected, he took off in a run for a hundred ft., stopped to see what was bothering him on top of the cage, and left, walking around the moat to see what was going on. He found the open door, walked upstairs and joined the others on the top. The crew lifted up the cage with me on it, loaded it in the back of the truck and I headed for the Miami zoo to load a giraffe.

Finding my way to the zoo in the dark was one sizable accomplishment; getting a small male giraffe loaded in the back of a furniture van loaded with animals was going to be another.

The van was seven ft. wide inside and about 10 ft. tall, and there was about 4 ft. inside the door that could be used. The director of the zoo had rounded up 4 or 5 people to help load, lights were found for the job, but I could see that it was going to be confusing for the giraffe. The hippo was just inside with his cage crosswise and above him were other cages. We nailed lumber and put bales of straw up against the back so he could climb the three ft. to get up and in.

One door was left open—all got around the poor little guy and pushed. Luckily, he was tame and went right in gracefully. He was so nice! If Ralph wanted a good working giraffe this should be it.

Thanking everyone, I pulled out, drove out of the city 'til there was a quiet spot and went to sleep. The next morning I got on the phone with Ralph and talked. No, he said, we could trade this little one and some money for a female at Memphis. Go and trade. OK...

It was morning of the second day out of Miami when the zoo in Memphis came in sight. Everyone was waiting, for the telephone had been warm between Ralph and the zoo. The small giraffe was quickly and easily unloaded. He ambled out of the trailer very unconcernedly then I backed up to another gate where they had thrown up a temporary fence for a catch pen to load the big one. Everyone was inside and gently herding her to the section where she would be enclosed and herded into the truck.

She went in to the catch corral and then panicked from the animals in the truck. Giraffes have long legs but really can't climb much, so she simply bulled her way through the fence to freedom into the main giraffe area. She started to run, turned, and then fell in an awkward heap and lay there. We all walked over and examined her. She was bright eyed but wouldn't try to stand. We all grouped around her, lifted her to her feet but she didn't seem to care whether she stood or not and wouldn't hold her head up. If you can imagine six to eight grown men standing under the belly of a giraffe attempting to hold it on its feet and talking and yelling to it all the time to "get with it baby."

Finally a vet was called. It was the zoo's job to get it on board. All afternoon we worked on it. It was hot and humid and the sweat was running off everyone in streams. Later, it was decided to take another small female. This time we found a large crate that we could use for the small one. It was about 8 ft. high and just large enough for the animal. She also got excited and knocked more fences down but finally she was loaded on the truck. Everyone was worn out and later Ralph said the large female had died. Broken neck.

Lana still wasn't home, she stayed at the YO in Texas for ten days at the behest of the ranch owner to see how many of the injured deer would survive. Finally, she left for Waco to pick up some alligators. Talking by phone with her left me shaken. She listened but I knew she was already plotting how she would do it, *her way!* They were 7-8 footers, big ones, and would have to be tied up for the trip, just right!

Two days later, while going in to feed the animals, I found the giraffe dead. It had not been eating well or drinking too well but then most of them are like that until they learn to relax after two or three days. It was a blow, and Ralph wasn't at all happy about it. I got back to California from the trip—unloaded the animals, including the dead giraffe, which went to Art Bryants and everything else was in good shape. 9,400 miles in 40 days. Some trip. Ten days in beds was all I could find receipts for.

Ralph called me a couple of days later and talked to me about a young hyena that I had picked up along with everything else. He started hemming and hawing over the phone.

"Now Dick, about this hyena."

"Oh? What's wrong?"

"Well, it's his dingus."

"His what?" I replied.

"Well, you know...his dilliewacker....."

"Oh...well...."

"Well, when he walks, it touches the ground sometimes!"

I said, "Hhhhmmmmmmmmm."

He said, "What am I going to do? I can't have him filmed like this—you know he's ah, funny-looking."

I was hardly controlling myself but he was serious. I knew it was something the animal would outgrow but Ralph was a little naive sometimes.

"Well," I said, "if you take a needle and thread and stitch it up for filming it might work." He seemed satisfied at this, but it was a source of much amusement for the crew and me for some time.

Ralph put in for an insurance claim on the giraffe, $5,000, and blamed me for hitting an underpass on the way home, scaring the giraffe and causing it to die. I had to sign a statement for the insurance company. I wouldn't say anything that incriminated me and it made Ralph a little mad but he did collect for it. He was pretty sharp with a dollar. He hardly ever came out on the short end; also I must say his taste in women was for real good lookers.

Two days later came another headline in the local paper.

"WOMAN LOSES ALLIGATORS"

Seems Lana stopped to sleep in a motel in Dallas and the alligators took off. Fortunately they were spotted and the police arrived. They didn't know what to do but they found her trailer, woke her up, and found she didn't know what to do either. She called the man in Waco, which was 150 miles and waited with the alligators 'til the crack of dawn when he arrived. She showed him how to tie them up properly this time, as I had instructed her in the first place, and with everybody breathing sighs of relief, Lana headed off into the sunrise.

She picked up a lion cub I had located for her and when it got sick they stopped at a vets in Kingman, Arizona for a week. A week after I got home she finally arrived. What a costly trip!

Gradually our animals were being moved to Jungleland in Thousand Oaks. They let me rent an area in the far back by some large barns that would work out well for me. There were some sheds that I rejuvenated. They had been storage sheds so new concrete was laid in for floors, the cages were put in on blocks so we could hose them down and keep everything clean. A new pool was made for my pet hippo and everything cleaned up. This gave me a whole new outlook by being legal, for the thought of losing all the animals with one slip at Sylmar kept me from doing much in the way of improvement. Being nervous all the time while gone was not my kind of life and Lana and I were gradually separating on a friendly basis. Tim would spend many late evenings at the ranch keeping her entertained for I liked going to bed at 10:30 after the news and she at one or two, so Tim would play cards with her half the night. She was really getting large by this time and the baby would soon arrive.

One evening when I got back to the ranch I found that one of my fallow deer had escaped during the day and was wandering around the neighborhood. Around Los Angeles these deer were used as Christmas displays so people were aware of what they were and called them reindeer. Tim, who had come home with me, had fixed a syringe onto the end of an arrow so we could shoot and capture something if we had the right drug and could figure out the dosage. He was a nut for bow hunting and the inside of his pickup was covered with skins, claws and claw-necklesses, with bows and quivers of arrows in the back windows. He put on his camouflage suit, fancy hat, and got all the paraphernalia ready with the arrows.

It didn't take long to find the deer but then it was hard to get close to, and we ended up chasing it through olive orchards, horse corrals, and back yards. Finally, on the edge of the road, peering into an olive grove we could just about see him. Both of us got down low and started to stalk him.

"What're y'after fella's—deer?" a huge voice behind us boomed out.

Both of us jumped from the sound of the voice and looked around. There stood a red-faced cop stooping down behind us peering out into the orchard to see what we were looking at. The two of us were so intent on the deer we didn't even hear him pull up much less see him. The deer was gone.

"Well!" I said to Tim, "we've got enough practice for tonight. Let's head for home."

The cop shook his head as he got in the patrol car and took off.

We headed for home as fast as possible and hid out again. Got a call the next day. Some people had the deer in a corral. They knew some friends who knew us and got our telephone number. What luck!

9 / Snakes eat on Thursdays

One of my best friends in the animal business was Ray Folsom of Hermosa Reptile and Animal Farm in Hermosa Beach, California. He had a large store crammed with reptile exhibits, animal cages with all kinds of reptiles to sell and animals as he had them. He'd been in business for years and, before that, had a colorful career of flying and odd jobs for odd people. Ray had done a lot of flying in Central America hauling all kinds of things including government agency supplies into Cuba.

When working at Ross Allen's Reptile Farm in Florida years before, I had seen a picture of him and his Lockheed Electra.

He was what you would call slightly stout and had a beautiful red haired wife that looked about like Tina Louise. He also had one of the most beautiful rattlesnake collections in the world in his bedroom and that really impressed me. He had forty-three out of approximately forty-five kinds of rattlesnakes and that was really something.

Thursday night was feeding night at the shop. He had such a large collection that he would have to provide a lot of live food for the reptiles; so, once every week, the feeding was done after the customers had left for the evening. Some people would get very distressed at seeing snakes eating live chicks and mice but there were a few select people who liked to come to see this ritual.

70

Never Kick A Bear in Your Bedroom Slippers

One slightly inebriated visitor leaned into a rattlesnake exhibit and fell in. He barely survived the trip to the hospital where he stayed a month. His arm was badly crippled but he acknowledged that it was no fault of Ray's and that he would be better behaved after that.

Ray had met his wife, Ginny, at a party in Panama where she had lived with a husband, then subsequently she split, cleaned out the bank account, took her children and everything she could carry, came to Hermosa Beach and moved in with Ray. He was not too hot about the kids but Ginny stayed for months 'til she talked him into marrying.

Ray and I traded animals, and bought and sold animals together, and went on trips for a little excitement once in a while especially if we could do some business. We had traded for years for he was one of the best contacts for foreign animals for the WK shows, and others that I worked on and, when he told you what an animal was, its condition and how tame it was, his word could be believed.

Ray knew a man who had a small zoo on a tourist pier in Redondo Beach, which catered to charter fishing boats and tourists that were sight-seeing on vacations. They had some good eating places, souvenir stores, and the zoo.

The problem was that not quite enough people were coming through to handle the pay roll, food bill and the management's salary. They had a 10%-of-the-gross deal with the owners, or a minimum of $300 a month, and it was hard to make it. He sold off most of his animals then we took over, keeping the same man that he was using for clean up and feeding, and we put our own animals in for exhibit, for we were just keeping some 'til they were sold. I used my little hippo which was tame; used this with a miniature horse, small goats, chicken and ducks and a small pond for them to play in. The little hippo was in love with the horse and would go around carrying the horse in his mouth 'til the little horse got tired of it. The goats would all stand around on top of the hippo and play king of the mountain. Hippos are herd animals and enjoy being around others.

It was hard to find someone to run the place for one reason or another. While we were gone Ginny would take over and bring the food, do the banking and see that some things got done but with

71

the shop to run she couldn't do everything.

One fellow we had as manager was spending more time running a private harem than the zoo for he would always be propositioning women that came through and then didn't show up home at night so his wife would come by the apartment looking for him. Both of us knew he'd be down in the office at the zoo with the lights off and refusing to answer the door or telephone. We went down a couple of times, unlocked the door, walked in, and ran him out of some compromising situation. Ray would keep telling him to leave the dollies alone, but no.

Finally there was a big explosion or rather a non-explosion. Ray was always looking out for me and trying to find a woman for me and one Sunday afternoon he got talking to a nice lady at the reptile shop, found that she was looking for someone just like me, was very attractive and lonely. He told her to go down and talk to Dick at the zoo and gave me a real build up.

She got there, asked for me and was told that I was gone. Instead this creep took her for himself, left the place with her and disappeared. When I got back from coffee there wasn't anyone around. Later I called Ray to find what happened to the man and if he was around the shop. No. Then he told me the story. Ah hah.... Later the man's wife showed up looking for him. The visiting lady must have been really something for no one saw him for months. Ray and I kidded about this for some time.

Lana went to work for Ray in the shop after she had her baby and had left the ranch. She moved in with her mother in Compton and then started in the shop working at cleaning cages and selling reptiles.

She and Ginny were at odds all the time woogying at each other. Lana wouldn't come to work on time and was often an hour or two late which upset everyone. Someone gave her some mice. She bought some cages, then got more mice and became a full fledged mouse-rancher. It took up half of a garage and an hour's work in the morning before she could leave for her job. The two things just didn't work together. Lana was not in tune with her job so she quit to work for herself.

She and Tim had given up their relationship and now Lana had a new boyfriend. A couple of months later they got married. Lana found that feeding and selling hundreds of mice was hard work and very time consuming so she left mouse ranching and decided on pottery. Later she moved to Nevada and disappeared as far as I was concerned.

One of my big problems at that time was Ray's wife. She and Lana had argued about who had the best figure and whatever women argue about. Ginny knew, of course, that Lana and I were not living together anymore and that Lana had had the baby and now had a new life. Ginny had a crush on me. I was living at the apartment when I was in town so I was around a good deal of the time. She would call the shop in the morning and ask Ray to have me come over and check the books with her, so I'd go over there. Everyone knew that book-keeping was my downfall. There wouldn't be anyone there but Ginny and I, and invariably she would be in a house coat that would be revealing to say the least. She would get talking about how much better her figure was than Lana's and ask if I didn't think that her breasts were nicer. I'd just grunt; my throat was dry.

It was difficult but I never once gave her a tumble; I knew that Ray was aware of what was going on but whether he cared or not was not the question. It was just plain no; not with my best friend's wife. This went on 'til she got mad! When Ray made a trip to the Far East and I went on a TV show out of town, Ginny got her revenge. There was a trailer load of my animals that was being fed close to the zoo. I arranged with her to have one of the fellows feed them every day. But she turned me into the ASPCA. She told them I abandoned the animals. They got me on the phone and told me what happened and I arranged for someone else to look after them.

From then on she bad-mouthed me for years about one thing or another. Makes you wonder sometimes about which course of action you should take. Ray would listen to Ginny talking about me and he would shrug his shoulders. We never needed to talk about it. We always stayed friends. A year or two later, Ginny took a bunch of snakes to Alaska for Gene Holter's circus and ended that trip by

DICK ROBINSON

running off with the drummer of a band.

We had the zoo for 8 or 9 months, then the owners decided that they could make more with a souvenir store.

10

Pinch her tail and make her snarl

Movie work was the exciting part of my career. Also the hardest. "Wild Kingdom" had another show to do on mountain lions in Tucson, the typical show with the dogs chasing a cat, capturing and taking it to a zoo. It did have one funny part though.

Warren Garst, with whom I had worked in Texas, had brought along his VW camper, and had the side door open and the canopy out so we could have lunch and refreshments in the shade. It was running 110° out and it was hot! A couple of hundred yards away we were filming with the cat up a rock, and by this time the cat had been working so hard her paws were bloody from wearing them on the sandstone; she was uncomfortable, so when the dogs closed in on her, she headed for the camper at full speed.

When that mountain lion and 6 dogs disappeared inside it was quite a sight. When we got there we found the cat crouched on top of the engine compartment in the back where she could comfortably fight the dogs off. Everyone grabbed a dog while I got the lion back and leashed up. I asked Warren if he had filmed it, and he replied, "No," that he had been laughing too hard. Well, why not do it again and film it?

We did, but Warren chickened out. He thought Don Meier might not appreciate it. Warren's wife wasn't on location, but when he took the camper back to the motel and she saw it, she threw a tizzy. She was extremely fastidious, and it took a couple of days to wash the blood stains and dirt out of the camper. She was very ticked off. We finished a good show, though.

Another show was waiting for us as soon as the Wild Kingdom show was finished. It was only a two-day job at Kanab, in SE Utah, where they do a great many outdoor western flicks.

The story was of a burro in the Grand Canyon, and, of course, many people. Joseph Cotton starred. We found we were going to work on a ranch about 10 miles from town where the rock structure looked like that of the canyon.

My main job was to stage a fight between the cat and a burro, have the cat jump off a ledge onto the burro and supposedly attack it. That was all right. The movie company had a father and son team, mountain lion hunters, in from around Bisbee, Arizona to bring a wild mountain lion and have it chased by the dogs, run up a tree and be caught. They arrived just as I was going to have my cat attack the burro from on top a small cliff. The son ran up to me at the top, asked how he could help, and I showed him.

Take one hand hold on the skin of the neck and one at the base of the tail and I would do the same thing from the other side. We swung it between us and at a signal it flew through the air on top of the burro and there was general pandemonium. It worked great; we did it again and everyone was satisfied.

We worked the next day with the cat doing a fight with the wild burro under a huge cliff. Worked fine with one of Art Bryant's phony burro legs.

Now the next day I would stay and see what happened with the wild one. These people had never done this for a movie before so I helped them figure out what to do. They were to get some shots of their dogs chasing and treeing the cat using their wild lion.

The photographers set out their camera for the cat to run by, and then follow them as the dog's tree'd it. Everything worked great! The cat streaked out, ran a quarter mile in nothing flat and tree'd. He sat in the top of a juniper tree and snarled his best. Only one problem; just a streak went by the camera. We filled in by using my cat posing here and there, snarling at the dogs, running back and forth, so it worked out well. Everyone went home happy. I could always make the cat snarl by pinching her tail so I would pose her on a rock, get out of sight and pinch. Great snarls. Everyone liked the action.

11/ Wild Kingdom Jaguar Show

Don Meier contacted me about another WK show in Arizona using my jaguar and another whole group of desert animals that I would put together. It sounded good. Not only did I need the money but the work was satisfying and showing me some direction for my future. Learning how to move actors back and forth, which direction for cutting, what a neutral was, new words to find understanding for, and how to build a show to make it interesting for the public. I took the offer.

Screen credits started to make sense to me. They wouldn't tell people that they were using someone else's animals so I became an "ASSOCIATE PRODUCER" with my name at the end of the show. It was getting to be well earned too.

Missie, my jaguar, was a great cat, but slow and bull-headed, never listening to anyone and really rough at times, but then, if you put her in the right situation, she would react accordingly and you could get some great filming. A local pet shop had a couple of jaguar cubs, 4 months old and extremely playful, that could be bought and then sold back to the owner, besides some other animals: small spotted desert skunks, lizards, a mountain lion, coyotes, a badger and others. The Circle Z ranch, close to Patagonia, was chosen as headquarters. About 20 miles north of Nogales, it was in the hill country of the desert. It was beautiful.

Never Kick A Bear in Your Bedroom Slippers

Marlin Perkins, Jim Fowler and Don Meier, the producers and owner of the show came, along with Ralph Nelson, the photographer, and a couple more. One of the characters in the show this time was going to be John Lilly. He was married to Gail Lee, who came from a famous family of mountain lion hunters and John was a great nephew or something of old Ben Lilly, the famous bear hunter. John rode in the show mounted on a white mule. He talked a great story but really knew little about movies and animals which we all recognized. The cat was supposedly in trouble and Jim Fowler and Lilly were to catch it and to take it to a zoo to keep from having to kill it. They were going to drop a large rope net over it and put it in a box.

Lilly always was high on this riding mule and one day everyone was standing around the camera with the jaguar lying, resting underneath the tripod. John, on his mule, was standing about 50 ft. in front of us in a rocky patch. The cat got her eye on the mule, moved swiftly on her stomach and then rushed him. She jumped clear to the front of the saddle where John got a whack at her but the mule panicked. It went up and down about as high as any horse I ever saw with the cat just sitting on the ground watching. John, after the first couple of bucks, went flying into the rocks. Slowly he got up to much laughter and kidding.

"How come you got off, John?"

"Jumped," he said, "didn't want the mule to get hurt. Falls over backward sometimes."

He never heard the end of that episode, even his wife was laughing.

That afternoon one of the Mexicans came charging up in a pickup and asked to see Mr. Robinson. He was from the ranch and announced that I had an important phone call, an emergency. I jumped in the pickup along with the Mexican while the crew started working on some shots that would fit in without my help and we headed for the ranch at top speed. We flew down the highway, into the gravel drive of the ranch and screeched to a halt in front of the lodge where there was a large group of dudes. Great show! Going inside I was handed a number which wasn't familiar to me at

79

all, but I went to the phone, and had the call put through. It rang and rang and finally, a bank came on. I said this was Dick Robinson and they said to hang on. In a short time a female voice came over the wire and said a name. Ah hah! A woman friend that I knew, but what could she want?

"Dick,... there's a little problem," she said.

"My God...you're pregnant?"

"No—no but I think I might have contracted something."

"Whatdya mean think?"

"Well, I know."

"Oooooooh...."

"You better get a shot."

"You too."

With this we terminated the conversation. This was indeed an emergency. What about my other girl friends? What was going to happen to my relationships with all those beautiful and interesting women?

"Any serious trouble, Mr. Robinson?" the girl from the office interrupted my thoughts.

"No, nothing that can't be cured." Oh, what a terrible pun, I thought.

The man came back and met me at the door to take me out to the set and he was very concerned.

"Hope everything is all right, Mr. Robinson."

"Oh, sure, just a small problem at home."

We drove back to the filming and I jumped out quickly and went back to the crew where there many questions and I told everybody that I'd have to make it into town for an hour or so. There were more questions that evening but I steered around them for they had made a big thing at the ranch about it.

The next day I took the truck and headed off to find a doctor in Nogales, Arizona. There were two Nogales, one on the Mexican side and one on the American side. Finding an office through the phone book, I came to the edge of the downtown district and a clinic where I went in and told the office girl that I needed to see the doctor. She asked for what? I told her. He didn't waste any time on me.

"You think you need a shot? You been with the girls? Across the river?" he asked, all in one breath. They had a large red light district across the river where the Americans went.

"You'll have such and such a strain," he mouthed off an exotic sounding strain of VD.

"No, this is LA," I mumbled.

"Well, doesn't make any difference, Nurse, give him a million units of penicillin."

With this I dropped my pants, got my shot, paid the bill and headed back.

Either I never needed the penicillin or it worked overnight.

We would sit at large tables at the Circle Z to eat boarding-house style and I got to meet many of the guests this way and had a chance to talk to them. There was a German girl from the east who had come by herself on an arranged package tour. She hung her head and blushed any time someone talked to her. Once someone made a kidding remark and she just jumped up from the table and ran out of the room. After that everyone was careful what they said. Usually, after dinner people would rest, go for an outside walk or get together socially. One night I got talking to her and found that if she got away from people she would talk a blue streak. She told me all her troubles, went with me to feed the animals and followed me to bed.

The show went well; the two little jaguar cubs were the best part of it for they did the main part of the work with their antics and playing with the other animals, also showing their curiosity toward everything. They seemed to develop a real affection for me and would follow me anyplace. We had a river about 15 ft. wide that ran down a wash and, when I would run and splash through it, they would follow. They'd leap the first couple feet and swam as hard as they could, holding their little heads up and paddling with their front paws, getting washed down the creek sometimes twenty feet or more but they never failed to follow and were great to film.

The actors didn't stay long, for each one would just come in for his part and would leave after 3 or 4 days; and then the camera people and I would do the rest of the show.

As Cheeta now was big it was tough to fit him in an act so he could work. Breaking in four half grown lions for a cage act in my arena was keeping me busy, but I decided to give Cheeta a try and see if he would still work with the whip and a cat. These lions were 150-200 lb. cats, good size. We moved Cheeta's cage up to the arena, put a cover on the top so he couldn't climb out, and turned him loose with one of the cats which was very tame. Cheeta used the whip, the cat roared and Cheeta, throwing down the whip, grabbed the cat by the tail and stopped him from running and then moved to the front end.

Grabbing an ear with one hand so the cat couldn't bite, getting a hold of the lion's two front paws with his own feet, he then proceeded to poke his finger from the one free hand into the eye of the lion. Of course the lion got furious but Cheeta wouldn't let go and the cat couldn't do anything but roar in frustration.

Some act! I picked up the whip and flicked it at Cheeta who then got mad at me. He ruffed his fur out straight as he glared at me. That would be a fight it wasn't worth getting into, so carefully moving them apart and getting them both back in their respective cages was a very sensitive job. Both of them just wanted to tussle with someone.

One old lion lying around in a transfer cage was waiting to go on a Tarzan show in Mexico City. He was about 15 yrs. old, hardly any teeth, but big! When I'd first seen it at the Salt Lake City zoo and had been told that they would trade it for a young cub and some other trade, I decided I wanted it. I could reach through the bars of his cage and pet him and he loved the attention. He'd been someone's pet before he came to the zoo and had never been abused. When I went to get him we couldn't get the cage close enough to get him in so, putting a chain around his neck, I just lead him to a cage and he jumped in. My cage was 4 ft. high and he just came to the top. One of the fellows who worked chimps for the Tarzan show was in Burbank buying animals for the Mexico City Studio. He was getting an elephant and buying a truck to haul animals down so I made him a deal if he would take the lion. We would split the price, $250 for him and $250 for me. He agreed if the cat was tame and workable. I assured him it was!

Would I show him? Of course. I pushed the cage up to the arena and turned him loose inside. The lion walked around a few minutes and lay down about 19 ft. from the door and with his back toward me. Taking a leash chain and going through the arena door, chirping to the cat to let him know I was coming, was scary. Damn scary! but I needed the money and wanted the cat out, to a better home. Leaving the door unlatched and opened an inch left me with an exit for a quick get-away in case something happened.

Talking all the while, I walked up quietly behind him and patted him on the mane. He was big, especially kneeling beside him. Slipping the leash around his neck quickly and making it look casual, seemed easy, but I left it unlatched on the end. Getting to his feet to attack me would take time, and I could be out of there before he could get far. Petting him some more just made him more contented and he lashed his tail, then turned his huge head, looked me right in the eye and let out one of the loudest, most earth-shaking roars imaginable. Deafening! I quickly slipped off the chain, slowly nonchalantly walked to the door with the man looking approvingly on. Good cat, huh! Sure good, I'll take it. What a relief and it meant a drop in my food bill when he left!

I heard later that the cat worked well but had a tendency to chase Mexicans who interfered with his way of acting. He really couldn't hurt anything for his teeth were all worn off but I imagine he could gum pretty hard.

12/ *Toe-Toe toes the mark*

While scouting around in the valley for animal traders one day, I ran into a situation where some animals that needed attention were being disposed of. It's nice to have animals but there is a responsibility for their upkeep on a daily basis and these animals weren't cared for. The people who kept them were publicity freaks who used the critters for raising money. So several of us bought some animals to help out and that started more happenings.

I ended up with a chimp. One dealer and owner of a pet shop sensed that there was something in it for him and sued me over it. I had $700 in the chimp and it would be a chance to make a couple hundred for a little basic training that I could do. The chimp was young, spoiled, but nice looking and had possibilities. The law suit didn't bother me much for this individual sued everyone in sight, had a reputation, and would on occasion get a little money on a settlement. Later Ralph took the chimp from me for $900 and started to have some of the girls work it. In "Daktari" it was called "Toe-Toe."

I had spent three days just teaching him to stay on a chair on command, and to obey. He would do things but had his own mind that needed changing! It was hard work for he needed to learn to respond everytime there was a command given and he fooled around for a couple days before he got the idea. Of course it took my belt for awhile but then he was great. Tender Loving Care with discipline!

This chimp was moved from one minimum security training compound that had a garden type setting, with a place for snakes, to the old hospital at Africa, USA, where they had cages, work areas for feeding, and facilities for semi-sick animals that needed attention. The chimp was put in a cage with these and a woman by the name of Louise became the trainer for him. She was in her early twenties, interested in the animals and was a very responsible woman who worked hard at her job.

One day I stopped in to see how she was making out, and she was telling me her problems of making "Toe-Toe" toe the mark. She couldn't get him to go back in his cage. I laughed and asked what she was doing for discipline?

"Well," she said, "I take a piece of paper, newspaper, roll it up and tap his face."

She was so serious I had to laugh. That was no way to train a chimp.

"Look, I'll show you what you need." I picked up a big heavy mixing spoon about a foot long. "This is the type of thing you need to impress him."

"But, Dick, what would Mr. Helfer do? He forbids this sort of thing."

"Yeah," I replied, "but Mr. Helfer doesn't get bit and he only looks for results. You show him the results! Let me show you about chimps," I told her, and went over to the cage, opened it and took the chimp out by the hand, led him over to a table and sat him down.

"Let me show you what you have to do to impress a chimp." I took his arm up to my mouth and took a bite as hard as I could on the meaty forearm. When I let go you could see a ring of teeth marks and the skin puckered up. The chimp took his other hand and with his finger pointed to the marks and said,

"Ou Ou Ou..."

Then taking his head in my hands I pulled his ear over and bit it as hard as I could, then let go. He reached around and felt his ear and looked at me.

DICK ROBINSON

"Ou Ou Ou...Ou?"

I then took the spoon and gave him a hard whack on the head and told him to get in his cage. He did so with alacrity and even closed the door behind him. Her eyes were round.

"What you have to do is explain clearly what you want. Gesture with your hands along with the words for they learn from the movement and gradually from the words. You haven't got time to give them a reward everytime they do something on a show so they need something else to convince them. Maybe this spoon."

I saw this little chimp many times in the series and he worked great.

When it came time for the lawsuit over the chimp, it was dismissed. It was just blackmail by a greedy animal dealer and his lawyer.

13 / *An odd smell*

A visitor came by one day and asked if he could buy Cheeta from me. He had been shopping around for a male chimp and someone had steered him to me. This man had a difficulty talking too well. His face was scrunched a little to the right and his mouth had an "O" to it that made talking a problem. He told me that after a few more operations he'd be all right. Naturally this aroused my curiosity and I asked him what the problem was.

He told me that he'd bought this zoo in South Dakota, where he was from, and that he'd always liked African lions, so...since he owned the zoo he had walked into a female lion's cage and petted her. She didn't like this so she expressed herself. She had his head in her mouth and was holding him when a tourist came by, going through the zoo. The tourist asked what was going on and the new owner shouted that the cat had the wrong attitude so would the tourist kindly call the deputy sheriff for help. This was done with great haste and some minutes later when the sheriff appeared, nothing had changed. When the deputy entered the cage, things took a turn for the worse, the cat dropped the man's head and turned for the deputy. He killed her.

The victim and his brother owned a truck stop and, even after all his time in the hospital and several subsequent operations, they still wanted the zoo. We made a deal for $300 and a llama which I would pick up when I delivered Cheeta to the zoo in South Dakota. I had been by the zoo several times in the past, before he had it, and it was getting old and run down and was a marginal operation at best.

Loading Cheeta's cage in the trailer was a terrible ordeal. We had to get a crane to pick up the cage and drop it inside the wire walls, then, loading up some other animals, we headed for South Dakota. I traded along the way, used the "ding jar" and, as Cheeta was quite a show, it was kept amply full.

When we got there I was amazed at the sight of the place. The owner, after his attack, had a taxidermist mount the lion, who now looked like a greyhound, on top of the false front which hid the zoo from the public. Underneath and across the whole front, a sign painter told the story of this tragic affair. On asking about the shape of the lion, he replied that the job was cheap and, even if it did look like a greyhound, that the people who came by thought it was exciting. I always wished there would have been a picture of this sight available but we couldn't find one.

The llama was loaded and then, taking Cheeta by the hand, we walked back through the zoo to his new home. The owner took me back to a large chicken wire pen with a rickety gate and I looked inside with amazement. There was a large female chimp.

"You mean, this is where he's going to live?" I said.

"Sure."

By this time Cheeta had caught on and was going out of control. He was screaming, jumping up and down and just starting to bite my hand to make me let loose when the owner opened the gate. Turning Cheeta loose so he could get to that mountain of female pulchritude was a sight. He ran on all fours through the gate and straight for her. She was sitting down and didn't even bother to get up. She took it calmly. She just sat as he sat down beside her, put his arm around her and used the other one to pat her arm and start picking on her. They started to oh and ah. I said goodbye to him with little notice, closed the gate and we headed for the office. No long goodbyes.

The owner gave me my check and I left for the south fast, cashed the check in the next town. Never did hear what happened but, if

Cheeta ever got tired of that female, what then? He could just walk through the pen any place and this was one time I was guilty of doing the wrong thing with an animal.

On the way to South Dakota, I had stopped in Jackson Hole and done a little trading. At the outskirts of Jackson was a little zoo with some temporary cages on a grassy meadow; after looking around, I found the woman who was in charge. She was deep in conversation with a couple and explaining the zoo to them. There were cages, mostly of native animals and deer, and I wondered if maybe they just spent most of their time wandering around for the cages looked like they weren't used to being occupied.

Finally the woman came over, introduced herself, showed me around and then went over and looked at my collection of critters. Mostly they were for sale or trade except Cheeta so she invited me out to their place at Wilson, which was 7 miles, to view some more animals that they could possibly trade.

She introduced herself as Darcy Gloy and told me something about themselves. Darcy was about 32 at that time and several years before had come to Jackson from back east. It seems she had met some people who were going to make a Disney movie at Teton Marsh about thirty miles away, and had talked them into hiring her. She had assured them she had a vast knowledge of wild animals. She managed to cover her ignorance and survived, met Fred Gloy, who was a game warden at that time and worked on the picture also, then soon moved in with him. He had left and finally divorced his wife and now they were living at Wilson in a hand to mouth existence such as mine.

She guided me to an old farm house in Wilson where they lived with the animals they had collected. Where was Fred? Naturally, if we were going to do any trading, shouldn't her husband be around? No, he was out drinking somewhere and would be in late. She showed me around and about the only thing that interested me was a jaguar with half a tail. I had an African Cape Hunting dog with me that really needed to go for there had been several surplus around Los Angeles. No one wanted them, and this was my last. They were smelly! An odd smell! Darcy looked with interest. We finally struck a trade. I unloaded the dog, and exchanged it for the jaguar. What a relief. It was hard to get away from Darcy for she was really a talker but I thought that there ought to be a good distance between all of us when Fred got home.

Sightseeing was fun in Northwest Wyoming and on into Montana. I pulled into the zoo at Red Lodge, Montana, which was also a private one, and met the owner. He was a very gracious host and I spent the night talking about the zoo business with him. When morning came, we made some trades, and I got rid of the jaguar in exchange for a tame bobcat and a wolf. All in all, it was an interesting trip to South Dakota and so, on my return, I decided to stop and see the Gloys again, on my way south.

When the Gloys' farm house rolled into sight at Wilson it was about five in the evening and several cars were around. Fred must have got home for the evening, I surmised. I knocked on the door and heard a voice holler to come in. Everyone was sitting around the kitchen table drinking. Fred immediately let it be known that he was really burned at the trade, that he didn't like the cape hunting dog, didn't like the smell and would like to have the jaguar back. Sorry, couldn't do it; I traded it already. Too bad. Well, have a drink. He didn't just pour me a drink but half a glass of scotch. The rest, Darcy, Fred, and an Indian by the name of "Chief", were busy drinking and soon we smoothed the whole thing out.

The place was a shambles. A deer fawn standing around bleating for a bottle, a beaver rooting around through the garbage and Fred getting rapidly under the weather.

The bottle didn't last long. The Indian went out and came back with another half and they finished it. I was still having trouble finishing my half a glass.

They were going down into Jackson for a steak dinner at Darcy's cousin's so everyone loaded into Fred's old car and we headed erratically for town.

Darcy's cousin Dolly was from a well-to-do family in Philadelphia; she had a nice log cabin and also had a game warden for a live in. We had a good time, more drinking and at eleven decided to go. "Chief" dragged his feet and didn't seem to have any intention of going.

Gradually everyone left but "Chief", and we would go and come through the front door trying to get him to move. Finally, we were all standing in the back yard and "Chief" flew through the door about 3 ft. off the ground in a horizontal flying position, clearing the small back door stoop handily but not quite achieving flying speed. He made a great landing, flat on his face! This would have been a stunt for a movie.

Fred calmly walked out and picked him up by the belt, dragged him to the car, levered him into the back seat and got himself into the front seat. Fred was smashed, Darcy was smashed and got in the middle, and I sat on the outside. Waving adieu to Dolly we headed for home. Fred opened the car up to fifty and headed down the road for Jackson, flying across bumps and through the heart of town, never slowing down, thru stop signs, dodging traffic, and for 4 or 5 blocks just barely missing the parked cars on the right hand side. I was petrified! How we missed them all I'll never know. When finally we made it into the yard at Darcy's I swore it was my last ride with Fred, drunk or sober, and felt lucky to be alive; I was!

Next morning everyone staggered in and talked about being hung over. "Chief" came in; he was the only one feeling good. He had a few scratches on his nose where he made the crash landing but was laughing and joking about last night. The last thing, as Fred was leaving for town, was a reminder from Darcy to be sure and pick up a couple more fifths for that night. What a bunch! I worked with them again later on some filming and, when things got bad for them in Jackson, they moved to New York City where Fred got a job with the Bronx zoo. They lived in a tenement somewhere and I visited them for an hour one night. Still drinking. Later, a couple of years, Fred died. If it was from overdrink I can understand it.

14 / *Alligators ride in sedans*

A year earlier I had met one of the most fascinating couples in the animal trading business; they were different, Evelyn and Doug Sturmer. Doug was a blind animal dealer living in Texas out of Fort Worth. Young and charming, Evelyn drew most of the hard work, as Doug bought and traded for animals over the phone and by letter. Evelyn would do the work of boxing and shipping the animals at night because she was holding a day job at the Fort Worth Zoo to keep things breaking even.

When I met them at home, her father and mother were visiting, and her father was also blind. I visited, traded a wolf for some small snakes and my first big boa. It was 8 ft. long and, not knowing anything about boas, it was a new thing for me but it wasn't long before I was picking it up and handling it.

People would be looking at my animals and naturally asked to see me handle it and I never did find out 'til later that it was a wonder it didn't bite me. I didn't know at that time that boas have a whole mouthful of teeth that could really make a mess of someone even though they aren't poisonous. It made a nice pet though.

I much admired Evelyn and later, when Doug and I met at Apache Junction in Arizona, where he had an alligator ranch that was a tourist attraction, he told me they were now divorced. The way he talked about her made me want to see her again.

Never Kick A Bear in Your Bedroom Slippers

Doug proved a good host for me. He would come outside and inspect the large animal trailer, listen to the animals, have someone guide his hand to a cage where he could feel the animals and stroke them and, not so strangely, would never get a bite. They seemed to understand the spirit of this man.

I was waiting for Karl Junghans, a German refugee who had become well known in this country for his still photographs and who had been a famous movie director in Germany before World War II. Mutual friends in Santa Fe had introduced us. We borrowed a little money and the two of us were going to film a mountain lion show.

Doug's alligator farm had a group of buildings for the tourist, rooms for souvenirs, rooms to look at small animals in cages, and walkways to look at various displays of the alligators. The farm itself had offices, living quarters for various people, and ample room for the storage of the large animal trailer, while Karl and I filmed our movie.

It was winter, January, cold even for that time of year, a bad frost had come and devastated much of the citrus crop. The farm, situated 20 miles north of Phoenix, was on a busy highway with many other tourist facilities but its now run-down condition brought few people even at the height of the tourist season.

Doug said he had put $10,000 down on the purchase of everything but the land and the buildings, and it looked like it was going to go down the drain. We had great evenings together, talking about the old times, and what the future would hold. For me, with only the responsibility of my animals, the future wasn't a big problem for I could move anyplace, put the 'ding jar' out and take something in. For Doug, well, there had to be enough tourists coming through to keep him going for he had no reserves.

Fritz, a friend from back in Missouri, had a pony ride there which could be used in various places on weekends, and he would help take care of Doug's reptiles and animals, keep the place half-way clean and generally help Doug out.

Karl and I soon finished filming, ran out of money, and Karl left for California to get the film processed. Being broke, I decided to head out on the road for something to replenish the treasury.

93

Later in St. Joseph, while visiting Doug, the story was told of the ending of the farm.

Things got tougher and tougher and there was just no money coming in even at the height of the tourist season. These kinds of attractions had died. The alligators were turned loose, which later created bedlam in the neighborhood, and the one valuable thing that Doug had left, in the way of an animal, was loaded up. Fritz had a big trailer, that had been a moving van, where he carried his ponies, so Doug's prized possession, a tiger, was loaded in a crate and put in among the ponies. It was a good Bengal, well bred, and just a young one, and worth $1200 or $1500 dollars. They took everything they could pack but it wasn't much.

They headed for the east and when they reached Oklahoma, Fritz had a bad feeling, stopped, went back to the trailer and looked in. The ponies were milling around and screaming and hollering and there was the tiger loose, and just starting to make a dinner on a pony as soon as he could catch one. Doug was sitting in the cab of the truck when Fritz came running up, reached in and went through the jockey box, found his pistol and headed back for the trailer. Doug had no idea what was happening and slowly climbed down from the tractor. He heard the roar from the 357 magnum and called to find out what had happened. Fritz told him what he'd done and Doug was devastated. They dragged the tiger out and put it on the tailgate of the trailer and wrapped it on with rope and headed for Missouri.

Doug figured they could at least pelt it out and get something out of it. Finally, when they did arrive at Doug's parents in St. Jo and unloaded his things, the aroma was getting quite strong and his mother protested vigorously but to no avail. Fritz was leaving it behind!

Soon after, his brother set him up in another animal business and he was back working again with a girl to live with and to help with the business.

Doug was a woman chaser even if he was blind and Evelyn was a big topic of his conversation. What a poor wife, how frigid she was, and much more. They finally had their daughter and Evelyn had moved back to St. Jo to get away from him and get a divorce. Now they were both here.

Well, of course, sooner or later I had to see her. I unhitched the big trailer and went looking for her. Eventually I found her in a small brick duplex with her daughter and it was exciting. We talked over old times and all the problems of animal trading and soon became very attached. Her parents had some oil interests, were reasonably well off, and had helped Evelyn get back on her feet. She was now teaching in a Montessori school and was getting her head on straight. Leaving the next day was hard, for we were very interested in one another, and later she told her folks about me. That was the kiss of death, another animal trader! No! Especially bearded! From now on it had to be all secret. It was telephone calls, an occasional letter and a month later, when I got back, it was worse. Now we started love making and both of us hated to part again.

It was easy to listen to each other on the phone and run up huge bills, then we agreed to meet in Texas when I had to come to get some alligators.

Taking the load of animals home to California and disposing of them took a couple weeks, and my continuing big problem was doing something with my surplus animals that couldn't be sold.

Monkeys were a cash item so they went to local research organizations which paid in 30 days. Surplus deer and hoofed stock were to be taken to Texas and sold for cash, and small animals went to the pet shops for anything I could get for eating money. When I got back there was stock that went to Africa, USA, and hoofed stock to be picked up at the LA zoo where aoudads, eight of them, had to be caught.

They would furnish men to catch them in a 2 acre fenced area on a steep side hill. As these beasts got older they would grow huge sets of curved horns and would weigh about 300 to 325 lbs., the size of a pony. There was one big tame one that was to be taken. He was roped and usually two men could stand, each with one horn and steer one of them into a pen. We took the rope off, I climbed on his back and took the handlebars and started to steer him into the catch pen. He forced a turn and headed for freedom. I decided to stay on. It was a mistake. I had my legs wrapped around him hanging on for dear life and when he went straight down the hill, around trees, around the side hill at full speed it was exhilarating but I knew that it was going to come to a bad end. I was right! He ran to the top, gave me a big heave, I sailed over his head and down the hill through the eucalyptus trees. That really put a dent in my ego and a crook in my back.

Everyone was getting a great laugh out of it and it was fun for a few moments. Later I spent several trips to the chiropractor to have my back adjusted.

I had quite a reputation at the zoo for my roping ability because, on one trip to get fallow deer, everyone had been having bad luck when I arrived. Grabbing a lasso, I got one on the first throw and then another one. I knew when to stop so it left me on top. That's half the fight. Know when to stop.

Making a deal with Ralph at Africa, USA, for alligators, I loaded and headed for Texas where I met Evelyn at the airport at San Antonio. We wandered around for two days at the zoos, making love and seeing the sights.

I had made contact with a young fellow who was an alligator hunter and poacher, whom we were to meet at a little fishing village southeast of Victoria. Later that afternoon we found the place and his relatives. John, his name was, had hunted alligators with his father and uncles for years and he was only nineteen. Alligators now were protected in Texas so we had to be careful.

A few months previously there had been a large alligator brought into a zoo at Waco that I had traded for. It was a major undertaking for that baby was 14 ft. long and must have weighed close to a thousand lbs. It had to be loaded into a hidden compartment underneath the floor of the deer compartment of the trailer and we built a ramp up to the side of the trailer, roped the alligator and put a pickup on the far side to drag it up the ramp and into the tank.

Even this took several people, the tank was only 12 ft. long and with a couple of others in there made quite a load.

I was rather curious where this had one come from and the story came out. Two men had caught and tied up this alligator out in the swamps, dragged it in and loaded it into the back of a car. A sedan! They brought it to one of the fellows at the zoo and sold it for a hundred dollars or something. It was worth a thousand. Everyone was amazed at how two people could work that hard and load this creature.

Seems that while they tied up his head that they would let it use its feet to do some of the work and then they folded it up in the back of the car and tied it in. When, in due time, I got back to Jungleland and got him unloaded, it took a dozen men just to carry him from the trailer into their pool. John was one of the two that had captured this behemoth, along with an uncle.

Evelyn had no old clothes so we outfitted her in some old khakis and tennis shoes and a GI hat. Because of the chiggers our legs would have to be covered with medicated grease and we had to cover the rest of ourselves with mosquito repellants.

All three of us got in a skiff with a small outboard, tote sack, plenty of rope, and headed down the shipping canal. After several miles we came to a set of huge locks where we went through with a large freighter. It was scary. It was nearly dark and after a couple of miles we turned the skiff up a small river and we went into the swamps. I never knew there was any place like it in Texas. Huge fields of saw grass, some of it 6 to 8 ft. tall. After a couple of miles John steered the boat into a small hidden cove and dragged it up on the shore.

He said we'd have to walk a couple miles so off we went. It was now dark, the water knee deep as we sloshed along. Evelyn asked if we were going to be on dry ground and John said, there was very little of it.

We found only an occasional island of sand. The light of a partial moon and a flash light was all that each of us had. It was nothing but swamp and saw grass and the occasional cow that would be frightened at our approach. Something else I never knew, the mosquitoes were terrible and soon my legs got sore. The two miles stretched to three and at last we reached a bigger island. The object was to get a big female alligator which John knew of and anything else we could catch. John went back and forth around the island and could find nothing. Sometimes the cows splashed like an alligator, but nothing.

We rested. Evelyn said she'd gone far enough. The island was only about a couple of hundred yards long, had a couple of pine trees on top, and John said it was covered with rattlesnakes. Evelyn said she'd take the rattlesnakes and if we found the island coming back she'd be asleep on the top. There were still a couple miles to go and we didn't have an extra flashlight to leave her but she said she'd make it. She had worked around so many snakes that they didn't bother her so off we went.

After a mile or so, John hollered to me from a distance that he had found the nest we were looking for, a big one. It was 4 ft. high of scraped up debris and leaves, warm to the feel, and we dug down. It was filled with alligator eggs. Now, alligator eggs are about the size of turkey eggs, and the shells are soft so it was easy to pack them with no fear of breaking.

The nest was torn down and 27 eggs were slipped into the tote sack. We ranged all over and didn't find any sign of the mother. The fields of grass all seemed the same to me and had me lost but finally after an hour we found the island and Evelyn. She said the biggest battle was with the bugs. We started back on a different route to see if anything else turned up but it didn't. Evelyn was pooped. It was getting dawn when we got back to the little skiff and started the motor. Bam! John stopped the motor and searched over the stern and felt the prop. It had sheared the pin but hadn't quite broken off.

There were no extra pins and no oars. He started the motor and slowly started down the river. There would be at least ten or twelve miles to go and at this rate it would take quite awhile and now in the light there would be the chance of a warden's boat checking us for it seemed that John was well known to them.

Slowly we pulled into the open gates of the lock, the gates were closed and the water level rose. This was really something to me. All that work to let one skiff through. These were government locks on the ship canal that went around S. Texas for the large freighters. Slowly we moved out of the locks and up the canal toward the village. We kept the top loose on the tote sack for if anyone got close it was going to be dumped over the side. Evelyn and I were exhausted from the night's work and dozed in the boat as it crawled along. When we arrived it must have been ten and the sun was up high; we split with John and I made a date to call him in a few days, and the two of us headed for the motel.

Putting the eggs on the floor of the truck so they'd stay warm we went into get some sleep. Evelyn got in the shower and suddenly started to scream. What now? I ran and brought her out of the shower with her hands covering her eyes like she was afraid. What was wrong?

"I forgot to take out my contacts last night and now my eyes are on fire."

The door started banging. I didn't have anything on and peeked around the door as I opened it. The landlady! I explained and asked her where the nearest doctor was. 50 miles to the north. When she left I took a quick shower, got Evelyn dried off and clothes on her. She was still holding her eyes and crying hard. Everything was loaded up and I headed for the hospital.

The people at this hospital were so kind and understanding and the doctor soon appeared, examined her eyes and pronounced his decision. Three days in bed! The eyes were ulcerated underneath the contacts and there were going to have to be pads on them with medication. Well my only job was to turn the alligator eggs once in a while and take care of Evelyn. We enjoyed ourselves, the alligators hatched in the warmth of the burlap sack and soon there were 27 little ones crawling around.

Evelyn had to catch her plane in San Antonio on Saturday to have dinner with her parents in St. Jo. on Sunday. She had no regular glasses and with the medication, couldn't see. I guided her to the plane and sadly bade her farewell. It was going to be quiet with her gone. We had talked about getting married but she couldn't make up her mind. She told me later the story of Sunday. Her daughter was a very precocious five year old, and so, when sitting around the dinner table on Sunday, with Evelyn wearing her glasses, the daughter piped up:

"Grandma, guess where mommie was this week?"

"Where?" her mother said.

DICK ROBINSON

"She was down in Texas with Dick all week."

Well, Grandma had one of her classic heart attacks. She was packed off upstairs to be put to bed for a week. Ma Bell made many a dollar off the two of us for there were many tearful telephone calls and, after a couple of months, I got an airline ticket for her to come for a weekend in California. It wasn't too good for I was having a big attack from my brain surgery and felt lousy.

15/ Gator aid

After Evelyn left me in San Antonio to go to St. Jo, I picked up John and headed for Victoria, Texas where they had a small zoo and did a little trading and I made a deal to catch alligators for a split of 50/50 if the zoo would get the permits. There was lots of cooperation. We hunted 10 miles from the city in a swamp that was right out of the movies: live oaks with moss hanging, swamp grass and lots of alligators. John and I worked by ourselves except a helicopter would come over periodically to check on us.

What an education that kid gave me about the swamps! I could handle alligators from my days working for Ross Allen's in Florida but never had I caught them like this before.

A pole was cut 15 feet long with a 3 inch hook wrapped to the end, like a gaffing hook for fish. We waded thru the grass and knee deep in water 'til we would find a trail. Following the trail we would come to what looked like the center of several trails.

The alligator holes would usually go down at a 45 degree angle. John would plant reeds in the water in the mud about a foot apart so they would stick several inches out of the water and about 15 to 20 ft. around the hole.

Then standing by the hole he would run the hooked end down 10-12 ft. and if he could feel anything he would hook it. Now if he scared it, the alligator would swim out and leave, when you watched the reeds bending or quivering you could guess what was happening. If they bent over and disappeared you knew it had left. If they quivered and stopped it might have gone back in the hole. Often standing there you could feel them touch your leg as they swam by. They wouldn't bite underwater but it gave you goosebumps to think of what could happen.

If you hooked one in the hole and brought it out it would only be a few feet from you and the first thing he did was stick his head out and see what had him. At that time you could gauge what size you had, then his head would go under and the struggle would begin.

I had a capture stick, about a six ft. long aluminum rod with a cable making a noose at the end. Finding his head I would slip the noose around his nose or head and tighten it up. Then I had control of him but he would start fighting, spinning and doing everything to get away. All this time we would be trying to get the hook released from him. When that was free and things quieted, one of us would jump on his back, grab his snout, yank his head back so he couldn't spin on us and tie him up. His mouth would be tied up in a neat way, then his legs behind his back and you would have perfect control of him. In a couple of days there were about ten 6 to 8 footers, but I still needed a big one.

A nice 8 footer was pulled from a hole under a bank on a little island and tied up and then John said he'd try the hole again just in case there was another. AH! got another! Now you can't tell the size of what you get because you ease him out slowly and when John pulled it up and the head came out I about flipped! I swear the mouth and head were 3 ft. long. A big one! What a battle we had. I got the noose on him and he would spin one way and then back and fight.

Finally John jumped on his back and got the jaws together. When you jump on their backs and grab their necks they can't bite but can they ever roll over! You run your hands forward along the side of their jaws and you can close it as they have only small muscles to force open their jaws. Clamping the end shut, you tie it up with two half hitches in thru their teeth and then around the neck.

But alligators have tremendous muscles to close their mouths and, if you get something in there like an arm or a hand, you'll have to kill it to get it out if you still have it. It's one of the reasons we all carry a knife handy.

Eventually we got it tied up and sat and rested 'til the helicopter came, looked at the alligator, shook his head and left. It was at least a mile to the track along side of the swamp where we could get help so we took turns dragging it and the smaller one. Alligators float but still it was a job. When we made the road we dragged the shoulders and head out and that was all. A crew came shortly, half a dozen men from the zoo and it was all we could do to load it in the back of a pickup. It measured nearly 11 ft. long when I sold it and must have weighed 600 lbs. What a day! Everyone was impressed and even a man from the paper came and got a picture.

John came back to California with me and stayed a few weeks at the zoo but life wasn't exciting enough so he returned to Texas. The next time we heard he was in the pokey. He'd gone back to the same place, poaching, got caught and lacked bail. Unfortunately not all of life is excitement. Alligators had to be hauled at that time in a hidden compartment under the deer pen in my trailer to get into California and this time it was a real load. I had the one big one and about 6 seven and eight footers. The big one went to the Los Angeles Zoo and the smaller ones to Africa, USA.

16/
Lions and snakes in a day's work

Working occasionally for Ralph Helfer of Africa, USA, was different and interesting. He bought a great many zoo animals which were tame and could be used in animal work on different movies. Normally, Ralph was short of money but he had just been bought out of a partnership by Ivan Tors, who was making it big with the "Daktari" series, and now Ralph could buy some new animals and put more money into his compound.

Ralph was a real bargain hunter and, sometimes, instead of putting a few extra dollars into something good, he would pick up a bargain if he thought he could get one. Such was the case when we both heard through the grapevine, about the sale of a small private zoo in Lubbock, Texas.

The zoo was run in conjunction with a Western Village and some rides a few miles from the outskirts of Lubbock, and it wasn't really doing very well. The village had fallen on bad times and news of the animals being sold was making the rounds. There were some of them I would like to have had, and a friend had invited me to come and see what was available. I was looking over the animals when Ralph's big van and tractor pulled in. My friend in Lubbock, who just handled native animals, had told me that Ralph's man was coming for an elephant. Ralph had some cowboy jockey driving the truck; he could drive all right, but didn't know beans about an elephant and, in this case, Ralph was purchasing an elephant from these people mainly because it was cheap.

They tried to entice the elephant into this huge furniture van with a bucket of oats and bread. She would go up the ramp and back down again for nobody knew exactly what to do with her and everybody was afraid of her. Finally my friend, who was only 19 or 20 appeared and watched the antics of the people trying to load her. He had hung around the zoo and was fairly well acquainted with the animals so eventually he said,

"Shoot, I can put that elephant in there."

He grabbed her by the ear and walked her right up the ramp and into the van, told her to give him her leg, and then put the chain around it. There she was. It made everyone look a little foolish.

I have often wondered about the trip back to California with a truck driver up front and an animal in back who could take the van apart with a few swipes of her trunk, also how they handled her at the other end. I didn't hear anything more about it but I always remember the incident when I pull alongside a van. Whew! The cheap way is no way to go with an elephant.

All the zoo animals were available for junk prices so a few days later, when I got back to LA, I went over the inventory with Ray Folsom. We decided it was worth buying some of the zoo so that week-end we took the list of animals and packed snake-sacks in his suit cases, which consisted of a large 4-suiter, and three smaller ones in a matched set. Our minds were made up to bring the snakes at least back with us on the plane.

We jumped on a Continental jet and, upon arriving took a cab down to the zoo to meet with the zoo director. We looked over his list of animals but, of course, the best thing to do was to see the animals themselves and find out how they were. This was a large Western Village with the zoo at the side of it. There were rides, western stores and a big exhibit area; also a snake house.

The exhibit area was set up so that the visitors saw the animals from the inside of a large oval and the outside was the service area. There was a big alleyway in the back where the cages could be serviced and the snake house was on the far end of the zoo.

DICK ROBINSON

We started walking around the service area looking at the various animals and, when we got to the lion cages, we looked in to count the number of lions; there were only two big cubs. When I say big cubs, I'd say 200 lbs. Both of them were up against the wire fence looking at us. I said,

"Well, where are all of the big lions? You have five on the list."

He said, "I just don't know what happened to them."

Obviously he knew, but he wasn't going to tell us. He said,

"These two are tame and you're going to get a real bargain with them."

He opened the door to pet one and it pushed out. The lion rubbed up against me and against Ray, then walked over to the director, stood up on his hind legs, put his paws on his shoulders, and cocked his head like he was going to kiss his neck. The man started to scream! I saw that the lion had him by the throat then threw him on the ground when he started to fight back and tried to push the lion off. It was all so sudden and unexpected that we were taken by surprise and it took a second to start reacting. I jumped over and pried on the cat's mouth, stretched his mouth open, one hand over the top and one hand down on the bottom, and pulled the cat off. The director tried to scoot away a little bit but the cat which was bigger than I was, and extremely strong, went after him again. The blood was starting to run.

The cat never took one look at me. He stared straight at the man and went right back at him. I told Ray, seeing that I couldn't handle the cat, to grab a steel fence post I saw and we'd try to pry them apart.

The post wouldn't work. I jumped on the cat again. Bill Slate, the director, had blood pumping out of his neck in a stream the size of a pencil and gushing at least 4 inches. Getting my hand inside the lion's jaw behind his big fangs brought some relief for Bill for here was a place that you could stick your hand, take the pressure off from the bite of the lion without getting hurt, and still retrieve it.

I took one quick look at his neck, still gushing. The cat now had him down on his back and all of his claws into him, trying to bite him, trying to get his fangs into him. I had my one hand in the lion's mouth and I stuck one finger of the other right into Bill's neck where the blood was streaming. I told Ray to run back to the house which was a good block away, call for a doctor, an ambulance, the police, and get a gun if one was there. Away he went. Ray was rather in poor shape with a big gut sticking out in front of him but he took off on a run for the house. Meanwhile, the cat was dragging Bill across the alley to the far side. I was still with them with my hand in the cat's mouth and my finger in Bill's neck.

There wasn't anything more I could do. The cat had him about 4 feet from a telephone pole and I kept watching for a way to leave safely when he finished off this one just in case he decided that I was next. If he turned toward me I was going up the pole but the cat for some reason never looked at me, and never made a move for me. Now I was waiting for Ray.

Ray ran to the house, ran upstairs where they lived, told Bill's wife to call a doctor, call an ambulance and police quick. Where were the guns? The wife, who was 7 months pregnant, went into immediate hysterics. She pointed to the closet out of which Ray grabbed a shotgun and rifle and took off running. Then she got on the phone with the operator but couldn't talk. She was in absolute hysterics by this time, but, as luck would have it, the operator who answered recognized her voice. They had been school friends. She didn't know what was going on but knew something was wrong and called the police and an ambulance.

Ray in the meantime headed back to me. He was so excited that when he reached the service gate he couldn't get the latch open and climbed over it.

When he got to us, we were over on the far side of the service area with the lion crouched down holding Bill's leg. The lion had changed bites from his chest section down to his groin area. His mouth was so big that he had it around his leg and groin together and I'll never forget the tearing and popping of the tendons when he chomped down on that leg.

When Bill started screaming from the pain I told him that if we stay quiet the cat will just hang on instead of chomping, and will wait for him to die. Bill immediately stopped.

DICK ROBINSON

A lion usually takes his prey down and suffocates it by grabbing the throat. He'll hang on to a water buffalo or other big animal by the neck and choke it to death. Here I was crouched over with my hand in the lion's mouth and my finger in the man's neck when Ray came running up with a rifle and shotgun. He lay the shotgun down and was trying to lever the rifle, but it was a 30-30 Winchester which he was unfamiliar with, and had a levering action he knew nothing about. I told him how, he levered it and got a shell in the barrel. He was standing about 10 ft. back and was going to shoot the cat in the head. I panicked!

"Wait, wait a minute!" I yelled at him, knowing that he could shoot my hand while it was in the lion's mouth, then I said to Bill,

"Here Bill, you must put your finger in your neck and I'll hold the rifle barrel." Taking my finger out, moving his hand and finger into the hole I took the rifle barrel in my left hand and put the muzzle to just the right spot above the eye where it would kill the cat immediately. I said quietly to Ray,

"OK, shoot!"

There was a tremendous explosion in my face, the cat just twitched a few times and rolled over dead. There was blood spurting from the lion's mouth and the bullet hole and it was running all over Bill. Also there must have been 150 claw and bite holes in the man. Blood soaked out of all his clothes where he had been mauled. Ray stood back and I said,

"Lever it, Ray, and we'll shoot the cat again if we have to."

Ray levered it again and again. There had been only one shell in the rifle and we had used that one to shoot the lion.

"Try the shotgun."

He picked up the shotgun and broke it open. No shells!

I was lying on the ground with the cat lying over my legs and I was holding Bill for he was really in pain. He turned and said.

"Dick, I'm dying. I'm going. Hold onto me."

"No, you're not dying, all you've got is a lot of blood all over you. You're just chewed up a little," I replied.

"No, no, I know I'm going," he moaned.

"It always looks worse than it is," I said.

By this time the shot had drawn the guard from the main gate. He came running down through a huge castle-like gate at the end of the service alley and up to where we were.

Bill looked up at the guard who was a nice Mexican man and said, "José, I'm going. Say a prayer for me."

Poor José didn't know what to do. He thought Bill had had it also from all the blood around and he started to cry. Here I'm holding this man in my arms, José is crying and the man is telling me that he is going.

"No, you're not going anyplace but to the hospital. They'll have an ambulance here soon."

By this time we could hear the sirens, and one man, a police officer, stuck his head in the gate, looked around and asked,.

"What's going on!"

"Nothing now! But you better get a stretcher in here!" I called.

"Is it safe?" he asked.

"Yeah, we have a dead lion right here. Can't you see him?" The lion was still lying across my legs.

"No, I can't see him. You're sure he's dead?" the officer really wasn't convinced. Ray walked over to the gate and told the ambulance driver to come in. We pulled apart, got the stretcher up beside Bill and loaded him. A reporter was right behind us now wanting to talk. I was covered with blood. Both Ray and I looked at each other with quiet understanding; we knew that anything like this happening around a zoo is bad news for our business so we told him it was just a minor accident and let it go at that. We left with everyone taking Bill to the hospital and we walked to the house to clean up and to avoid talking to any strangers.

Ray said, as we walked along,

"We came for the snakes, what'll we do?"

"Let me clean up, and then let's get the bags and get loaded," I said.

Upstairs in the Slate's apartment were clothes in his closet; slacks and clean shirts, so I took a shower and put on what there was that could be worn. He was taller and skinnier than I, so his pants were tight but with the cuffs rolled up I was presentable.

DICK ROBINSON

Now for the snake house. It was filled with a variety of poisonous and non-poisonous reptiles and snakes. There were all kinds of snake sacks in the suitcases, so the non-poisonous were gathered first with just our hands and stuffed into sacks, then with snake hooks the poisonous ones were harvested. The larger went into the middle-sized suitcases and the smaller were stuffed into the smaller suitcase and into all the spots where there was room. The poisonous snakes went into one box inside a suitcase except some of the copperheads who went into the middle-sized bags. Three of the suitcases were now filled; there was just the large one left, and one snake, a reticulated python, seventeen feet long, big!

With only the two of us it would be tough, but fortunately both of us were unafraid of snakes and knew how to handle them. There was a large burlap sack in a corner so I grabbed the front end of the snake with the head and Ray took the middle. The object was to stuff it into the burlap sack. It now started to thrash around, trying to get a coil on something, but both of us had too much experience to let this happen, for if it could get one man started with a loop on him it would be next to impossible to extricate him without killing it. The snake wasn't used to being handled so it raged at being pulled about. Ray had the tough job, holding the sack and trying to feed the tail end of the snake into it, still holding the snake free from us with the other hand. This was worse than the lion. What a hell of a job! Gradually we worked the snake in and the last thing was turning his big head into the sack with a quick snap and popping the top closed. We found a piece of wire to secure the top and the bag was dragged to the large suitcase where it was rolled in and the top brought down, but it wouldn't close. The snake was jammed tighter. No good. The lid was forced down with both of us on our knees on the top edges bouncing in rhythm; we forced the air out of it and the lock snapped shut.

Well the lid was fastened but how about the snake breathing? Our eyes were glued to the case, it started to bulge. Ah hah...we hoped no one looked too closely. All this would have to go into the baggage compartment of the plane when we left.

We called a cab and loaded the suitcases carefully as we told the cabbie to get us to the hospital so we could check on the director. There wasn't any doubt in my mind what his condition would be but it was a shame that it all had to happen.

There wasn't any trouble finding Bill, for everybody had heard about the episode by this time, big news in a little town this size. They had him all washed up, pumped full of pain killers and evidently had cleaned all the holes. His wife could talk to us now so she told us all about what had happened from the time they had taken him.

Just as I thought, there were a lot of claw holes in him and he had got a pretty good chew at his groin but they couldn't find the hole in his neck! There I was the whole time during this ordeal with my finger buried in his neck and yet the doctor said absolutely there was no hole. Bill was groggy but managed to greet us with enthusiasm. After thanking us we started talking about that hole again. Looking carefully where my finger had been inside his neck brought no sign of any type of an opening, not even a scar line. Very peculiar.

Apparently the cut was on a line in his neck and it fastened together so quickly that they could never find it and it "healed." This is still a cause of wonder and introspection to me.

The meter was still running on the taxi so we thanked everyone, made arrangements to return the clothes and set a date when we would start picking up the other animals. The cabbie rushed us to the airport for we wanted to make the Continental flight back to LA. We went directly to the counter with our luggage and asked if there was any extra charge for the large one. It took both of us to carry it, and when we put it on the scale we held our breath, 98 lbs. The man at the counter said that the law allowed four suitcases. Good!

The flight left in 20 minutes to LA so they started loading our bags at once. Everything was great, a little Mexican fellow came running up for the large suitcase, grabbed it, flew up in the air and landed hard. He thought it was light and he didn't even phase it. It took two of them to put it on the conveyor and the belt chugged to a stop and they had to hand carry it to the cargo section of the jet.

The counter man asked what was in it and I said,

"My wife's biscuits."

"Come on, quit kidding," he said.

Ray got serious and said,

"Ah, it's just his barbells for weight lifting."

He accepted that story and we glanced furtively around as we strolled for the plane. Of course, every law in the world made it a no-no to carry poisonous snakes on airplanes.

"Do you think we ought to sit next to each other?" Ray asked, when we went up the ramp into the plane, "just in case they catch us or something happens?"

"Naw," I replied, "there's nothing more going to happen today."

It was not too long that the plane pulled into the ramp at Los Angeles and two rather tipsy animal dealers debarked and slowly made their way to baggage claim. Ray said, "I'll get the car and keep the motor running."

"Ok, but if I come running just be sure you let me in 'cause it'll sure be an emergency."

I stood inside waiting at the back of a large group of people wondering if the big bag could stand the bounce when it came off the carousel. If it broke open, well, it would be hard dragging out the python in a burlap sack. That girl at the check out door would sure be surprised. Ray had been worrying on the flight back about working on the Lassie show tomorrow but this could prove a little bit more exciting.

Missie, my jaguar, was to jump on Ray for the TV show and he was to fight it, for he was to double for Arthur O'Connell. He was upset!

Our two small bags came down the belt and dropped onto the rotating wheel. I took those two over to the girl and checked them through and then outside and into the car. Ray was parked in the 3 minute loading section watching for patrolmen, and I scooted back inside.

Well, no excitement, and there was another bag going around. People were thinning out, and there became an air of expectation. Bags stopped coming, and people started to fidget, maybe something happened? I got ready to run. All of a sudden my rabies shots started to itch. They were shot into my stomach area or anyplace they could find a good clear patch of skin that wasn't inflamed. My hands and feet would swell and these days it was hard getting my shoes on. Now I had an itch. Gads, I wish something would happen. The belt started and stopped a couple of times. Looking out the door I could see that Ray was still there.

It came up! Now it dived down for the bottom and hit with a slam! I pulled it off the edge and over onto the floor. Taking one bag and dragging the big one, I headed through the check stand and out onto the sidewalk. Ray jumped out and helped me put the big one in the trunk, jumped in and we took off.

"Whewuuuuu...that really takes it out of a guy...."

"Let's go home and collapse," Ray said and I agreed. "What a day!..."

17 / "Dick, are you alright?"

The next morning we loaded the jaguar and took it to Chatsworth for the Lassie show. They had a large fifty-man crew. It was hot in all the rocks and sand where this was going to be filmed. Lassie shows were enjoyable. Nothing had to be too authentic and they went fast for they had tight schedules. Ray was doubling in this episode and was going to have to fight the jaguar. They were going to have the tussle and then a few other shots for us. Ray got all the make-up on and the clothes he would be wearing.

Our first stunt was to get the cat up on a 7 ft. rock and wait for Ray to come along and then throw the cat on him pretending that it was attacking him. Missie wouldn't jump on anyone by herself so I would have to throw her. The crew was getting things ready and I was trying to keep Ray calm and interested. The Lassie crew always shot the animal work first and fast so that they could get on with the people work as they had only a 3½ day schedule. I kept talking while standing on the rock with Missie.

"Ray, when you're around the jaguar, the one thing you have to be careful of is that these cats, rather than rub against you like mountain lions, will butt you to show affection. She'll take her head and give you a poke."

Just about that time the jaguar gave me a nudge with her head and I went sailing off the rock on the back side. We were on the

114

edge of a cliff and down I went. I saw myself going by this open spot and all of the crew watching. I went down 15 ft., hit a sand ledge, bounced, went another 15 ft. bounced, and flailed my arms and legs in every direction so when the next one came, I stuck. I was on my back looking up at the crew whose faces where starting to appear over the edge at the top. It was funny for I was safe now. One of them hollered,

"Dick, are you all right?"

"Great. Throw me a rope."

Then, looking around to see where I landed, brought a surprise that really shook me up. It was 600 ft. down to the next ledge which was the bottom! My knees turned to rubber. Down came the rope which I tied securely. They pulled me back and I climbed the rock where the cat was still standing. Casually I told Ray not to worry. Everybody was sighing in relief thinking I had been a goner for sure.

The cameras were ready. When they called "action" the cat flew through the air, knocked Ray flat and then she walked off. We did it a couple times. It looked great and by this time Ray was getting over his fear that the cat was going to hurt him.

Our next big shot was a struggle with the jaguar on top of Ray. Both of them would be thrashing on the ground supposedly after Ray was knocked down. It was now getting so hot on the ground that it was as hot as grease. Jack Hively was directing, a man in his early seventies, who was one of the old time directors and had done many of the Lassie series for the Wrather Corporation. He had a large straw hat which was his trademark and a very useful item here in the sun. When everything was all set and the jaguar was lying right on top of Ray, the director called "Action."

Ray was lying on his back with the cat's mouth close to his and he had the cat's neck between his two hands. The cat would growl a bit and snarl; Ray would lift the cat's head up from the ground, then both would wrestle 'til the director would say, "Cut!" Ray would fall back and the jaguar would collapse on top of him. They would lie there and rest until the director would call for action again, then both would go through this wrestling bit once more. The cat would growl and snarl, Ray would hang on, thrashing around. When they had done this a half dozen times, it got to be old. It worked well and they were both ready for a cool drink and some shade. We finally finished the shooting for the morning, had lunch, and now waited for our afternoon shots.

It was hot, I was in terrible pain from my rabies shots, my teeth were hurting by this time, and I have never seen them film so slowly in my life. Arthur O'Connell was now at bat. He was a real pro but he had to do one scene 17 times with a little dog. It was so boring that I counted. The dog had to jump up into his lap and he had to go through his dialogue exactly right. Jack Hively had him going and going. Boy, were we glad when that scene was finished. Then we could get home and get out of the hot sun. Ray, by this time, had all of his confidence for the cat was really good.

The next week Ray took off for the Far East on a buying trip. I took off on another WK show and headed for Texas while Ray pointed for Tokyo.

Our national publicity was minimal with regards to the lion incident back in Lubbock; but Ray had told one of his friends in Tokyo about it by phone since there had been a short news clip in their English-language paper. His friend called the press about Ray's visit and when Ray's plane landed at Tokyo airport there was a mob of newsmen. His coverage was half the front page of the English language paper.

18 / A hyena and a hippie

In order to prepare a show on tigers I had to get a hyena and I finally found one in Colorado Springs. It was half-tamed but to me a hyena was just not the animal to be cuddly with. When I went back to Jungleland, I took it along. It needed a home and, out of the blue, a woman drove into my gate in a little sports car saying she heard I had a hyena. She got out and introduced herself, Julie McDonald. She was tall and thin and all the jokes about tall people who liked small cars seemed apropos.

She told me she was an authoress and sculptress, lived in Pasadena and needed a male hyena as a mate to hers. Great! But didn't the neighbors complain? Well, sometimes, but then she would tell them her dog was sick. She had a yard all fenced and very private. Now hyenas moan when they call and it is disturbing if you're only used to wolves and other animals.

We haggled about price and she said she'd think about it. A few days went by and I visited her at home. It was a big old fashioned shingled house, really old, with beautiful wood work inside, but smelly. Seems she'd had a baboon in a cage upstairs on a landing, had written a book about the experience, but the residue lingered on. She had a couple of children who were grown now and the book had been about a baboon in the family.

We started going out together. Julie bought the hyena and

chained it up in the backyard to keep the other company. Julie was different! She was an excellent sculptress, but only when she needed money. When she really got broke, she would buy a block of Indiana limestone, get an air-hammer outfit and knock out a semi-modern animal. She had no problem selling them and would live on the proceeds 'til she started to starve again.

I tried to get her to do a little piece or something for me, but no, not even a smile on a round rock to look like a clam. She thought that it was a funny idea, but no good! One time, Ray, Ginny and I were visiting Maggie Taylor's house and drinking when Maggie put a wooden cat under my arm to take home. Maggie had heard some of the wild carrying-on of Julie and me and knew that I loved cats. She had six of Julie's works and, we were all laughing so hard at my attempts to get a piece from Julie, she couldn't resist. I tried to give it back when I sobered up but she wouldn't hear of it. Just said come get another. It was one of 2 wooden ones she had ever done. Our romance gradually fell apart. I had to drive a hundred miles a couple of times a week, and the hangovers from our drinking were hellacious. Besides, Julie's hyene died and she thought that mine had caused it. That's the way of romance and animal trading.

After staying several months at Jungleland I was given my notice to move. They were working on the picture "Dr. Doolittle" and needed all the room they could get so I became the victim of progress. Finally I found an unused animal research compound on the top of a ridge in Topanga Canyon in a beautiful location. There was not a house in sight and it had a group of great chain link cages that UCLA had used for years. It was owned by a very nice couple, and the rent was right. A few of miles from it was a man who would work for me and he and his wife had an extra bedroom for me to stay.

Moving was no problem as it was only about 30 miles from Thousand Oaks and much closer to Los Angeles. Topanga is a heavily wooded canyon covered with giant oaks and scrub trees, and at that time the long-haired hippies were just moving in. It was very secluded and you could do your own thing.

No sooner had I moved in than I got a call from "Wild Kingdom" to do another Jaguar show in Arizona. Loading my large trailer with other animals and the jaguar, I headed for Arizona leaving my helper to take care of the remaining animals. There was one pressing problem. I needed someone to work with me on the show and to help with the traveling animals. I went a couple of miles to the junction at the top of Topanga Canyon to head for Los Angeles when I saw a long-haired hippie in sandals, beard, with a flowing and flowery shirt, carrying a bag. I stopped and asked where he was going? Anyplace interesting! Well, how about Arizona and did he like animals? Great! Let's go. That's how I met Bob Gruys. He could talk, drive a truck, anything. He was a tile setter by trade, split with his wife, made so much money he couldn't afford to work all the time and was a downright interesting person. Later I found out he couldn't even read but his personality made up for it plus his native intelligence.

We made it to the Circle Z Ranch in Nogales, where I had stayed before on the previous jaguar show, and got the animals comfortable.

Now the Circle Z was an upper crust dude ranch that catered to about forty people, mostly from the East. We were furnished all accommodations by the production company so we were guests like everyone else except we were movie people and, of course, mildly celebrities from our association with "Wild Kingdom." Now most of the people had only heard about hippies at this time and here we were: me with a beard and Bob.

All the people were interested in what we were doing and seeing the animals so they naturally gathered around and soon forgot that Bob was a "hippie." After two days the crew arrived, Marlin, Don Meier the producer, the photographer and Jim Fowler. I'll never forget our meeting. The ranch had a lovely Spanish dining room with tables holding 12 people and, of course, waitresses serving everyone.

They all came in and we sat down at a table. Bob was sitting at the next table deep in conversation with a retired admiral and his wife when both Don and Marlin looked over and said quickly,

"Who *is* that man?"

DICK ROBINSON

Very nonchalantly I replied, "He's my animal handler."

Big silence and many looks back and forth. They thought I was crazy from all the unsaid remarks glancing around. Fortunately, after a short exposure to him they felt the same way everyone else did. Bob was a great guy! When we finished the show it was back to Topanga for me and Bob left for Mexico. There he did a year in a Mexican prison which boosted his repertoire of stories.

19 / Patrick Frawley, Jr.

Ray had a customer who would come in from time to time and buy animals, Patrick Frawley, Jr., a multi-millionaire, who lived in a mansion in Holmby Hills with some animals in his back yard in cages. Gregarious, now anti-alcoholic and now anti-smoking, he talked about it incessantly. He would pay cash in hundred dollar bills for what he bought and ordered. Ray took me up to his mansion on a delivery one day and introduced us. We found we'd both been in the RCAF at the same time before Pearl Harbor, except I had returned to the U.S. Navy six months after Pearl Harbor and he had stayed.

He left Nicaragua where his family still resides and enlisted in the RCAF about the same time I had. Later he met a girl from Vancouver, married her and moved to the States after the war.

His cages were at the back of his estate which bordered on the fence of the LA Country Club. We sold him South American animals, foxes, deer, birds, monkeys, and more. The animals just kept disappearing, some killed by his dogs, some by each other and some escaped. I heard that some of the golfers complained that a red fox would run out, grab their golf balls and carry them away. He never did have any trouble with animal control which was a miracle. We became good friends and he would call me to come up and watch movies in the theatre behind the house or just talk.

DICK ROBINSON

Meeting people through him was interesting and an opportunity to learn from others. At that time he was in control of Technicolor and Schick Razor Co. and was really flying high.

Ray and I were working more and more in TV: a couple of shows for Wild Wild West, several on the Lassie series, and other miscellaneous ones. They were jobs we didn't seek to get but they were nice to do. There were a couple of agents who got part of the take, and people at the studios to be paid off, but it seemed to be part of the system. It was something I disliked and, if I ever got away from it, I didn't want any more.

One day Jim Fowler from Wild Kingdom contacted me and asked me to help a friend out. He was doing a commercial on a tiger and his company, which was based in Chicago, needed help, so after much talking about what he wanted and how to do it; it was agreed for $650, that he could film my tiger and another one I could get for a morning from the Derbys, and that I would find a location for the filming.

Hunting around for just the right area was hard but finally a place was located in the mountains southwest of San Bernardino which entailed driving over a Boy Scout Ranch of some 1000 acres or so and then finding just the right spot.

There were scattered small groups of tents with kids in some so we went back about a mile from them. The production company brought 3 people. I had two to help, and so we started with the Derby's cat after things were set up. Ted, the owner, was busy so his wife brought the cat, a big Siberian kitten, about 350 pounds.

When it was turned loose in front of the camera, the cat just panicked from the whirring noise of the camera, and would run straight away into the brush. It was too big for Ted's wife to handle, so I would drag it back and go through it again. Boy, was it hot! The idea was to have the cat weave around at full speed; but then, they really didn't know what they were looking for.

It was to be a commercial for Enco. No luck. It was near lunch, so the cat was loaded and taken across the little valley to an open spot on a ridge and was turned loose. It ran and ran, with the camera-man riding in a station wagon filming it. It was great on running. That was it for that cat. Ted's wife took the cat home; and now it was back to work with mine.

A half-compound next to the brush was quickly erected, and my cat was turned loose. Honey, my tiger, had only one thought, same as the other one, get in the oak brush and get in the shade. She went around the compound and took off for the brush. Now this cat you couldn't chain up with a leash, like the Derbys', but had to herd. But first, find the cat. We all walked over the hills. I got my capture gun out of the back of my truck, loaded it, and, having only 2 darts, knew that it would be touch and go.

All of us worked the hill sides all around, and no "Honey". Gathering on a ridge, we tried to decide what to do. If the cat moved very fast, she could make it to a scout site, and I could see a tiger walking through one of these. I told Tim, my helper, to take a truck, get to a phone, and call for a helicopter out of the San Bernardino Field to get to us right away. We started the hunt again. An hour later, I found her. Everything was covered with small oak trees and oak brush about 6 ft. high. Walking into a clearing about 20 ft. across there was a sight for sore eyes. She was sitting in the middle of an opening, saw me, and raised her head and purred a "Hello" to me. Tigers have a peculiar short purr for greeting when they lift their heads.

She got up, headed for the far side into the brush. I shot for her back leg with the capture gun. It had a half-inch needle for cats, so as not to go in too far. They used to make it look easy when they used a capture gun or threw a dart at something to immobilize it, as in "Daktari", but it's really quite a process to load and use one.

The syringe is a heavy casing, 50 caliber diameter, with a screw-in needle on the front for different kinds and lengths. An elk would use a 1″ or 1½″ with a short casing. When you had the needle out you could insert the drug and screw in the front. In the back, you loaded it with a special 22 caliber blank which fired the syringe when it hit the target, and this activated the injection. You had to estimate how much the animal weighed to figure how much material to give. It was easy to kill an animal, or not give it enough of the drug to put it down.

123

DICK ROBINSON

When I fired at "Honey's" rear end, I missed the leg, where there's much muscle, and hit her about 6 inches from the base of her tail, but right in the tail itself. There's not much but bone and nerves, so I could really be in trouble from this shot from damage to the tail. I hollered for help and followed her slowly, herding her for the cage. She moved slowly. The drug hardly worked.

We finally got to the compound, and just then the helicopter came in and landed. What was the problem? Well, I told the pilots, we were going to film a tiger, and would they stand by in case it got loose? We sure didn't want to tell them it had been wandering around and let it get back to the press.

After an hour and a half, the drug was working and the cat was acting goofy. We got some shots of it dodging around and running. I figured it was a terrible day. Later, they used the footage of Derby's cat for the commercial, and for me it was a lousy day's work. But, at least it ended well and it only cost me a couple hundred for the helicopter, so all in all I about broke even.

20 / Amor amor, the snake loved the waterpipe

After a W.K. tiger show in Texas, the Wild Kingdom people found that there were some extra sequences that could be used. Warren had gone to India to film Marlin doing the outside shots of getting into the howdah of an elephant, taking out his binoculars, searching around, finally seeing a pair of tiger cubs and saying,

"Oh look, tiger cubs, the mother must be around." Then he gets out his trusty Bell & Howell camera and starts filming the show. Like a serial, this leaves us an opportunity to start another show and use the extra sequences (which I didn't get paid for) and just film a couple more for an entire new show.

They had gone to the Gir Forest, which was in the middle of a drought, to film an Indian Lion show. There were only 50-60 animals (lions) in the whole preserve and the only real filming they got was a monkey scampering over a female lion suckling her young, and a tied up water buffalo being casually grabbed by the throat, slowly throttled by the lions, then eaten tail first which was pretty mucky. All together about 5 to 6 minutes out of a show of 24.

Chicago was windy and hot when I went into the offices of "Wild Kingdom" and watched the work done so far in India. We struck a price on doing the shows and then I was shown what needed to be done. Now it was my job to finish it.

Finding the right terrain was the next task. Because of all my travels up and down the west coast, I remembered various sections of country in which a show could be done. Paso Robles was one. It was hot just then, the grass had turned to golden and just the oak trees had color. Taking a plane I flew to Paso Robles, landed at an airport a few miles from town, borrowed a car and went to look for locations. The coloring was great, just like the drought in India, and finally, an hour after talking to some people, I found a ranch. It was ideal: good shooting locations and a place for a compound with a little lake. This was it! Everyplace you would walk here was covered with gopher snakes and I figured Ray could use a few. I took off my socks and stuffed some in and tied them, then, my shirt came off. Next my T-shirt. Snakes were everywhere. Even my brief case was full. I didn't have much on when I reached Los Angeles but sure had a load of snakes.

Ray furnished more animals, and especially a large Indian reticulated python that was one of his prized possessions. It was strictly on a loan basis and the python was to be guarded with my life. A local man had a large European blue boar, such as they had in India, which could be rented. There were 3 of my big 150 pound African lions that were tame and that I had been training for an act along with all the others. Tim and I put up 1500 ft. of fencing and waited for Warren to fly in. He had been in the hospital for a month recovering from the trip to India and was still a little shaky for lack of exercise but recovered quickly once outside and moving around.

Tim returned to LA to look after the animals and it left just Warren and me to do the work. Nothing went right! The tiger picked up the boar by the head and dragged all 300 lbs. of it off, the owner got mad and we had to pay him double. Ray's good snake got out of its sack in my motel room, went into the bathroom and crawled up under the sink, got entwined around the pipes and refused to come out. It had been put in a sack with DDT powder to delouse it and it had got the top open.

The black lady who cleaned would throw the towels into the bathroom and slam the door. It was lucky she would do my room. The lions acted crazy and would be a real nuisance with their playing with each other, which was fine for awhile, but got annoying when they started seriously chasing people. One needed to look like he fell off the cliff in the water so I rigged a box on a platform over the edge of the cliff that would trip and dump him in. It worked, but when he dropped onto the steep slope near the water, he would come to a screeching halt just before going in.

Every day there would be an hour spent trying to work the snake out from under the sink. The manager would come in and watch giving me directions for I'd get one end free and then the other would take up. We decided that if we couldn't do it the next to last day of shooting, we'd call a plumber. The snake was about 8 feet long and loved the warm pipes.

Warren and I worked for a couple hours along with the manager on the critical day and got it free. What a relief! The snake had to work with some small animals and did great! The show was wound up and Warren left, off to film another great adventure on Wild Kingdommmmmm...I found a man to help me wind up wire fencing and posts which took a couple days and headed home. This show was work....

21 / "Don't worry, I'm not violent."

We did lots of animal trading in Texas and one of the characters we had to deal with was Ralph Brown. He owned an indoor zoo which was well-kept, did well financially, had a good variety of animals and was an interesting place. Ralph just wasn't honest with people and unless you got your money or trade when you made the deal, you were out of luck. He was worth trading with for he had things in his kids' zoo, for instance a nice little tame buffalo, that couldn't be found other places and he would trade.

One night I pulled into Big Springs where the zoo was. There wasn't time to do anything, so I got a motel room and parked my trailer and animals in front of the door. I went in and went to bed. Deciding a book was the cheapest entertainment for awhile I lay in bed reading. A half hour later there was a ring at the door. Opening it a crack to see who was there, brought a real surprise. A pretty blonde in a bathrobe. She said,

"Hi, Mr. Animal man, mind if I come in?"

"Come on," I said, going back to bed again, pulling up the blankets, stacking the pillows and waiting to see what would happen.

My clothes were stacked on a chair in front of the bureau where I had taken them off and the hunting knife I habitually carried was on the dresser.

She had eyed the knife as she came in and looked around. She

128

came to the side of the bed, sat down on the lower end and started talking. She talked about how she had left the hospital, walked through three miles of corn fields to get to town and then made me promise not to turn her in..

Now I was surprised. She rambled on talking and telling me about her problems. She was the daughter of a Colonel at Fort Bliss. She looked at the knife and said,

"Don't worry, I'm not violent."

This went on for an hour. I was getting bored. She was sitting at the edge of the bed. When she leaned over toward me, I thought she was going to kiss me, instead she gave me a hell of a bite just above my hairline. I reacted instinctively and knocked her across the room. Wow! Did that ever hurt my head and finally the blood started to flow. She didn't seem upset but said it was time to go back to her room. I got some merthiolate out of my first aid kit and, after washing the wound, put some on and went back to bed.

The next morning I went to the zoo and was talking to Brown and a couple of helpers when I mentioned,

"The craziest thing happened to me last night," and they laughed and said,

"A blonde bit you on the head?"

I was floored. How did they know? Seems it was a regular occurrence. Now human bites are dangerous compared to an animal and it took a month before it healed.

Brown kept up his dirty dealings and finally a man came in to collect one day. Brown said he could go to hell. The man pulled a pistol and shot him in the head! Dead! It was a terrible mess in more ways than one. If they did put the killer away he sure deserved a care package.

22 / Willie, what a bear!

Willie was born about the 11th or 12th of January at the Los Angeles Zoo, and I just happened to be there that day and watched Dr. Gale come from the den with this small bear. It was about 10-12 inches in length, brown with soft fur, probably weighing a little over a pound. I felt that it was a real thrill to see this, and wanted it in the worse way. It gradually became the mascot for the opening of the new zoo, was much photographed, and was being bottle-raised by the girls in the nursery of the kids' zoo. But he started to get aggressive and became too much for the girls to handle because he loved to play rough.

As the trading relationship built up, there were more and more animals that were surplus, and I was starting to find how to go through channels of the city bureaucracy to get them, and who to talk to to speed the way. However, Dr. Gale was the key man.

Jaguars were another of the animals that seemed necessary to have, and eventually there were 11 tame cats. A jaguar show was partially done. They were used in all the shows, for they were bright and colorful and would work. Several more bears came from the zoo as year followed year, for now the new cats and bears went to me every year.

Not everything turned out well at the zoo, however. I remember needing all kinds of game animals at the YO ranch and it kept me looking for African animals, which were scarce with the kind of money that I had.

I found one old zebra surplus at the zoo which brought on immediate action. It cost $900 cash before delivery, and I bought him in the pen. It was 11:30 in the morning and several of the keepers were working hard at catching him. It was hot work. The vet drugged him to quiet him and we roped him, dragged him into a crate and loaded him on the truck. We all went to lunch and waited for him to quiet down. When we returned, there was a dead zebra, so, instead of going to the YO, it went to Art Bryant's for the hide to be removed. Eventually I got $100 out of it.

You never know until you have the animal delivered! Capture guns were the big thing and the drugs were readily available through the zoos. The big problem was that a lot of the time you would kill as many as you would get, so it was a case of catching animals, if possible, without harming them.

This meant good catching facilities, such as catch pens and loading chutes for hoofed stock, and squeeze-crates for cats and other smaller animals to get them in for loading and doctoring. It was an education by itself. A trader needed a large enough markup to cushion himself when he had losses, which everyone had, and then he needed a good collection system, for some zoos were terrible about paying. The directors could always use the excuse that the city council hadn't furnished the money yet, or the zoo society hadn't met yet, or their fund raising hadn't worked, or something. At one time the more business I did, the poorer I became. At least the movies brought in cash sometimes.

Living on top of Topanga was a boon for all of us. Going west on the highway brought you down the hill to Malibu, Santa Monica and around to west Los Angeles. Going east down the hill brought you to the valley, where you could go north to Jungleland or east to Africa, USA or find convenient freeways to the zoo or about anyplace you desired. Los Angeles was only twenty-five miles and the freeway was only a mile and a half from the house where I lived. The country was beautiful and the compound with all the cages was isolated from all the civilization around it. You could stand and see no houses and nothing but hills and valleys. In short, it was heaven for me and, while the animals didn't realize the significance of it, I did.

Alas, I was only going to be allowed six months for this sojourn. The fire marshall came along one day, looked the place over and told me we'd have to move. Why? He decided that if there was a fire I'd turn all the animals loose. It was an arbitrary but final decision. I had 30 days. I tried to appeal, but no. There had been fires, would be many more, and the fire people had complete control. I started to look.

Tony Bauman and his wife had a leopard act, an arena, cages and trailer situated in a wrecking yard in Sun Valley just north of Burbank. There was an extra building and some pavement. I could join them. There was nothing else to do but move.

Everyone was nice. It was convenient for everything and I would just have to make do. This is a business that I went into for the love of it and I had to accept what came along.

One thing about living at the wrecking yard was the availability of a welder and someone to help rebuild my trailer with the alligator tank in it. I built a house on it over the tank by siding up the deer pen with cedar boards, mounted a generator on the side for 110 volts and put a freezer in the front to hold 500 lbs. of meat. It could now be lived in, and carry animals and food for a good trip or a couple weeks in the woods on a picture.

Buying a big 1½ ton truck solved the problem of handling the trailer better and it could handle a load of cages also.

My biggest project was to trade for a cub grizzly they had at the Los Angeles Zoo. I still had the desire from being outside the cage when the vet., Dr. Gale, came out with this day-old bear. The cub was going to be put on the surplus list and it was going to be expensive. I had to get it at just the right time and I did. The cub had been used for extensive publicity and was on the emblem of the zoo. They had a good exhibit of bears, had cubs every year and this was my chance to move.

A deal was approved by the Los Angeles City council to trade between Dick Robinson and the Los Angeles Zoo: 1 hippo (female) and 2 Cape Hunting dogs for 1 cub Grizzly bear. The bear was getting too big for the women guides and keepers at the children's zoo and he could go. His name was "Willie" and what a bear! He was the best natured bear there was, loved to play and get into trouble but could take discipline. We spent much time together getting acquainted and now Pat Frawley and I were working on putting a deal together for a short show on a boy and a grizzly cub. 10,000 feet of film was to be shot for this TV story and the pay would be $10,000 for my work. It was to be handled through Jack de Nove, a commercial producer. Renting an Arriflex camera and outfit, hiring a cameraman, Mike Hoover, and finding a boy to play the part in the film took but a short time. I loaded all the native animals that were needed on the trailer, loaded all the gear and supplies and headed off for Jackson Hole, Wyo. It took several days with the big truck and the rebuilt trailer for we were heavy and slow. Rather than stay in the trailer in Jackson, we found some cabins outside the town about ten miles in an area called the Gros Ventres.

We spent four or five weeks filming, getting all kinds of footage with the boy being lost and finding the grizzly cub that was supposedly lost also. There was lots of animal action with the boy and grizzly cub together. I was broke all the time and had to take the film back and really argue for any of the money that was coming.

I brought back my car and a few more animals and after looking at some of the film at de Nove's, I could have cried. It looked so bad, out of focus with bad lighting, that it really took the wind out of me. Mike got all the blame for his filming and Frawley had the film stored and nothing was done with it. Several years later I looked at it again at Technicolor and it was perfect. The equipment I used when I was at Jack's was so bad it looked rotten but with a good projector it was fine. I owe Mike a large apology.

Finally I managed to get $8500 out of the deal so someone got the rest. It was really a bad deal and Frawley always accused me of wasting the money, but it wasn't so. That film could be used right now.

A couple of weeks before shooting was finished a fellow came by and wanted a job. He said he could do anything, that his name was Rod Allin and he impressed me for wanting to work. He told me about the filming experience he'd had with Warren Miller, the skiing movie maker and what he'd done on his own. Putting him to work cleaning cages, carrying cameras or whatever was necessary brought out the realization that here was a man worth helping. He really impressed me and we started a lifelong friendship. Rod turned out to be a first class camera man and could always be called on to do a first class job. He always seemed to have back trouble but took it in stride and would never falter no matter where you went.

After we finished the film for Frawley, I had to come to a decision on a turning point in my life. From now on it was to be films or nothing. The animal trading had been good for a background, but my real life was to make my own pictures someday. I had bought my own Bolex 16mm movie camera and tripod and now I would do what I wanted.

23 / *Wild Kingdom*

Contacting "Wild Kingdom", I went to the Don Meier Productions in Chicago and laid out my capabilities for a couple of shows. They had me prepare a script outline on two shows for Jackson Hole which were approved by the sponsor. Fifteen hundred apiece for furnishing the animals, handling, and directing but again I was learning. This time, Ralph Nelson, a photographer for them would come and Rod would be a cameraman, help me and I would do everything else. We would start in a few weeks.

In the meantime, an Australian cameraman by the name of Des Bartlett had been introduced to me and we had started doing a little work together. He was filming for Anglia TV in England and was working on a beaver special. I worked some of my animals with the beaver and made a few dollars from him and got some more experience. His wife and daughter were with him and all three traveled in a Landrover and a station wagon when moving. They were first-class photographers and we all got along well together.

It was well into the fall when Ralph Nelson arrived with the camera equipment and film to start "Wild Kingdom". These were going to be different shows, special shows showing a piece out of the life of an animal and to be narrated by a real narrator instead of Marlin, who was going to be used on the commercials only. Ralph Nelson, at that time, was big and overweight and really didn't like to go far or carry his equipment any distance. I assumed the responsibility for picking locations and deciding on the action. This didn't sit well with Ralph at all.

I was a contractor and Ralph worked steadily for them so he figured that put him in a special category. He didn't like to take any direction from me. Staying in a motel on company payroll was great for him. Rod lived at home and I had to feed animals first, pay my expenses and didn't have much left.

Winter was coming and going so the filming was discontinued around the valley and Rod and I decided to film up behind Teton Village, a ski resort, before it was too late. It was straight up for 8 miles. The truck was loaded with animals and gear and we started. The nose of the truck seemed to be straight up. We made it a mile but then the wheels spun out and we had to back down and turn around. Everything and everyplace on this road was straight up and down. When we got to the bottom there were several men waiting and watching us, part of the ski company's crew. They said they didn't think we'd make it so were going to wait and see what happened. We pulled out the chains, got them on and started up again with the gallery of men waiting to see the fun.

Some of the turns were so short I'd have to back up and go forward a couple times to get around a corner and then spin out, it would be so steep. On one particularly bad one Rod said to heck with it. He'd walk. It was scary, but we made the 8 miles to the top. It was right at 10,500 ft. and the scenery was spectacular. We set up camp, erected tents and unloaded cages. The next day we filmed around camp. It was the most beautiful mountain country you would ever want to see. We were camped on the upper edge of a bowl, probably a mile across with the far side going up another thousand feet to the top with the only snow around.

I decided that the place to film for the next day was the top of the snow. It should be cute to have the grizzly cub sliding down from the top. It was steep! Ralph, who finally got up there, didn't think it was at all cute.

The next day, the four of us headed off. Rod, Ralph, Willie and I. It was all rocks up and down and finally after an hour we reached the snow-line. Ralph was still a long way back. Rod and I took to the edge of the snow and started climbing. Half way up, Rod stopped and sat the camera down, said to have the bear slide by was the best. I went on to the top dragging the grizzly behind. It was work!

Trying to hold the bear was a slow pain and finally Ralph made it to the bottom. Rod had a habit of having his camera ready the moment he sat it down while Ralph stood around playing with his for five minutes before he could get ready. It was a bad habit.

I couldn't wait any longer and was going to throw the bear off. Ralph got mad and started to scream and holler from the bottom that he was directing this and it would go when he said. I guess I told him to stuff it in his ear and threw the bear. Willie went down part way and I had to take him back up again and do it over. Ralph must have got the idea, for he was filming also. Rod's film came out great.

The bear went down in great style the next time in a beautiful slide for several hundred feet. Rod pointed out that if you filmed as they went by and had the mountains in the background that it really looked steep on film and you got that impression, but filming up, it looked flat. He taught me many tricks that he had learned from ski-filming with Warren Miller.

Ralph was really upset at having to work at my say-so and there was a big confrontation about it. He called up the office in Chicago and got the final word: we were to work together, but my decision was final.

On our portable radio there was news of a storm approaching so Rod and I decided to go into Jackson. It wasn't safe to drive that day for the road was covered with mud so we were going the 8 miles to the bottom on foot. Ralph elected to stay. The eight miles to the bottom didn't take long and then we caught a ride to town. Boy, were my legs cramped. It snowed and blew for three days before we could get on top again. As we plowed into camp we decided Ralph hadn't been out of his tent since we left except to feed the animals.

The tram could be taken to the top and then a hike of over a mile downhill to our camp. Some of the shots we took there were great, with the fog swirling around the points overlooking the valley. Both the bear and mountain lion were used.

Getting down ended up being serious business. The snow melted and the road hung on some cliffs that slanted down and out, and were muddy. As far as I was concerned, we couldn't do it alone with the truck without sliding off, so I made a deal with the ski company to take down their big bulldozer that day, chain my truck up to the back of it.

Even at that I kept the door open ready to jump. It was a slow trip to the bottom, and one I really wouldn't care to make again at that time of year.

We moved the filming 35 miles from Jackson to another area called Granite Creek, a beautiful little valley in the high mountains, with beautiful scenery, moose, deer wandering around, and the prints of one big grizzly.

Camp was set up in an area about a mile from a set of waterfalls, which we filmed around. One section of the river was about 20 to 30 ft. wide and a couple of ft. deep, very swift and choppy as it ran down by a cliff and the edge of a mountain. It had little 2-3 ft. rapids that boiled, and I wanted to have my mountain lion washed down this river and over the falls.

I now had a tame half-grown lion and 2 wild ones that all matched color and size, so it was planned that the tame one would do the work that was easy and yet hard for the wild cats. The wild cats would do the hard work of diving off the falls. First we needed a way for the cat to fall in the river.

A tree across the river would be good, maybe meeting the grizzly half-way and having the mountain lion jump in, but first I had to get a tree across. I found the perfect place and a tree to fall. Having logged in the woods for years my experience with trees was considerable and in my judgment there was just no way this tree could be sawed down with a chain saw. It was dead, tall and looked like the top would break off and hurt someone any minute. They were called "widow makers" in the woods.

We made a trip to Jackson when filming was done and purchased dynamite and fusing. The next day I carefully ringed the tree with the dynamite sticks tied together, lit a long fuse and ran! It went off with a terrific roar! Bark flew everywhere along with dust, dirt and pieces of wood. The tree just quivered. We filmed again and went to town that night and got more dynamite. I changed the direction of the sticks and arrangement, 12 sticks but with the same results.

I caught Ralph pointing his finger at his head now when I wasn't looking. The next day I got the blacksmith to weld on an extension and a handle to a wood auger the size of the dynamite sticks.

We got another supply and tried again the next day. This time I bored holes through the tree and filled them with the powder.

It was the answer. It worked great! Blew the tree down and over the river in just the right place! Only one problem. It broke up in six ft. long pieces. We got the mountain lion out onto the pieces of log in the river and he did fall off conveniently and did a creditable job but the effect still wasn't right.

One side was a cliff twenty-five feet high with the river running at the bottom, and several small ledges. Now, if the cat could just fall off a ledge into the river.

Putting the camera on the far side from the cliff, I had Rod help me get the cat and a hand held camera to the ledges. It was straight up, around on the side of the hill and then practically straight down thru a crevice onto the ledge. I had a hold of the cat's chain but he managed to fall on me while coming down knocking my pipe out of my mouth and it dropped on down into the river. I was furious! My good pipe! Getting the cat down onto a ledge where he couldn't get off was the object and I found one.

Rod headed back for his camera and I petted the cat while I waited for Rod to get set and then turned him loose. Then taking the hand held camera I climbed up on another ledge and filmed him walking back and forth. I had bought a new mouton winter hat and taking it off to film brought on another catastrophe. Lying on my stomach with it beside my elbow was all right 'til I had to turn and then I knocked it off the edge into the river during the action. I wondered if I could cost expense this off somehow.

I left the camera, jumped down on the ledge, patted the cat and saw a little dead tree laying against another ledge and picked it up.

DICK ROBINSON

It was about 12 feet long and with the cat standing beside me, ran it from the ledge to a rock that was sticking out about 10 feet from us. It was parallel with the ledge we were standing on and about 15 ft. above the river.

The cat was curious and walked the dead tree over to the rock while I held it steady. Rod and Ralph were filming the cat. When the cat got to the rock I let the end slide off the rock and then the whole thing dropped into the river leaving the cat stranded on the rock. He either had to jump in the river or jump back to the ledge and I quickly put 3 or 4 rocks on the edge so if he tried to jump back they'd slide in the river along with him. I hoped! I scooted back so they could film.

Rod was ready with his camera but as usual Ralph was standing fiddling with his camera when the action occurred.

The cat made a flying jump for the ledge, caught a couple of the loose rocks with his front feet, gradually slipped in the river with a big splash and got washed down the river. He went about 50 feet, walked out, shook himself off and lay down to wash himself. Quite an adventure. I climbed back the way I came, waded the river, got back to the cameras and put the cat away. Rod got a great shot but Ralph got none. He was mad because we wouldn't wait the action till he was ready. For the next few days we would throw the cat into the river 2 or 3 times a day, let him swim and fight the rapids, then walk out.

Willie was to be on a ledge high up in the snow while he was looking for a cave to hibernate in. I took him on a chain and Rod with his camera outfit and mucked through two feet of deep snow up a steep mountain to a ledge which took a half hour to make. Ralph fell far behind and we had to wait half an hour for him. It took five minutes to film.

While we were sitting waiting we looked and saw a beautiful snow slope that went down for a thousand feet to the highway. When it was finished we gleefully headed to the top of it. Rod went first with the camera gear, sliding on the seat of his pants with the camera tripod over his shoulder. I followed with Willie on his chain, sliding right behind me. My feet were pushed into the snow for brakes at the bottom after this exhilarating ride down the side and we climbed off the shoulder at the edge of the road and walked a couple hundred yards to the truck.

Ralph slowly climbed down and it was another half hour before he made it to the truck. He left a couple of days later for another shoot for WK and Rod and I finished the show by ourselves.

A fence compound was put up about a mile south of our campground where we had an elk killing scene with the lion and cubs feeding off the carcass. We used all the animals in different combinations and it did get bloody but to me it was real life in the woods. While Rod was filming, I was taking stills which Rod laughingly called my killer pictures but later, through my agent in London, the pictures were published in practically every animal and nature book printed in Europe for years. They were part of nature.

There was a good sequence of the mountain lion falling off the cliff, being washed down the river and now we needed the shot of this cat going over the water falls.

With Rod and I left to do the work it was going to be touch and go. The river was wide and fast with a cliff on the far side and the waterfall cascaded down 60 to 70 feet. I had to convince one of the wild mountain lions to cross the river from the far side and get swept over but first I had to get the cat across and into position. Rod was going to film from a cliff on our working side and couldn't help me if anything happened. I put a rope noose on a hoe handle and, putting the noose over the cat's head to keep him from biting me, I went across the river. It was just below my hips deep, probably 3 feet and 30 feet across and very swift!

I fought my way across with the cat without getting washed down, got my rope tied to a rock and let myself down the edge of the river against the cliff for a hundred feet with only the rope holding me.

I had the rope in one hand and the noose and cat in the other. I stopped about 20 feet above the falls, turned the cat loose and waited for him to get washed over, only he just walked out in the water, as fast as it was going, without a slip. Then, turning, he came back and attacked me. Jumping for my throat, he came after me time after time. I would put my arm up to let him bite at it, and move up the rope to get back to a little point of dry rocks. He was still after me. I had blood all over my arm and now I had to catch him. One last jump on the point of rocks and I took the stick, clubbed him between the ears and knocked him cold.

I put on the noose and when he woke, I went back across the river and put him in his cage. Then we went up to a hot spring about a quarter mile from us, soaked my arm for half an hour in the flowing mineral hot water and headed off for the hospital in Jackson to get my arm stitched up. It was so sore that it would be several days before it could be used.

Next time I used the other cat and I clipped off his claws (for I figured that the cat was using them to hang on to the bottom; I was wrong). I let myself and the cat down to the top of the falls, with the rope tied around my waist, then took off the noose, grabbed the cat by the base of his tail and the scruff of his neck and, with a wild heave, threw him in right at the brink of the falls. Over he went!

I never did see what happened until I saw the film. He went down part way, hit a rock, went on further and into the pool at the bottom. He finally came up and I saw him climb out, walk off and lay down to wash himself. We had a forest service man watching who pitched in and helped. I made it back to safety, crossed the river, and got to the bottom of the falls and caught the cat. I kidded Rod that, if I ever got swept down, I wanted him to be sure and film it all!

Rod got the shows of me being chewed up but Don Meier never would give them to me. When the film was finished everybody agreed it was the best show ever done like that for Wild Kingdom but the results from the public weren't good. Too many people complained about the cameraman not jumping in and saving the cat from going down the river. It looked so real and close that they wanted the cat saved before it went over the falls. (And the cameraman?)

Most of the work was done with my good tame cat; it was easy for him without serious jeopardy. (Something about cats always landing on their feet.)

We moved down 10 miles and did a den sequence with Willie going to bed for the winter. We used an overhang of a cliff by the main highway. We put a black plastic up to partition it and got lights and a generator. It turned out great for Willie was drugged, sleepily made a bed, curled up with steam coming out his nose from the cold and went to sleep.

They didn't use it, but I saw the scene later in Chicago. It was things like this that soured me on working on contract. I really worked hard for something that wasn't used and then, sometime in the future, it would show up in which case I would get no pay for it. It would be prepared for TV and then it may be used in a full-length movie without remuneration. Don promised that he would let me have this piece back but when it came time there were excuses.

24/ "Bolt the horns on that elk!"

As the winter came on and it got colder, the filming slowed for few wild life photographers would brave the elements in such cold weather and now it was below zero much of the time. During the day when it warmed up the cameras could be run for a little filming. Willie was used in as many scenes as we could for he was the star of this show and the mountain lion of the other. There were scenes of Willie playing and chasing on the ice of a pond and going out in a field with me to inspect a bull moose. (We were both crazy for doing it and he chickened out first).

We climbed around ledges where mountain sheep and deer could be found and then Dave Currant brought an eagle over from Laramie, Wyoming. It was used to sit on a deer carcass and then would get chased off by the bear or the mountain lion. Teton Marsh in the park was a good location where the trumpeter swans were filmed and then we got slow motion shots of them flying. Boy, did it get cold! They would roost right on the ice.

On Christmas day, Des, the Australian, and I had found an elk carcass on a ranch and decided to film it. It was a half mile into the field so he with his Land Rover and I with my 1½ ton truck headed down thru the snow to the carcass. The snow was hard and deep and, even with the chains on the back duals, it was a battle to make it. This was going to be done with both the grizzly and the mountain lion which were in their cages on the truck.

We took a pair of horns and bolted them to the head of the elk for it was a cow and the horns would give a better effect, even if they were the wrong color. It started to snow. Both of us were filming. The bear used the carcass first and then we turned the cat loose. He rushed in and decided that it belonged to him. They played and snarled 'til we had got plenty of film. It started to snow, which added to the feel of it, and then we developed a slight problem with the horns, as they started to wobble when bumped by the animals, so we got a wrench and tightened them. It really looked good.

The animals were loaded, and both the trucks started for the highway. Des engaged the four-wheel drive on the Land Rover, which made it to the road, but the truck just couldn't fight its way through, for it was uphill. We had several inches of new snow, and the chains on the truck wouldn't pull. By this time it was 2 o'clock, and we were hungry. Some yuletide!

Des went to town, and an hour later showed up with a bright red tow truck. It looked like Santa Claus had come. They threw me a cable, three hundred ft. of it, and pulled me to the road. Des had pursuaded an acquaintance who had a tow truck to leave his Christmas dinner and come after me. That's a friend!

Finally getting to the Wirth Hotel, after putting the animals away, and getting a hot toddy and turkey dinner did it for me! Merry Christmas!

Moving into a boarding house instead of the cold trailer put me in social contact with more people. It was always hard, when working, to find a girl or woman who was fun to be with and to enjoy life together.

There was Janice who was nice, but after we had done a little drinking and went swimming in a hot spring at 10 degrees below in the middle of the night, she thought better of it, and discontinued our relationship.

I had my eye on one very good looking girl, much younger, and would talk to her occasionally but I never had the nerve to ask her out. I finally got to the point about a week before I left, and it surprised me when she said yes to dinner. It seems she was as much interested as I all the time, and we ended up in bed. It taught me a good lesson, at least; always ask. Now I found out, after 6 months and with only one week left. Some romance!

The shooting ended for Wild Kingdom and still I didn't have enough money to leave Jackson; but a week later I made a nice deal with Bud Wiser, of Metromedia in Hollywood, to do a short piece for a TV special called "Big Cats – Little Cats". Soon a couple of men arrived at Jackson, did some filming on it, and headed back. It was March and cold! I took a kid from Jackson to help me, and we headed for Tucson. It would really be nice to get to the warm weather. Des and his wife also went to Tucson.

25 / Rastus, javelina, enforcer

The first thing on arriving in Tucson was to get organized, find a place to stay for ourselves, and a place for the animals. Several miles out from town was a deer park that hadn't been a financial success and had been sold. I managed to make a deal with the old owner to have a place for the animals, and to buy some of the animals that were left before the new owner took it over for a housing development. He had two tame javelinas that we could use for filming, which delighted me.

I got the animals situated, found a little apartment for me and immediately had to finish some of the shooting for the hour special that we were working on for Metromedia.

Getting a mountain lion to stalk and knock down a deer and, obtaining some grizzly shots with the mountain lion, were the remaining things that had to be done.

The cat-deer shots we did at a little lake called Rose Lake, on Mt. Lemmon which was down from our camp area and rather isolated so we thought. These deer shots were done one evening when all was quiet, and then the next day we started working with the grizzly bear at the lake.

The lake covered about 2 acres, was surrounded by trees, and there was a little road on one side that came down from the parking lot at the campground. At this time my grizzly was a year and a half old and very playful. He liked to run and jump and just have fun when he was turned loose.

There were several people from the game department looking at something at the south end of the lake while we were filming on the north end with the bear, who was just playing around. The game people started to walk up the trail around the lake, talking to each other and pointing here and there.

The little road coming down from the parking lot was too steep to walk, and at the bottom Willie was running and playing with a stick, which I was filming, when down the road came a young couple from the parking lot. They were probably in their early twenties, holding hands and laughing and talking. I put my head up from the camera, put my hands to my mouth and shouted at them to turn around, go back to their car as fast as they could for there was a grizzly bear down here.

They giggled a bit and kept on walking down the road. I hollered at them again and they giggled some more. About this time Willie stuck his head around, saw them, and started walking up the road toward them. They really couldn't believe their eyes. This time there was some action when they heard my voice for they turned around and started walking. Now Willie loves to chase people so the faster they walked, the faster Willie went and by the time they got to the top of the hill they were at a dead run, and believe me, that bear was at a fast run right behind them.

Dropping everything, grabbing a chain, I took out after them. They just made it to their car in time, jumped into their bug, and when I got there Willie was looking in the windows and scratching at them with his claws. Everyone got a big laugh out of the bear trying to play with them through the windows. The game department people followed us up for they had seen and heard it all and got quite a laugh out of it, and took some pictures of the little bear trying to get in.

Actually the bear wouldn't and couldn't have hurt them. He was small at this time and probably was only 150 pounds in weight, although he looked awfully big because he had a lot of winter hair on him.

Willie was still walking around trying to get in when I got there and put the chain around his neck. He'd had his fun, but it really scared me in its own way. As an animal man I am responsible for the people that are close by, and even a bear that wouldn't hurt someone nevertheless could scare someone so badly that he might fall over a rock or fall off the side of a hill, or anything could happen and it would be my responsibility. This is one of the things that I spend a great deal of time thinking about, worrying about, and planning for in case something should happen.

This was some of the first film work that I had done independently, so after getting the film together and sending it off to the people in Hollywood I waited on pins and needles to see what happened.

Happily, a check came back in a few days so there was enough money to keep going on, and, they thought the film was all right.

Des was working on some desert shows and still doing some beaver things, so the animals went to work again. Working with Des was certainly not very profitable, but it got me further into my own filming. He would pay me a little money and give me a little film so that there would be something in my bag to show for it. More than anything else this was a whale of an education. While Des was getting well-paid, he certainly didn't help out in comparison to my financial needs, but no matter. Whatever we did seemed to earn us just enough to keep from starvation.

When filming animals, we would put together a compound if we had to contain the action for good shots. To do this we usually put up a six-foot wire fence on steel posts and wound it up and down hills to lay out the shooting area so that it got the best light. This was necessary because there were usually two animals in a confrontation, and sometimes they would get excited and run away.

An area was usually picked that had a little valley in it, so that a cameraman could stand on one hill and film across that valley, using a long lens, so as to see the action on the other side without getting too close and interfering with what the animals were doing. This was likely to be one hundred yards at the very most.

Possibly there would be two camera locations, so that we could get down in the valley and film up the hill or up the valley to vary the shots and not look like it was all in the same place.

Des had a little house about 10 miles from town, and the compound was only a short way from it. Of course, it was nothing but desert, with lots of cactus and small bushes. Jon and I put in about 1800 ft. of fencing, which was a typical area for filming. The left hand fence facing away would run down into the valley, up the side hill and around behind a small ridge, back around the far side, down a little valley and a hill, making a full circle around behind us.

There was a gate in the fence where we could drive the trucks, slide the cages off, and put them inside the compound. Here the cats, or javelina, or whatever, could be released. In this case we used the coyotes, skunks, badgers, mountain lions, or combinations of these animals. We would turn them loose inside the compound for filming, and then have to catch them again and put them back in their cages. If they were really wild we would use a catch wing on the outside fence for they invariably followed it and would go into their cages when they got to them.

At this time there were four mountain lions, one of which I had traded from Fred Gloy. This cat had only half a tail so it hadn't been used yet and Fred said it was only half tame which could make a dangerous situation. A cat like this wouldn't hesitate to go after someone. There were the other two wild ones that had been used to go over the waterfalls in Jackson and of course my tame one that could be turned loose anyplace.

At the first of the shoot with Des we had four javelinas (wild pigs), two very tame and full grown, with long tusks on them. Des promptly named the big male Rastus, who was super tame.

Now Rastus was very friendly and would come up to you for attention and although he didn't have any tail to wag, he did about everything else but throw his arms around you and his favorite trick was to jump in your lap if you were sitting down, and nuzzle your face. He must have weighed at least 60 lbs. and was quite a lap full.

Strangers were warned for it was scary if you weren't aware of what was going to happen. The female was also tame and she would come up and put her head across your knee if you were sitting down, but she might also inadvertently bite your leg (or deliberately) so we kept her off at a distance. Rastus was really our pet and we would turn him loose with half a dozen others that were semi-tame, which had been borrowed from the Desert Museum. They were used in mob scenes and they could be worked close in the compound for we had Rastus to keep them around close. On the first day of shooting, we had a man from the Game Department, who was supposed to catch some javelinas to move to another location and put on them some colorful collars and radio transmitters for tracking. There was great footage being filmed with the javelinas and mountain lions. The mountain lions would be eating on a javelina carcass when the "mob" would come up and drive the cats off and protect the body. Some sight.

Evenings we would drive around picking up road kills with the permission of the game dept. and of course all the animals out in the desert had no scruples about eating other animals or road kills so they became very important to us for filming, especially when we had mountain lions involved and they needed to have a victim. We had a great deal of good footage with all the creatures. Good ol' Rastus was so tame that he had no fear of the mountain lions and this pig would just wade right in.

Rastus would slice at the mountain lions with his front teeth and tusks which were so long that they would stick out of the side of his jaw. He would keep them sharpened by the opening and closing of the mouth and when a javelina started to clack his teeth you knew he was mad and all the animals knew too. He thought it was great sport to chase the lions and cut their throats before we were aware of his game and it wasn't long till he had the two wild cats unusable so we had to keep them caged for healing. It now got down to the last half-tame mountain lion I'd gotten from Fred. In this hot desert country we could film only once a day and that was usually from 7 o'clock in the morning when the shadows were long 'til 9 when it became too hot. The temperature would reach 110 and it was too hot for the cats.

Now was the time to use the half-tame lion. He was turned loose and went over the hill so I told Jon to go and shoo him down the hill toward us so we could turn something else loose and get some action going through the cameras. Jon disappeared behind the hill and soon we heard a holler from him.

"The lion's going to grab me; the lion is going to get me!"

I said, "Oh, baloney," and leaving my camera went up on the hill. Most of the times we carried pick handles along with everything else so, if we had problems with an animal, or if it chased us, we had something to fight him off with. Des left his camera and followed me and sure enough, when we got there the lion was crouched down, swiggling his way through the cactus on his belly getting ready to charge. He had a couple balls of choya cactus on his face and Jon was right. Usually he would yell before anything happened but this time he was right. The cat was still making little jiggles forward, one or two inches at a time and what he was doing was trying to make up his mind whether to go or not.

Sure enough, he went right at all three of us but only with little crouching springs that took him right through some more cactus. Some huge choya balls of splines covered his face and slowed him down. Our pick handles were up and ready for action. Fortunately, he stopped to try and get some painful splines off and slowly we backed off without being jumped while he was working on the cactus. We moved back without being attacked and the cat ran and crouched under a low mesquite. It now became clear that getting him back in his cage would take all our ingenuity for it was obvious we wouldn't be able to work the cat. Des suggested,

"Why not use Rastus?"

He was right. We knew Rastus's tusks could solve the problem if the ruckus didn't embroil all of us in battle.

Jon ran down the hill, turned the pig loose and ran back to us with the pig right behind. We tried throwing some rocks at the lion under the tree but he would just look and growl at us and get ready to attack again. Now, Rastus was standing beside me and Des leaned down and spoke to him.

"Rastus, get in there and get that mountain lion."

That lion's eyes opened wide when he saw Rastus starting to snort and, when he heard those teeth clacking, the hair standing on end and the squealing, he started to move! Rastus took after him at full speed 'til the cat made another low mesquite and moved his position 150 ft. closer to his cage. Rastus came back just wiggling all over. We petted him and thanked him and then went walking down to the next tree. At him again!

We were all laughing tears, for it was the funniest thing I'd ever seen. Nobody thought to get the cameras and record the action.

Twice more. The last time he got a nip at the cat's tail and, when finally the lion saw his cage, there was a streak as he got into it. Rastus came panting back to us, looking at us like he was saying, "Hey, how did I do?" That was one proud pig! I don't think we ever used the cat after that and finally swapped it off for something else. Des would tell Rastus,

"Good Ol' Rastus, let me tell ya, ya really did a job." I think that pig did get a pride out of doing this job; of course it was rather hard on the lions.

Finally the time came when we ran out of uses for the compound and that type of terrain. We needed to change so we moved with some of the animals to a spot about five miles away along a little creek. We took along my tame lion and placed Rastus alone on a nice green patch of grass in the middle of a water seepage and let him feed. He was really enjoying himself eating the grass and not paying attention to anything when we turned loose the tame cat. Now the cat was really playful for he was still only a year and half or so old, but of good size, so the first thing he did was to crouch down in the grass and very carefully stalk the pig. He made it about ten feet from him without detection, then quietly pussyfooted up to the back of the pig, put out his claws and banged him on the back. It didn't hurt the pig but, when those claws went to the skin, Rastus became unglued.

He jumped straight up in the air, looked at what had hit him, turned in air and went right after the lion when he hit the ground. Now the lion knew what the pig was all about so he took off in a run, jumped over a high bush and headed off up a hill expecting the pig to fall back, but the pig didn't bother with jumping over anything, he just went through the bush and straight after the lion. We

• could hear the bushes popping back and forth, all kinds of noises, the pig and the mountain lion both hollering.

The attack was filmed with Des using the 'cine and I shooting it with a large still graphic camera. Des got all the action with the 'cine and there was a possible still in it for me and a good vet bill. Following the action I found the fight and the wounded mountain lion. He had a gash in his back hip that you could just about stick your hand into. Rastus followed Des back into his cage feeling very proud. This made the third mountain lion that had been put out of action by Rastus. What he needed was a medal. I picked up the lion and carried him back to the truck and took him to the vet where it took 18 stitches in the side of his leg to close up the wound. That pretty well incapacitated the lion for a couple of weeks.

Working with bears was really giving me an education and Des was teaching me much about filming, what lenses to use and apertures to use. I had a windup Bolex 16mm camera already, and some lenses, a motor, and new fluid tripod that didn't work too well for him or me either. It wasn't that good but at least it got me started. This basic film footage was the first film footage we used for the "Desert Show" that I put together later on. Eventually I shot about 25,000-30,000 ft. of film in the desert during the next few months and the education I got with Des really paid off.

In the mornings we would film from 7 to 8:30, pick up our gear, load our animals and go back to his house which was a quarter mile away, sit and drink a shantie, which was a drink he'd picked up in South Africa that consisted of ginger ale and beer and, by golly, for a really quenching drink in the morning, or for just sitting around the pool, it was great!

Jen, Des's wife, would spend her time cataloging slides and doing their correspondence. Des did most of the movie filming and a great many of the slide shots, while Jen did most of the filming of birds. She would organize the slides and send them to their agents in New York and England and she did a great deal of the writing on many of their articles. It was interesting to see what this kind of life was doing to their daughter who was 12 at this time and had been following their ways from birth.

They ordered a correspondence school course for her from Australia where both of the parents originated, so she had the same course that the kids from the outback were taking. Aside from getting all of her required education through books, she also learned so much more by being along with them; and was a very well educated little girl of 12. Eventually when she got a little bigger, her parents put her in a private boarding school in Australia where she got the rest of her education. It was hard for her to part with her parents with whom she'd been traveling and living for so many years. Eventually I saw her when she was 17 or 18 and she was a very mature person.

26 / A ring for a stirrup

Late spring I did another show with Willie starring again. He was fast growing and acting more settled although he still enjoyed clowning around and playing. We remained great friends. He was to be roped and caught by Stan Brock. It was typical. Watch with the field glasses and go and catch.

Stan Brock had taken Jim Fowler's place on the show and was called the "barefoot cowboy." He had obtained a job in England to run a ranch in Guyana and down there it was hot, so the cowboys didn't wear shoes and used only a ring for their big toes when riding, instead of a stirrup. Stan had gone native with his job, was an excellent rider and roper, having done this for several years after leaving England. He had met the WK people on a show they had done there, and would work for the price WK was willing to pay. By now he had done a lot of their shows.

He had a very long rope made of leather such as the natives in Guyana use and he had roped many other animals with it in various WK shows. This was to be another first. He was good but not with a bear. He was mounted on a good roping horse, but it would have to get to a full gallop to catch Willie for the bear could really move out. Then he would hear the rope coming, duck his head and keep his head from being caught. Finally the guide, who owned a working cattle ranch, asked to be given a try. He wasn't any better. Finally they gave up and did it in pieces.

Never Kick A Bear in Your Bedroom Slippers

Wild Kingdom specialized in drugs, ropes and a few traps and spread the shows over the world in the role of saving the animals from danger, however that was. The idea was excellent and kept people interested. My work was mostly in the stories about animals having the adventures of growing up or facing danger.

The problem with the desert setting was the splines from the cactus that would go into Stan's feet. He had half inch callouses on his feet and they were tough, but when he got a cactus, well, it had to be cut out and it left a hole. He had to be careful and there were times when he would be seen sitting on logs or rocks, working on his feet with a knife. It was hard keeping one's feet in shape in modern civilization. There was a story going around that he used to walk down Michigan Ave. in Chicago to work, wearing GI boots with sand and gravel in them to keep his feet tough. It sounded logical.

We filmed several confrontations with the grizzly bear and dogs and then with a mountain lion. We had used a huge black bear in Wyoming, in the WK show. It came from a private zoo near Boise. It was a cage animal, not wild but then not tame. We had the dogs chase it in Wyoming, treed it for the show and then had to retrieve it. Using the capture gun worked out well in the end. The bear was hit, but only just enough to slow it down and at first we couldn't get him back in his cage. Then, everyone was trying to rope it but with no luck. A couple of old cowboys had come by and were watching all the carryings on and finally one of them said,

"Let me try it."

He took the rope, made a crazy swing over his head, and the loop sailed down from heaven right over the bear's head. Great! Everyone pulled him into the cage and loaded it on the truck. The old cowboy gracefully took his applause as the champ, and we all went home.

We used the same bear again in this show. We ran it around with the dogs and finally up a tree. Shot it with the same dose of capture medication as we did in Wyoming but it died in minutes. Capture guns were the pits. When they got the right medicine years later, they were better, but they were always dangerous to the animals. The guide took the skull which was later sized and rated at 6th in Boone and Crockett. It was a big black bear.

27 / Hauling bears to Alaska

Don Meier, the owner and producer of the Wild Kingdom show, and I had discussed doing a show in Alaska and, after several telephone calls about the project, decided to go ahead with two programs, one in Alaska and the other in the Wells-Gray Park in British Columbia. Both shows would be built around grizzly bears and cougars. WK had tried to film a show in Alaska but had never been successful, so now I would haul all the animals up there and try it my way. Rod would be the photographer, but the chief photographer, Warren Garst would come up, check him out, and then we would be on our own.

It would be my job to furnish most of the animals, transportation up and back for $5,000 a show. They advanced $5,000 and I went to work getting supplies, arranging for animals, permits from Alaska and getting across Canada. Rod would be going and another young friend, Clint Rowe would go along as animal handler and "gofer." Clint was 16, had worked for me before, and the trip would be good for him. There's nothing to beat travel to broaden a young person's education. He was good to have around if you could keep him interested and not let him get moody.

Alaska was going to be a long trip and, under my contract, I would have to furnish food for all three of us the first 60 days. Food was expensive along the Alaskan highway and especially in Alaska if

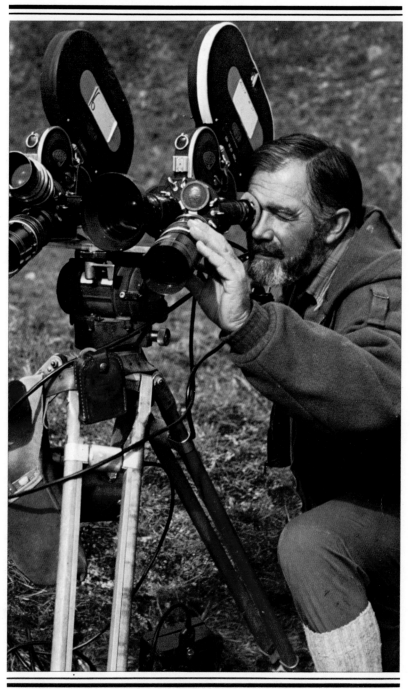

9 / Dick trying out Warren Garst's cameras in Alaska.

10 / "Honey," the tiger, and cub relax between shots for *WK* in Waco, Texas.

11 / Snaring the toothless monster on Lake Hi-huim in British Columbia for *WK.*

12 / The crew prepares for shot on *Bridie of the Grand Canyon.*

13 / "Willie" looking over a bull moose at Jackson, Wyoming.

14 / A friendly native wolf during *Wild Kingdom* filming in Alaska. Fall was there.

15 / Rod filming "Willie's" underwater scenes in a beaver pond in Alaska.

16 / Willie "lost" on a glacier for *Wild Kingdom* in Alaska.

17 / Glittering peaks of ice in an opposite view.

18 / Transporting a menagerie is less painful with a good rig.

19 / Dick and "Willie" taking a well-earned nap on a mountain top.

20 / Dick with Thiokol in *Friend of the Wind*. Spring of 1974.

21 / Carol with "Wilamena," the chimp and her pet javelina.

22 / Dick with mountain lion cubs at Cedar Breaks, Utah.

23 / Carol and "Missie" enjoy a quiet moment.

24 / Robert Redford, Sidney Pollack, Dick and "Willie."

all rumors were correct. I had one 15 foot deep freeze, bought another one especially to hold food for the trip. We bought large supplies of peanut butter, jams and anything that wasn't bulky. Also we bought several cases of Army C rations, filled the freezer with a hundred and fifty TV dinners and frozen foods that would last. The plan was to stop at night, plug in the freezers and keep the freezers frozen. The second freezer we filled with chicken necks all packaged for the animals, 800 lbs. of them.

Buying supplies, spare tires, tools, refurbishing everything took only a couple weeks and we looked forward to leaving the desert and the extreme heat. Extra drums for gas, which we would buy wholesale along the way, were loaded on forward next to the cab for siphoning.

Disposing of the extra animals was the hardest for me. Rastus had to go for there were no pigs in Alaska but we did manage to find a good home for him. Des would meet me there in a month or 6 weeks so the two of us could do some filming underwater if a good clear beaver pond could be found.

The second week in July we headed north for Idaho Falls where we were to pick up Rod. His wife "Chickie" brought him down from Jackson to meet us and load more materials. He wanted plenty of mosquito repellent and camera supplies and Wild Kingdom had forwarded all the cameras for us to carry. The truck itself had a twelve foot bed on it, was covered with cages two high and the trailer had a small living compartment that would hold supplies and had one bunk, for me. The rest would use sleeping bags.

Traveling with 3 of us in the cab got to be a drag after a couple of days. Rod would sit in the middle for he was the smallest but shifting gears regularly was an inconvenience. We soon reached the Canadian border where everyone was very courteous but why were we taking grizzly bears and mountain lions to Alaska? Our instructions were to say as little as we could about going to film for Wild Kingdom but after awhile we found a plausible, comfortable story and would lay it on people. "Experimenting."

Calgary was 250 miles north of the border and we immediately pulled into the zoo. We were to pick up a tame wolverine and a wolf and it would give us a chance to clean up cages, repair the trailer, get more supplies, gas and meet the people of the zoo, who were more than helpful. The wolverine was in their big cage but it certainly didn't look tame or even half tame. Now wolverines aren't large but they have a mean reputation and it is well justified. After getting the wolverine loaded, it promptly started eating through the wood floors in its cage which were 2 inches thick. Hummmmmmm, by adding to the wood maybe we could make it up there before the animal escaped. The wolf was excellent. I was to buy a couple of pups along the way so there would be a group for a supposed family.

Edmonton was another couple hundred miles north and the last big jumping off place for the north traffic. There were to be more animals loaded at their zoo when we went by. A hundred miles along the road an ominous grinding arose from the rear of the truck. With just enough money to get to Alaska, much less fix the truck, it was going to be necessary to do something. I pulled into the GMC repair depot in Edmonton, parked behind a big hanger where they had their shop, unhooked the trailer and took the truck inside where they could assess the damages. Sad news. Both the rear end and transmission were shot.

I called Don in Chicago, told him of my plight, and got the repairs started. A complete overhaul on both units. The crew was excellent from GMC. They worked on the transmission to make it as good as new, replaced the rear-end and, while doing this, helped us with the animals and furnished us transportation around while waiting. The money came in by wire for repairs, and I picked up the animals from the zoo.

There were all kinds of people around looking at the animals, asking questions, poking in fingers and trying to pet them. It gave me conniptions to think about what could happen so I just turned it over to Clint who liked to talk about the animals. I hid out. Clint was a great talker to older people but when it came to girls, well, then he became bashful. Rod and I were always trying to fix him up and it began to be a game to see what would happen.

After three days the truck was ready. There was pavement for a couple hundred miles and then gravel for a thousand. Up and down small but steep hills for days, dusty and hot, but there were beautiful mountains, moose and bears, trucks and tourists. We had tire troubles, but about everyone else had them too along with a broken windshield and always the question,

"How come you're hauling bears and animals to Alaska?" Pretty hard to explain. It was hard to keep our mouths shut about doing the show as everyone was supposed to think that Marlin Perkins actually went out there and filmed them himself. We had to try to keep the image. Going through the Yukon we got in an argument about how much Willie, the grizzly, weighed, so we stopped at a truck scale to find out. We off loaded him, put a chain on him and walked him onto this huge truck scale. He weighed in at 178 lbs. He had such a thick coat of hair that even some of the game officials thought he weighed at least 400 or 500 lbs. Now we knew for sure. But the operator of the scales turned us in as soon as we left, and down the road 20 miles a game warden stopped us. After checking our permits he allowed us to proceed.

Alaska came into view—the only difference was a narrow paved road instead of the gravel. We found a car wash at the first town, and washed off the dust and dirt from the truck and trailer, got ourselves cleaned up, and headed for Anchorage. There we were to get our permits, be instructed as to the locations for filming, and to find where a salmon run would be, which was our prime objective. Then we would wait for Warren to arrive from the States on a plane.

Seaplanes are fascinating to me, and at Anchorage was a large lagoon where there were hundreds of them to be seen. *One third of all the seaplanes in the world come through this small lake on the edge of the city.* What a sight! Of course they thought we were too. Hauling bears to Alaska!

There was lots of company. One fellow who owned a flying service came by and brought us a seven or eight pound smoked salmon out of his freezer at the airport office...just for Willie. He handed it to Clint, who started to chuck it into Willie's cage, but I grabbed it just in the nick of time.

"Don't give it all to him at one time," I said.

Then I broke off a small piece, with the man looking on approvingly, and I put the rest in the freezer. When he left, I told Clint that smoked salmon was $3 a lb.—a delicacy that we couldn't afford to give to a bear. After tasting a bite, he agreed that Willie should have the skin from it, and we should sample it slowly.

Anchorage was the place where most stopped to get fitted out. We bought climbing gear, supplies for a week on a glacier, along with our permits and animal feed. The game department officials directed us to a good place to film 75 miles inland at a glacier which was a couple of miles from the main highway.

Our camp was right at the base of the glacier, right where it came to an end. The days were still long, as it was the end of July and the sun didn't go down till 11 or so, and with the ice close to the truck, there were some nice cool evenings, for it was hot during the day. The glacier had a huge river of dirty ice water running out from the bottom of it, which roared by carrying a load of sand and small rocks, dangerous to cross and there were stories of people losing their lives trying to cross.

Crampons, a grid of spikes to put on the soles of our boots, were an absolute necessity, digging into the ice when we walked on it, and they made it easy to negotiate the hills of the glacier with all of our gear.

There were many crevices and narrow, worn valleys, sometimes with little ponds and melting water running through them, and the bear loved to walk through the canyons and swim in the little lakes. Everything was a startling white with pools of blue water.

Warren Garst flew in to work with Rod for a couple of weeks, checking out Rod's camera work, and, compared to us, he had it easy. He stayed in a nice lodge about 30 miles away, had great food and pretty girls, waitresses that is, and it was great! We were still on the C rations and TV dinners. Clint found out that by mixing several types of dinners together it changed the taste and was something new. Also I can recommend personally the mixing of scrambled eggs (C rations) and peanut butter, which makes an excellent breakfast food with some wholewheat bread around it. Very nourishing. There were many interesting natives at the lodge. One night Warren's credit card treated us to a dinner, which we all considered a luxury. Behind the lodge were mountains with white Dahl sheep to be seen and photographed.

After a week of Willie running around on the glacier it got to be boring, and I could see that we were wasting film. He was supposed to be lost and trying to find his way out before he starved to death. There was a collective sigh of relief when he eventually made it and we could get on to Paxson. This was an area where we could make a base camp at a hotel, and film at various spots close in where creek conditions were right for the salmon runs that were taking place.

About 30 miles short of Paxson was a large log cabin cafe with gas pumps, so we pulled in. It looked rather deserted, but on walking into the cafe we found a very courteous middle-aged Indian woman, who immediately waited on us. While sitting down at the counter my eyes lit on some delicious-looking blueberry pie in a case. Everyone starting ordering pie and my order was naturally blueberry, but she refused to let me have a piece. Why? It was a day old and wouldn't be good!

I couldn't believe it! At a dollar a slice this seemed to be crazy. Would she mind if I brought my pet grizzly in and he ate it? Kidding of course. It seemed a shame to let it go to waste, for only one piece was gone out of the tin.

"No, bring him in," she said casually.

Just as casually, I went out and jumped Willie out of his cage, put a chain on him, and then guided him into the building.

He was extremely well-mannered inside. There was a highway crew having coffee in a booth, and when they saw that grizzly go by them, they decided it was time to go to work, now! When Willie saw the pie on the counter he raised up, put one foot on the tin edge, looked at me for the go-ahead, and then literally inhaled that pie.

The Indian lady was duly impressed and said,

"My, he does like pie!", and put another full tin in front of him.

"Old?" I asked.

"Well, no, but he does seem to enjoy it," she said.

Willie soon finished, and we dragged him out and back into the trailer before he got used to the idea. I ended with fresh apple pie. It turned out that she was the owner, and if I would come back next week she would have some fresh blueberry pie I could take back. Very nice lady, and I ate many of her pies over the next month.

We went on to Paxson, set up our trailer in the hotel's private trailer park, and started looking for sets and places to film. Paxson consisted of a highway repair station, hotel, and service station. A few houses for workers and a few cabins were scattered around through the woods, as you find them all over Alaska. These were some very independent people, who live where they can find their privacy and still be fairly close to supplies.

Paxson was at a junction of the highway to Mt. McKinley and Fairbanks, and its greatest assets for us were the great scenery, the shallow creek beds where we could see and film the red sockeye salmon, and where Willie could fish. There were many moose wandering around that we could film in the wild, and hopefully some grizzly bears and wolves.

I had brought otters, wolves, coyotes, elk, badgers, snowy owls, foxes, deer, black bears, and a mountain lion, along with Willie, of course, and the wolverine, who had been steadily chewing on all the wood parts of his cage since we left Calgary.

Warren had arrived at Paxson a couple of days ahead of us, and was safely ensconced in a room at the hotel, writing on a book he was doing. He stayed for a few days to work with the wolf pups, for he was good with them and they liked him.

We built a compound with a 1,200 ft. fence around a little draw, with a beautiful mountain background. Our main object was to film several wolf pups and their mother in the compound, along with foxes and other animals. We were looking forward especially to using the wolverine, for they were seldom filmed except by one of Disney's crews, who had some tame ones.

We had the fence completed and had various kinds of animals ready to turn loose at appropriate times. Wolves were in cages wagging their tails waiting to be turned loose; two cameras were set up with Warren and Rod waiting for the action. I had the wolverine cage off on one side so that he would run by the camera and hopefully would play around out in front.

The wolverine bounced by the camera when he was turned loose, ran to the far fence, turned and ran along the fence for a couple of hundred feet, then stopped and scratched under in about 5 seconds and left. We watched as he bounced across the tundra until he went out of sight. Just think! A $350 dollar bill running across the tundra just like that! Don's going to be ticked! Outside of that, everything worked fine in our fenced area.

Willie was taken to a creek about a mile from the hotel and worked every day. To get to our area, we had to go by a dump where there there were 12 to 15 wild grizzlies that would come out at night, visit the dump, fish in the creek, then den up during the day. I never did see one during the day, and Willie worked without trouble 'til a tourist who went through the area shot and wounded a grizzly at the dump one night. We immediately moved to another area for a few days just in case, for we had no guns and had to be careful.

Grizzlies are taught to fish by their mothers, so I had to stand in and show Willie what to do. After several days he got the idea. Grizzlies catch salmon by sticking their heads in and grabbing the fish with their mouths, not by slapping them out as people are led to think. After he caught on he thought it was great. He found a pool with a hundred fish to chase. It was a dilemma. Which one would taste the best?

He would chase one after the other, with fish flopping and going in every direction. It made great filming. We brought an underwater camera to film the action and all went extremely well.

Alaska supposedly was short of women, but at Paxson there was a surplus. They had a large coffee shop and hotel, so they needed many women employees. All the waitresses, cooks, and other female help lived in the downstairs of the hotel so they could be close to their work. Practically all the trade was on a transient basis, and there were few steady men around. We regularly went to the coffee shop, but only for a big bowl of soup and an occasional piece of pie-a-la-mode—$1.25. It was heart-rending. We had little money for food with the average price of a meal starting at $8 or $9, but Warren would eat here, for he was on an expense account.

We did get friendly with the girls, though. They made pies for us, cut our hair, partied, and did all kinds of little things. Clint was so bashful that the girls would tease him, and that made him worse. Rod had one girl giving him the clothes her ex-husband had left when he moved out. Sometimes the parties went on all night.

Finally the owner of the hotel came and said we'd have to cool it. He was tired of having to break up fights downstairs over us, for the girls had come to pulling hair and fighting hand-to-hand to see who would get to party. Then we stayed away, but they would come to our trailer and visit.

One night we were in the bar with everyone drinking, when a man came in looking for me. Could I help him out? With what, I asked? He had been to McKinley Park, and his dog had a chance meeting with a porcupine. The dog was covered with needles all over its face and mouth. He was frantic, and was talking about going on to Fairbanks, which was 150 miles, for a vet. Gathering everyone together, we noosed the dog on the top of the mouth and got another noose on the bottom, and with flashlights for illumination we started pulling quills. It went on for a couple of hours. My hand was worn out from using the pliers, and all of us were under the weather from the drinks. When it was over he set up the house with drinks and headed back to McKinley.

The next day, sitting in the bar, I heard a familiar voice behind me. What now? Same thing! This time we sent him on to Fairbanks to the vet, for it seemed like a good time for the dog to learn a lesson (and his master).

By the 15th of August it had turned to autumn. The frost came quickly, and the colors were magnificent. Now we filmed a great variety of scenes. Our wolves were worked in front of the mountains, in the creeks with the otter we'd brought, and in the creeks catching salmon. There were many wild wolf tracks but no wild wolves to be seen.

Everyone visited around as we had time. Up the road at Big Delta was a crew from Disney doing a falcon picture. They were flying model airplanes by remote control, and had cameras mounted on them, and we were all very impressed. Frank Zuniga of Disney was directing, and getting some great film footage. It was good to meet other people in the same field, and we became acquainted with "Beaver" Nelson, who was to work for me later on a picture.

The hunting season started, and we were really careful when filming along the road, for we didn't want someone shooting Willie for a wild one. Crews came from all over to hunt. Big-tracked vehicles were every place, some so large that they had kitchens, bunks, and a bar to keep a half-dozen men in comfort. They clumped across the tundra shooting at moose, caribou, wolves, or whatever they saw. Planes would be called in if necessary to haul meat out. The parties raged for weeks in the bar. Thousand dollar bills weren't counted; it was the thickness of the stack that counted. Drinks were free from morning to night, and didn't slow down till the hunters went out for a few days to shoot. What a time!

Des and Jen showed up about the end of August, just when it was really starting to get cold. They stayed in a cabin behind the hotel, where they had a place to cook and sleep. It was small but comfortable, and we had a welcoming party with a bottle of red wine they had brought from home. They had brought their Land Rover packed with their daughter, cameras, and everything they owned. We decided to film some underwater shots in a beaver pond which was about 50 miles north of where the hotel was, towards Fairbanks. At Jackson there were few places to film underwater, because everything we touched disturbed the fine mud and clouded the water. We needed underwater shots of Willie swimming around on the surface and views of how a beaver pond was laid out for winter. The one we found was 10 feet deep and clear as a bell, 300 to 400 feet long, and had some huge beaver houses in it.

The pond was many years old and had a large dam to hold the water. Des had brought underwater scuba gear and suits, underwater cameras, with housings for them, to do this filming. This was strictly on a trade basis; he would furnish his gear to film for WK, and I would furnish the bear for him. This way we all came out.

After a couple of days all of us drove north to the pond, which was beside the road. Des put on the wet suit, loaded the underwater camera with film, and started filming with a snorkel for air. The water was so cold he lasted about ten minutes, and came out. Now I suited up and went in. It was great filming; the water was clear, and Willie took to it like a duck. He went to the middle, played in the water and then tried to tear the beaver house down. Fat chance. I lasted ten minutes and then came out. I got the suit stripped off, and got in the Land Rover in front of the heater. It took 5 or 6 shots of brandy, and 20 minutes in front of the heater to return to normal. Rod was now suited up, got the underwater camera ready, got all the scuba gear on with the air tanks, and away he went. He filmed Willie from underneath, wrestled with him in the water, and did a great job. All the film was marvelous.

No one could stand to go back in now, but Willie was still going strong. I did everything I could think of to lure him to shore, but to no avail. He paddled around, looked under the water, played on the beaver lodge, and then went back in the water. After an hour-and-a-half, he came over for a piece of cookie, and I jumped him. He had become hungry before getting cold.

At the end of the shooting I met Chuck Keen, a film maker from Juneau, who was doing a film about a Klingkitt Indian boy, and I tried to use Willie for a scene. Willie's feet were so tender by this time that he could hardly walk, and it was hard to get any action on the tundra. Chuck said he'd get us a ticket on the ferry to Juneau and also give me a couple of baby moose he had there for a little filming.

Great! I immediately took him up on it, as we were going to British Columbia to do the picture for Wild Kingdom anyway, and the ferry would save driving several hundred miles. Everything was packed up. We went back to Haines Junction and then to Skagway. It was tourist time, and the traffic was so heavy that we had to wait two days for a boat, so we had some trailer repairs done at a welding shop. There were loads of tourists and natives who were waiting around town. With the wash-board gravel roads things would always keep breaking loose on the trailer, so we became good customers of the welding shops wherever we were. Next time, there would be a welder-generator instead of just a generator on my truck.

All kinds of smoked salmon came to us from local people who came to see the critters once they found that the bears like it. You seem to get more attention from people where there are lots of animals, rather than the opposite. The ferry arrived to the cheers of all those waiting, and loaded. It took a day to get to Juneau and everyone took to us on the ship. The crew fed us well; the animals got all kinds of goodies from the crew and the tourists. There was a great party that night and sorrowfully we landed in the morning.

Chuck took us in for a few days. We viewed the edited work print of his movie but the show was much too slow for me, not enough action, and being the way I am, I told him so. He really didn't like my telling him but later it came out about as I predicted.

Chuck wanted me to do a piece in the picture for him and, as he'd done so much for us, I was happy to oblige. We agreed that Willie was to chew up a dead moose on the edge of a pond. The truck was loaded, Willie put in a cage on the back along with a stuffed moose, from the museum, that was to be junked. It was all hauled to a small pond. The moose was laid half in the water on the edge of the pond. It was huge and looked exactly like a stuffed moose lying partway in the water. Willie went up, played half heartedly with it, tore the hide off, exposing the white plaster, and generally made a mess of it. The plan didn't work too well. We loaded the bear in his cage, left the moose and started for Chuck's home which was about 10 miles. All of a sudden a pickup started following me. I couldn't shake him off and he wouldn't pass so I stopped finally and told him to butt off.

Boy, was he rough looking! Had a rifle lying between himself and a woman on the seat. He took off and I went back to Chuck's home and watched some filming in his back yard.

The next day I took Chuck's car and headed for Juneau to get a driver's license, for mine had expired. I had an introduction to the Captain in charge of the state troopers and spent half an hour talking to him. He said to come back at 3, take a driving test and pick up my license. I got a special number, 35, so I could get some help from the state if any was needed. When I came in at 3, the Captain introduced me to the Sgt. who was going to give my test. One look! Zounds! It was the man from the pickup when we were out working the day before. He was even rougher looking in uniform.

I was thinking, after the rudeness of yesterday, here goes nothing!

DICK ROBINSON

He just laughed and said that, after following my driving the day before, he'd OK me. Turned out to be a nice guy. He'd just been out to the rifle range and was coming back and was curious about us.

Chuck gave us a little mountain goat kid to take back, plus the two moose calves, which was great and very generous of him. Mountain goats were practically unobtainable and this one went to the Los Angeles Zoo when we got done with him, on a trade for some jaguar kittens.

28/
Wells-Gray Park
in British Columbia

The next day we caught the ferry for Prince Rupert in British Columbia. It was a two day trip and we had the same reception as before on board ship. This was really a large vessel compared to the other one with many more people and vehicles. We ate in the crew quarters again where they really had great food and for free. We partied all the time with the other passengers, had a wedding at sea, and got to sight-see at Ketchikan.

Prince Rupert, where we were getting off in British Columbia, was a large logging town with many mills and a small customs station. They told us to report to Kamloops for further customs inspection. Wells-Gray Park was our destination. It was eight or nine hundred miles through the mountains and desert of British Columbia to Kamloops and then north. Everyone of our contacts was cordial, the game department people, the park people and the customs department in Kamloops, for there had been several letters in advance and everyone there was expecting us. We soon headed off north, after getting supplies, for the 75 miles to the park. It is one of the most remote parks in British Columbia and has one of the highest waterfalls in North America which is 635 ft. high and has a large river that flows over it. The noise is deafening but when the river reaches the bottom it is nothing but spray. Only one road went into the park and it was mostly a one way gravel road, that had passing spots. After 4 miles we came to one of the scariest bridges I've ever seen. It was a wooden span, old, rickety, long, cantilever style over a 400 ft. deep gulley. It swayed, bumped, and how we made it I don't know. Then, slowly swinging around the corner of the road which was just hanging on the side of this steep hill, there was another bridge, only worse. We were heavy, 35,000 lbs., and we crept slowly across. The sight of solid road at the far end brought on a babble of conversation. The road went into the forest for another ten miles 'til we found the store and lodge that had been recommended. It also was hanging on the side of a hill and was so cramped for space that I had a hard time finding a place to turn around, much less finding a place to park the trailer which was 30 feet long.

The people who ran the place were very sociable, luckily, for we had to spend three weeks hanging around because of the weather which was rainy and foggy all the time.

One morning it turned bright and the blue sky appeared, so we rushed out to film. We had a day and a half of good weather but it wasn't enough. It was mid-September and there were few people around, mostly hunters and, while the falls were spectacular, it wasn't enough to waste time here. I had spent days looking over the country to find better filming country and finally decided that west of Kamloops was a dryer area, more picturesque with different types of trees. We moved everything.

We often discussed the bridges on the road in and one was considered so bad that the school bus would stop and let the kids walk across by themselves; so when we got down to the first bridge, we creaked carefully and slowly across, then, coming to the second, Rod asked me to stop and told me he would walk across. Clint said, if I was going to drive he'd go with me so we proceeded. On the far side a huge bulldozer was cutting out a place where obviously they were going to put a cut through the hill and put in some new bridges.

We stopped and talked to the cat skinner while waiting for Rod to walk over and laughingly told him about Rod walking. He got a great laugh about it for it seems Rod got out on the wrong bridge.

Rod got a great deal of kidding as we rolled down the road and eventually Kamloops came in sight. Suddenly I felt a bump and saw a wheel rolling across the road in my rear view mirror, narrowly missing a car coming from the opposite direction and flying into the bar pit on the opposite side of the road. I pulled off on the right of the road and went back to survey the damage. The whole wheel and part of the axle had broken off on the rear of the trailer. Now what? After unhooking the trailer and getting everyone settled we took off the axle and headed for town. Thankfully, we were on the industrial side of the city, and, having gone a mile or so, came to a machine stop where we stopped. Talking to the foreman was discouraging at first; he said it would take at least a week to replace the axle but why don't we just let him make another short one and weld it back on for $100? Great! The job took two days and we were back on the road again.

Needing cage material, I stopped at a steel yard on the edge of town and went in to get some prices. With old clothes and a big beard, I made quite a sight. An English girl, from her accent, looked at me and asked if I was taking the animals to a zoo?

"No," I said.

"Well, are you taking them to a game farm?"

"No." I again replied, not volunteering any information. I got really tired of prying questions so I would say nothing more than was necessary and would hope they would stop. She and the other office help promptly left to look at the animals while I cooled my heels inside. It was always like this. Thirty minutes would be wasted so I learned to be rather short with people and it saved time. Finally they returned. I found what I needed to know, talked to the girl a few minutes and left to buy supplies in town.

Our area was forty miles from Kamloops, called Deadman Creek, which was fifteen miles in on gravel road through the hills and then into the woods. There was a house and barn to rent so we took care of that, then we got settled, and started laying out plans for filming when the weather got better. Sparkling weather was all that could be used to film, according to the company, so it was wait 'til we got some. There was one place for a set in the high rocky cliffs where I'd need a cage for the mountain lion. I could walk the cat up to it but needed a cage to hold the lion for a day or two. There was only one way to get a cage up and that was by moving it piece by piece so I started designing the cage.

This show was to be a mountain lion show and soon a couple of small kittens came from Sue Pressman at the Boston Zoo. They were really small and had to be bottle fed so that got to be a way of life. Clint got most of the work taking care of them and it caused a little hard feelings for he needed to get up in the middle of the night and neither Rod nor I cared to.

The biggest problem with the cubs was their lack of hair. It was practically non-existent so they had to be carefully protected from the cold. My one young mountain lion was good and tame but the big female was fairly aggressive even though she had no claws nor front teeth. Whenever it had to be moved, this toothless fiend was in a cage for she wasn't leash broke and would bite even without her front teeth. It did smart!

The two moose calves had to be bottle fed so it kept Clint busy feeding. Rod and Clint lived in the house and I stayed in the trailer. But, with an electric heater on a cord from the house, it was delightfully comfortable. Winter was coming and going, cold one day and nice the next, snow one day and gone the next. Finally it broke out clear and blue, with no snow left and fall leaves. Everything was ready and we shot fifty per cent of a show in two days of fast shooting. It was sunny and we got the kittens playing with a marmot, also a mother mountain lion with cub on a deer kill (actually the tame cat), and in this scene we used one of the wolves trying to sneak some meat away from the mother. One of the cubs chased my red fox and then the red fox chased the cub. Turn about is fair play!

The best sequence was actually the easiest but worked best for film cutting purposes. I had my own Bolex 16mm camera outfit and now there was a motor on it so all the film could be run off at one time for longer sequences.

Being the director let me have my choice of shooting locations but there was the problem of how much film my camera could shoot (100′) compared to Rod's (400′) and the choice of lenses he had to cover the scene. Now we needed some real action for the show so, if we had the cubs being threatened by the black bear, well.....

The two cubs were put under some pine trees, the lion cage behind us, the bear cage to the left (all out of sight of course), had Clint run from one cage to the other and turn the animals loose on cue. We started the cameras running, turned the bear loose, who immediately went over to see about the small cubs, turned the mountain lion loose, who immediately joined all of them. He jumped on the bear who ran and started climbing a tree; then the cat came back, checked out the kittens, and resumed chasing the bear until he went all the way up the tree.

Now the bear went up thirty feet or so and the lion was right behind. Seeing that the bear was well out of the way, he came back down the tree, checked on the kittens again and walked off with them. Great!

The footage was extra good. We got all of it as planned, put the animals away, and then called for Cubbie to come down the tree. No! We called, pleaded, offered candy bars, and finally threatened. He just sat and looked. Rod and I finally left Clint guarding the tree so he could put the bear back in his cage when he came down.

We finished the scene with the mountain lion and cub with a deer carcass, and got back to the treed bear just before dark. Cubbie was still there. Getting out my chain saw seemed to provide the answer. Very gently sawing the tree off till it eased down on its limbs did the job. Cubbie gracefully stepped off as though getting out of a carriage in the 1800's. He quietly walked into his cage accepting a candy bar on the way. We roared home. We were tired but happy at the filming. We sent the rolls off to Chicago the next day for it had turned cloudy again and we started to figure out what could be done next.

We tightened up the amount of film we were using now. Not so much a question of waste but Don thought that 12-14000 ft. was about right for a show while 5-6000 seemed better to me. I just got more action and wasted proportionately less film but certainly I didn't want to give them any free sequences if it could be helped.

A few days later we got a call to go back on the set and film some more with the bear but refused. They couldn't understand it 'til we convinced them that there was a fallen tree in the middle of the set and certainly nothing could be done about that.

My education was coming by telephone from Chicago several times a week, after a period of filming, and my directing was getting better. If it wasn't right, I heard about it, so I was learning the construction of their type of sequence and keeping them happy provided me with a schoolroom in the forest.

Remembering was now my business for every bit of film had to be cataloged in my head. If they couldn't find a piece the editors would ask to have it shot again and if we'd already done it, well, why do it again? Editors get lazy sometimes. Everyone's instructions had been to let me direct and run a show but not to run a camera. Now that my film was going in, no one seemed the wiser. There was plenty of validity in the argument for not letting me learn to film. If I could do that maybe I would just take the animals, a camera, and shoot my own film. Simple.

All the pay checks and expense checks came in every week by wire from Chicago to Kamloops so we spent time in town for supplies and talking to the English girl occasionally and even having a date once in awhile. Buying the cage material had introduced me to her and we had hit it off well. Patricia, her name was, had lived in the States at one time but now had come to Canada to work, was interested in what we were doing and was going to come up on a weekend to watch us shoot.

Snow was now a constant thing for it was cold and most of the time the clouds kept the sun from shining so the snow just lay on the ground. The weather got no better, but we found a lake on the top of the mountains for filming. Pat came up and we headed for the lake that weekend so she could watch us. The weather took a turn for the better and it was nice that Sunday.

It was the Canadian Thanksgiving and we had dinner with the people who ran this small rustic fishing camp where we stayed. They had ten cabins built from the trees that surrounded the place, chinked with moss and only the crudest of facilities. The people were great to work with and the husband carted us all over the country looking for places to film. He had a four wheel drive station wagon and could go to places we couldn't.

Pat and I stayed in one of the cabins that night and it was really cold; it must have dropped to zero for the air was crisp the next morning and everyone was dressed in his winter wardrobe.

Our plan was to take my tame elk out on the lake, saw a large piece of ice free and let the mountain lion chase it around 'til hopefully it would fall in. We were going to use ol' tooth-less and had to push her cage out to the middle of the lake close to where the filming was to take place and Fred, the elk, would go any place for he was a great pet. The ice would moan and groan when we walked on it but it must have been close to a foot thick. Still it left everyone nervous about falling in.

All the people were to stay close to the camera. Rod got ready, the cat was turned loose and, hopefully, she would chase the elk around the lake on the ice, come close to us and fall into the section that had been sawed loose. It turned into a circus. It was a continuous riot of everyone going every direction and nothing happening. Fred decided he would be safe standing among the people so he would mingle with all of us and the cat would circle around wondering what to do. Pat finally broke the ice, figuratively, for she broke and ran for the shore and the cabin which was a couple of city blocks away. The creaking of the ice, all the animals milling about and people hollering instructions were too much for her. As she ran, Fred decided that he would be safer with her. The harder she ran the closer he ran behind her, like 3 ft. This scared her more and she flew across the lake, ran up on the porch, into the cabin and slammed the door. Fred followed her onto the porch and tried to get in the door. He stood and whistled for her but she was safe and wouldn't come out.

The laughing was contagious, the cat was put away and Rod went off to film muskrats who were building little dens on the ice with reeds. They drilled holes thru the ice and got feed off the bottom of the lake. We all went over to the cabin and put a rope on Fred and put him away. All of us had an enjoyable weekend finishing off the rest of the turkey, loading the animals and heading down the hill to our camp.

DICK ROBINSON

Rod packed up his gear a couple of days later, went to town with us and took a bus for home in Jackson because he was going to have to film ski movies as well as supervise the building of his new house. We were going to miss him.

Later Ralph came in to finish the show and to take Rod's place.

Winter was here and all the show had been shot in the fall so, after talking to Chicago, it was decided that we go south to find the same type of terrain and trees with the same type of foliage that already had been used. Utah, I decided, is where we'd find it. My animal supply was really crowded now. One of my moose calves had died of pneumonia, which frustrated me, for they were hard to keep alive and the feeding of them was so crucial. Bottle feeding the moose and trying to get them onto some kind of hay and oats for solids was hard. We scrounged all over for willow roughage. The remaining moose and the elk stayed in a stall in the back of the trailer. The elk was fat as a butterball but the moose just picked at her food.

The living compartment was in the middle of the trailer and I had 6 ft. in front of it for small cages and a freezer. We piled all of our wire fencing, poles, posts, and miscellany on the top of the trailer and everything else hung on the sides. The trailer was getting more cluttered and loaded down for it was a sin to throw anything away since it would just have to be bought again.

The week didn't go well, only a few shots could be picked up but then Pat came up for the weekend. Everything was loaded Sunday night and we headed for Kamloops in the middle of a raging snow storm. The little gravelly road was now covered with 6 inches of snow and was slow going. There were four of us in the cab which made it hard to shift and the visibility was next to nothing. It got more slippery as the snow piled up and when we hit the main highway it was just scary.

Traffic was slow and we were slower. The truck was just barely manageable. Pat was frightened and tired, the storm got worse; and then the truck stalled and stopped on a mountain hill and could go no further.

When I went back to look at things and see what could be done

I found a flat. Now changing flats on a big truck was bad anytime but in the middle of a blizzard with trucks and cars whizzing beside you on the highway in the storm was not good! The side was jacked up, the wheel taken off and changed, chains put on the wheels on both sides, and then the equipment was packed up. It had taken an hour and a half and it was now 3 in the morning. We moved on slowly.

When the lights of Kamloops appeared below us through the blowing snow and the highway became free of snow, I could have got down and kissed it. What a relief! The truck had been swinging with the wind, and now it steadied. We descended the two miles into town, found Pat's apartment, which was convenient to the highway, said a quick goodbye, for she looked like she would fall over any minute, and headed for the Okanogan Valley where we would cross over to the U.S.

Another fifty miles and the weather got better, and when trouble hit us this time it was right in the middle of town. Another wheel came off the trailer, this time on the right, and had to be replaced. We spent half a day getting it fixed, resting, and getting re-supplied for the next few days. My past relationship with Ralph and the long hours of the trip with three of us in the cab made it miserable for all of us.

We passed through the border easily, and we headed for Spokane with weather that got balmy. Wilbur, about seventy-five miles from Spokane, had a good cafe, so we parked the truck in a closed service station across the street from it, and we headed over for dinner. The three of us were sitting at the counter waiting for dinner to be served when a very happy drunk Indian came up and asked if we were going to Spokane, and we said yes.

"Could I have a ride in with you?" he asked.

"Well, not unless you want to ride with a couple of bears or a mountain lion," I replied. "There're three in the cab now."

He was lurching around, pulling at some cigars in his pocket to offer us as we were talking.

"Are they safe?" he asked.

"Sure," I replied, hoping this would scare him off, "but sometimes

195

they mess up your clothes and tear them up a little."

He thought a minute.

"OK, I'll be waiting."

We finished dinner and everyone headed for the truck. Halfway across the street we heard a shout, and the Indian came weaving across the street after us.

Oh no! I thought, well as a last resort, maybe we can scare him. "Clint," I said, "take off the side panel."

The panels on the side of the truck hid the animals from the public, and by showing him...well...maybe we could scare him off. Clint took off the panel and I looked in and said,

"Well, you can ride with these two if you want."

He peered in, for it was fairly dark inside, saw the bear cubs, which were half-grown and very playful. He called them and they came over sniffing. He looked at the mountain lion, then at the cubs, the lion again, and said,

"OK. I take these," pointing at the cubs.

Clint and I boosted him in, closed the cage door and put the side on, and headed off down the highway, Clint taking the flashlight and shining it back through the back window so we could see him once in awhile. The cage was six feet long and had plenty of nice clean straw for bedding.

He stretched out and was soon asleep. Cubbie, the little male, sprawled on his chest sucking on his paw, which many bears do; we call it humming. Mabel, the other cub, started to work on his shoes. She liked to take out shoe laces. By this time we were laughing and giggling about it and from time to time would check to see if he was all right. It was about 11 when we rolled into the heart of Spokane. We pulled up to the curb and got out next to a church. Clint took the side off, opened the door, and woke the bear cubs who were sleeping on top of the Indian. He shook him and called to him. No reaction.

He panicked and called to me,

"Dick, he won't move!"

I climbed into the cage, pulled him upright and shook him.

"Hey buddy, you want to get out at Spokane?"

He slowly came awake, looked around, was helped out of the cage and down onto the grass parking. The bears both watched with their heads out the door for they had just lost a good companion.

The Indian staggered around a little and headed for the back of the church for a quick relief. To put it mildly he was a wreck. His shoe laces were hanging out, the pockets were hanging from his jacket and shirt for they had been half pulled off, straw was all over him. What a story he would tell his buddies when he got to the bars on skid row where they all hung out! It furnished us a laugh for many days and relieved the monotony of the trip. He was a Colville Indian, one of the nicest groups of Indians I had ever been around and, even when drinking, were good natured.

Our next stop, Cedar City, Utah was a large town of 10,000 that sat at the foot of a high range of mountains that abruptly ascended to over 10,000 feet. The road went up from 5 to 10 thousand feet elevation in 18 miles. It was steep and slow, wound through the forest on top for miles, past lakes and lava flows to the log lodge where we were going to stay and finish the show. The weather was fall here and beautiful.

The moose take was the first sequence we wanted so Ralph and I set the scene at a little lake which still had snow around it from the last snowfall. We turned the critter loose and filmed it walking around, wading in the water looking for something to eat while we got scenics with the cameras.

Now we turned the mountain lion loose. The moose watched him lurking around the edges of the lake while he casually walked through the water trying to ignore this obviously threatening visitor. The cat stood around the edge hoping that the moose would come ashore for it didn't relish the idea of swimming at this time of year. The still camera was something we were allowed to use if nothing else was going on so I spent the time shooting off a roll of film.

Finally the moose wandered ashore, the cat chased it around with no results and they were both put back in their cages. Next it was the black bear's turn. Putting the bear by itself, with a little cookie to keep it interested, we opened the door of the cougar pen.

The cat waltzed up to the bear thinking it was going to go up the tree like the last time but the cougar got a terrible surprise. The bear was going to fight and it did.

Lots of smoke and huffing and puffing with the bear standing up at a tree, looking up to see if it was usable for protection and walking around it on her hind legs with the lion snarling behind.

A large half dead sugar pine was close by and Mabel, the bear, sprinted for it at full speed then climbed it. She was still going so fast that when she hit a large piece of dead bark on the way up, she kept right on going from the momentum and, when the bark came loose from the tree with the bear still holding on fifteen feet in the air, it was like you were watching everything in slow motion. The piece of bark was straight up and down and the bear was hanging on, looking around in utter disbelief. It gathered speed and hit the ground with a thump, bark going every which direction and the bear sat utterly amazed.

The cat rushed over to see what happened and inspect the scene of the accident. The bear thought quickly, "I've been punished for running up a tree!" It broke us up laughing and we decided that this was enough. PS. The bear never would tree after that.

Earlier, when we had left the Alaskan town of Paxson, the lady in the cafe where we'd been getting our pies asked us to take a couple of her young pups to the States. Certainly there was a motive as far as I was concerned for maybe there would be a trip back that way and we may need the pies again.

We brought the pups all the way back with us and now with all the animals there were in the trailer, it was getting a little stuffy. There were only a few people around perhaps to unload one of the pups on, but one fellow did have possibilities. He was an old retired cowboy that helped do odd jobs around the lodge and had lots of stories about the old days, had lost his own dog about a month before and was still grieving over it.

The dog was his best friend. It had fallen out of his station wagon and been killed. We talked to him obliquely about his feelings for a new dog. The lady at the lodge told us that everyone had found and offered him all kinds of dogs but he wanted to suffer awhile.

Everynight we had our little tableau going over the dinner table about the day's filming, what happened, all about the animals and the dogs. One dog was going to have to go; then the next day, one would have to be disposed of soon; then, finally, one was going to be taken out and shot tomorrow! The next morning it was cold and snappy. The old fellow passed by a couple of times as we were feeding the moose and elk, and then finally a big show was made of getting the poor dog, dragging it around to the truck, putting an old rope around its neck and tying it to the back. Disappearing into the lodge for a final cup of coffee could bring results.

In fifteen minutes we went back outside, and the dog was gone. Hummmmm, maybe a dognapper. Around the corner came the cowboy.

"Say boys, you don't mind if I just try out the mutt for a few days, do you?" he said.

I put on a frown, puckered my forehead, and said,

"Well, it's better than being shot. You can keep him around to try him, but you know I had to psyche myself up for this, and I couldn't do it again. Next time you'll have to do it yourself."

With this he disappeared, nothing was said, and in a few days he was back with Puca, the dog, in the back of the station wagon, and later, at the dinner table, he was beaming for he had found a new friend.

Ralph and I had been working the cat and the beaver, the little cubs and beaver, the grizzly, and the cubs playing around with their mother. The footage was excellent, my stills were great, but I couldn't use my own movie camera. The wolves ran around and we spent most of our time chasing them. One left while filming and we had to follow him for a mile, then we couldn't do anything with him, and ended up carrying him back. That was work.

Everybody left. The animals were moved to the fairground building in Cedar to get them out of the weather, and to let us get organized.

With everything done, there was a trip to Chicago that had to be taken care of. In the WK offices we straightened up what was coming with all the expenses and extra time that was put in. Don told me that they were the two most expensive shows they had ever done but were well worth it. Watching some of the edited work printed from Canada with a group of editors, I happened to exclaim how great that shot I got was and one said,

"You got?" It was the one where the bear had gone up the tree with the cougar right behind.

I was caught. It came out about my filming and it became hard to defend myself for breaking the rules. Later that night, Don took me to dinner and laid it on the line. Either I signed a three year contract at $300 a week and expenses or no more work. I declined. The two mountain lion cubs were supposed to become mine at the end of the shoot and some of the other animals that had been bought; and I was to get them at half of what the company had paid for them. But no!

They knew that my next show was to be for Bill Burrud's new series "Animal World" and they were afraid that the animals would be used on it in competition with them if I had them. Certainly it rubbed Don the wrong way and it left me feeling that his word was no good. but I could understand his actions.

29/
Two extremes—
"Bumpy" Bell
and Cameron Mitchell

With no more work from WK coming in, it meant that my world would have to expand so, after buying some camera gear in Chicago, and visiting New York City for some contacts, I headed back for Cedar City.

The grizzly show we had contracted with Bill Burrud was done, and then I made a deal to do two more jaguar shows. The two that we had done for Don had been excellent and Burrud decided to do a couple.

Pat and I had kept in touch by phone several times and at Christmas I drove the truck to Kamloops. It was a hard trip through the snow most of the way there and was even colder when I arrived. The first night there wasn't a thought in my head about antifreeze and I hadn't checked it for a long while. In the morning my motor on the truck was frozen solid. We worked on it for five days to get it going without cracking the block. What a job. It finally came up to zero and we got it started. Clint was taking care of the animals and, as the fairground was on the edge of the business district, he was close to everything and found plenty to do. It was cold there too and as soon as I got back we headed south to where it was warm.

Pat and I had decided to get together as soon as we could afford a ticket for her when something got going and the money came in. After arriving in Tucson, Clint split and stayed with some friends and started visiting his steady girl friend again. As for me, it was up to the mountains again, only this time to the bottom of Mt. Lemmon, at the end of a road, on a piece of ground that some friends owned.

The next project was to get a jaguar from a woman who had a pet one that lived in her backyard with an African lion. Borrowing the VW camper from Burrud's crew in Tucson, I headed north. These two animals lived in harmony until they were now nearly grown but then the kids and people would bother them and finally a man got such a good bite from the jaguar that she had to get rid of it temporarily so we could use it for this show.

I had contracted with the Kansas City Zoo to have a man come with 3 little jaguar kittens, when they were needed, so that, Sid, the name of the jaguar, could have three babies, for he was to be their "mother."

On arriving at Incline Village, finding the woman a well-to-do matron surprised me, especially after seeing this beautiful woman petting the lion and jaguar without any qualms. She helped load the jaguar and showed me how to handle him. When the show was done and, if the coast was clear to bring him back, we promised to spend more time together talking about the animals. Sid, sat next to me in the cab on the seat and immediately insisted the gear shift was his. It was a constant battle, hitting him, then a snarling fight and back to the gear shift, then getting up and looking out the window, then on my lap. What a trip!

Getting to Lodi, I chained him to the gear shift and went into the super market to get some chickens for his dinner. By the time I had returned with his din-din, he had chewed and mangled the seat he was occupying. Now I was going to get it! But I managed him.

By the time I got to Burrud's in Beverly Hills the next noon, sleepless, tired and hungry, for a story conference, I was a wreck. There was a discussion on where to put Sid, for of course there was no cage and, after much talking with everyone, it was decided to use the bathroom off the screening room. I headed off for Holmby Hills to see my friend Frawley for a little visit leaving his telephone number where I'd be.

Patrick had been talking to a TV interviewer who was just leaving so the three of us got involved in what an exciting life I lived. Pat was telling him about the time that I had saved the life of the man at the Lubbock zoo when the telephone rang. It was a call for me from Burrud's. Come at once, the jaguar had attacked Wolfgang Bayer who had been rushed to the doctor's office. Racing out, I jumped in the VW and shot out the driveway at full speed for the office. It was slow through the traffic of Beverly Hills and, screeching up to Burruds, I jumped out and casually walked in. What was the problem? A secretary quietly told me. Wolfgang Bayer, the head photographer had come in, brought some friends with him, let the jaguar out to show it off and then went to put it back in the bathroom. Sid didn't want to go! Wolfgang insisted. He was German with quite an accent, young in his late twenties and forceful. Also a little foolish at times.

He dragged it into the bathroom, which was small, the door swung in, and, once inside, both tried to get outside again. The basin was torn loose, the toilet was rendered inoperable and splashed much water, there was blood scattered here and there from some deep wounds in Wolfgang's leg for Sid had been quite insistent. The place was a shambles. Wolfgang made it out but his leg needed a good deal of attention. At the doctor's he was asked what had bit him and he finally had to admit it was a jaguar. They immediately wanted to have the cat quarantined for rabies for 10 days but Wolfgang told them it was his fault and the cat had already left the state.

The secretary handed me a slip of paper with an address on it. They told me to take the jaguar there, tell no one and come back tomorrow.

Opening the door to the bathroom brought Sid out with a rush. He acted as if he'd found a long lost friend. I put the chain on and quietly walked him to the van and hopped him in like we'd always been chums. Sid sat on the front seat looking and peering out the front window as we zipped through traffic. At last, finding the address, we pulled into their back alley and knocked at the door. One of the help let me in.

The place was huge inside, filled with cat cages big enough to walk into and many with different decors, like rooms in a house. They boarded cats and made them feel at home. The manager soon appeared and steered me to some hidden outdoor pens in the far back and told me not to worry. Sid went in quietly and made himself at home.

We spent a couple of days figuring out what shows were going to be done and what was needed in the way of a crew and animals. One was a jungle jaguar show and one a "hunt'm" jaguar show. There was enough advance money for a ticket for Pat so she quickly quit her job and flew to LA.

Pat had some friends there that she had known for years and she wanted to visit them, maybe even stay the night. But it became imperative that we leave on the same day. She was white with exhaustion, for she hated flying and always got sick. It had been a long flight from Kamloops to Vancouver and then to LA. After visiting a couple hours and getting the camper loaded right, we left and her friends followed along to see us off. We pulled into the back alley of Sid's temporary home, then we got out and everyone was inspecting the van, seeing how it worked and oh and ahing over its many new features. It was the latest in camping vans put out by VW and loaned to Burrud by the distributor. It was packed with cameras, lighting equipment and other supplies that had been rented and purchased in LA for the show.

Pat climbed into the van, took a quick look at the torn up seat she was going to have to ride in and closed the door. She rolled down the window and was casually talking to her friends when I walked out with Sid. Now Sid was a big cat, 150 lbs of sprawling cat; led on a chain, he headed in the side door, went up between the seats, grabbed the gear shift knob and sat in my seat.

Everybody was saying goodbye when Sid arrived. They looked in astonishment for no one could believe the size of him. Talking about jaguars seemed to give them the idea that he was some little pussy cat but then, with me, well, I didn't think anything about the size of an animal. Walking around, I got in the driver's seat by pushing Sid off as he snarled and I sat down ready for action. It was all in a days work. Pat turned white again and asked where Sid was going to ride. With us! She didn't say another word. Just went to her fate gracefully. She quietly waved as we headed for the freeway.

The cat had ridden in the front seat coming down and decided joint occupancy with Pat was the order. He climbed up and sprawled over her. She was petrified. How far did we have to go she asked? Well, I said casually, 600 miles. Oh...the freeway was full of afternoon traffic as we headed for San Bernardino.

Then Sid started playing his gear shift game again. Shifting was continuous in slow freeway traffic in the afternoon so it turned out to be World War II waged across Pat. Sid would put both paws and his mouth on the knob and look at me and growl. Then I I hit him between the eyes with my fist. He would growl and roar for a minute then let go. Of course, I was very nonchalant about it for by this time I was used to it, but Pat thought she was a Christian in the lion's arena.

It got hotter and hotter as we approached the valley and left the ocean behind. The cat was sprawling over Pat on the front seat, both exhausted and trying to relax enough to sleep. Later at night the bunk was fixed in the back and Pat thought she could get away but that cat was brought up by a woman and, by golly, Pat was his protection. The cat followed and went to sleep on top of her. It had been a hard day.

The next morning, with some rest behind us, everything started looking brighter after having breakfast and getting cleaned up. Arizona was only a mile away where there was an inspection station for plants and fruit and all the cars were stopped. There was no health certificate for the cat; maybe they were looking for us. Inspectors were not welcome in this situation. We put Sid down on the floor between us with his head being held down till he got used to it, then our little bus took its turn in the line at the station waiting for the inspector. Pat rolled her window down and the inspector asked us if we had any fruits or plants? No. Ok, thank you. Just then Sid raised his head as I started to move. "Hey," the inspector said, "What've you got there."

"Just our pet," I replied as I speeded onto the highway. Well, they hadn't told me to stop....

Holding my breath for an hour was hard, but no patrol cars appeared as we headed across the desert for Tucson at top speed, which wasn't much for a VW camper.

The heat really started getting to us crossing the desert, having no air-conditioning. When we arrived in Tucson, Pat was wilted. Having to weave across town, through the suburbs, and into the wilds seemed to take hours and then the bumpy road to our trailer for the last half mile was a little un-nerving for her and it *was* a little isolated. Pat looked at the trailer when we arrived and said, "Is this where we're going to live?"

It was a couple of hundred yards from a house, had a hose for water, an electrical hookup for power and, admittedly, it looked a little rough up this canyon, but then all the mountain country in Arizona was this way. Full of yuccas, cactus and mesquite trees, rock and sand, it was typical desert.

She had stayed in the trailer before at night, but having to live in it was something else. Where was the john? Out behind that mesquite tree. Where was the shower? See that hose hanging over the limb? You just turn the water on. The water from the hose is warm from the sun being on it during the day. You just turn the water on.

Just then a couple of hippies walked by. Who are they? Just hippies; a tribe lives a little way up the road. Oh? What do they live in? Oh, they have some brush huts and sleeping bags. What do they eat? Scraps from the grocery stores in town. Just then the smell of pot drifted down. What's that? Pot. OH....

Pat had no intentions of being caught using the mesquite tree in the daylight, so she waited for nightfall. I could see my next project was going to be an indoor chemical toilet and shower. Soon! Taking out a storage room and changing it to a shower and john was a job, but she was satisfied.

Three days later I found a place to camp at an old dude ranch called Aqua Caliente. It was an oasis with palm trees, had a lake with ducks, jungle foliage, a large creek fed from a spring, and a place for us to camp under a palm tree.

The family that took care of it told us to help ourselves, and they really babied this dainty, beautiful English girl out in the wild west. I hunted the country for snakes, gila monsters and anything that could be found for the show, and had my own animals shipped for the jungle show. It took every bit of our money to support the menagerie by this time.

There had been all kinds of animals coming in from Ray Folsom, and they needed to be caged and fed properly. Building sets and table tops took all the time there was. I'd take a piece of plywood and put it on sawhorses, dress it up like a piece of the desert, put snakes and lizards on it and wait for the action. I had a new lens for my camera, a 12-120 zoom lens that I learned to use; it had many advantages for close-up filming.

Doing filming like this intrigued me, for the possibilities of what could be done were endless. One scene that came through was amazing to everyone. I used a little spotted skunk, which was about 6 inches long, and a water hole, with a 4 foot long western diamondback rattlesnake lurking around it. The little skunk came in, was struck by the snake, and then grabbed the head of the snake, wrestled around with it, and proceeded to polish it off. Then it ate the head of the snake. The poison from the snake didn't affect the skunk. It was a fantastic scene to see and it was done repeatedly. Those skunks were really tough little devils but seldom seen. They made good pets, but were hard to find.

Pat's big problem now was the snakes. I'd spend time catching snakes and lizards, putting them in pillow cases or flour sacks, tieing them up and chucking them under the trailer in the shade. They would bounce out or crawl out once in a while, and it was her job to throw them back. All she had to do was to take the top of the sack, pick it up and throw it back. She hated it.

Crews came from Los Angeles and started to film. Clint would help work the animals while the crew and I filmed. This was film that could be used in the future, a far cry from the days of WK. Both shows were finished, both well done and well received by the editors and now Pat was becoming aware of the problems of making these kinds of shows for television.

The last of the work for the show was to film Bill Burrud doing the introductions for the shows, near the Circle Z dude ranch and at another ranch close to Nogales. After that was done, the crew adjourned to a motel and club in Nogales for a celebration. Milas Henshaw, who had been chief photographer on the bear picture he had just done with me, came by and said he wanted to introduce me to someone. I found that another company was doing a full-length feature about a couple of companies of black troops during the Civil War, and Cameron Mitchell was directing and playing in it; also, they could use some animals. In a few minutes, Cameron appeared, looking terrible, bearded, with his hands covering his face. He apologized for looking and acting this way, but he'd been eating garlic and was really hung over. What animals did I have? I told him. OK. How much to use them tomorrow morning? $600. OK. Be on the set first thing in the morning. What luck!

The next morning we arrived early from Tucson, where the animals had been loaded, and watched them film while I was waiting for my turn. It was horrible! Never had I heard a man use such filthy language in front of a cast and crew. There were probably 60 people, and many must have felt the same. I mentioned it, and a very kindly man said that Cameron did it purposely to impress people, believing they liked to be treated this way. I couldn't say that I agreed.

When it was my turn everything was frenzied. I ran about madly placing animals here and there hoping to get it over quickly. Now one of the black soldiers was told to carry a coyote to the big chief. I put it in his arms and he panicked and dropped it. Pat was close by and it attacked her without warning, biting her wrist and arm severely and tore her dress before I could get to it. She went faint with all the blood running. Someone brought a bandage and wrapped her. Another man, a visitor, volunteered to take her to the hospital in his jeep so away they went. I grabbed a mountain lion and went to work again. It took an hour to finish. They told me to get my money from a man sitting in a station wagon, which I did. Just then Pat returned, dress repaired with strips of masking tape, wrist and arm bandaged up. She was her usual pale self under pressure, so we loaded her in the truck and headed for Nogales to cash the check. It was about all between us and starvation. It cost a hundred dollars for tetanus shots and doctor bills, but it was a life saver for our finances.

Burrud's company kept me busy for some time with these shows, and one of the most interesting was with Willie. He was to be a Mexican Grizzly, which were practically non-existent then, so we had to devise a show around the south country, mainly Mexico, and use the bear threatening something. In this case it was cows in a corral. Our crew consisted of Milas Henshaw, head photographer, and his assistant, "Bumpy" Bell. Bumpy drove up the first day in an old pickup truck powered by a huge motor, dressed in old clothes, and immediately pulled out a large box of medicine. He informed us that he needed this in case of trouble, and, besides, we saw he was a hypochondriac after he began downing pills.

He couldn't find the belt for his pants, so we rigged up a piece of bailing wire over his shoulders to hold the pants up. Milas was a comedian, and the air was filled with jokes and gags all day with Bumpy often the butt of them. They had worked together on many underwater shows in various parts of the world, many award winners, and knew how to get along with anyone, anytime or place. Bumpy got out his camera and mounted it on the tripod. It was something extraordinary to see. It was an old Bolex 16mm converted to an electric motor drive, with a chain running down the side, and other gadgets hanging on that are now built into cameras. Bumpy informed everyone that this camera had never been used in the open air, only under water, so this was going to be a first.

The camera was all set up, a black changing bag was pulled out, slipped over his head and the camera, and he began the job of changing film in the dark. Willie then walked by, stopped at his backside to investigate, goosed him and then took his huge paw and started gently to pull down his pants. Bumpy thought someone was goofing around and hollered, then put his hand back to push them off. A hairy paw materialized under his hand, then the hand felt and found the claws. With that he started shouting and kicking backwards 'til people started to notice. It brought a laugh from everyone, Willie ambled off when he saw the look we gave him, and when Bumpy finally uncovered and saw all the fun he said,

"Give me a shark any day."

After that, Willie kept an eye out for Bumpy changing film and would come over to tease.

Standing on a street corner one day in Tucson, waiting for a light to change, I saw a strange sight. A big sports car pulled up, a Lamborghini, one of those fancy foreign jobs, and there was a man driving that looked just like Bumpy, dressed in a wild sport coat and rakish Scotish tam and when the light changed, he went varooming down the street.

The next time I saw Milas I mentioned it. He laughed and said it was indeed Bumpy who was probably going to his club. It seemed that he really just helped out for fun when Milas was around. Rumor had it that he was an heir to the Pittsburgh Plate Glass Co. fortune. He had a beautiful Spanish home on the edge of Tucson, which I visited later. His brother had a large cattle ranch between Tucson and Nogales, something like 10,000 acres, with a beautiful simple home where we filmed some of the grizzly show. They were really nice people and very hospitable.

Pat decided one beautiful and hot day that it was a good time to get married. She got her white suit on that she had brought for the occasion, got me into a suit, and we headed off for Nogales, the Mexican side, where we thought we could get married quickly.

We parked the truck in Nogales, Arizona, and we found a Mexican cab to take us to a Mexican judge for a marriage ceremony. The cabbie advised us that he could take care of the whole thing. Don't worry; these things are easy, he said. He parked the cab on a dusty, rutted street and led us into an old adobe building. We went into a large room filled with couples and children. All of us sat stiffly waiting for some action. It wasn't long in coming. Screaming accusations in Spanish hurtled from the judge's chambers, from both sides; then kids started screaming and a soldier sat slumped over on a bench pruning his nails. The soldiers were the police here so the arguing must not have been unusual.

From the sounds, the judge must have been adjudicating family quarrels. It became hotter and Pat unfastened her white jacket. The court room was oozing floor oil; it became still hotter and the fights louder. Finally our time came and we went in to talk to the judge and get the job done. He was very nice and explained that he would indeed marry us if we would go down to the border and get a tourist card. This would cost us $8 apiece at Immigration. Meanwhile, the cab had been waiting for us. Pat blew up in the taxi as we headed for the border and I didn't hear about getting married for several months after that.

30/ Three wolves
in the sunset

Des and his family and Pat and I decided to head back for the high mountains at Cedar City, where it was cool, to continue the beaver show. It was beautiful at this time of the year, for the mountains turned spring in July, the flowers came out, along with the little birds and animals. On the way, we stopped at Zion Park and visited with a friend of mine, Bob Davison. Bob had some animals: deer, bobcats, a black bear, and small animals. He worked for WK occasionally and did filming on his own. He had his own camera equipment and during the winter would lecture for the Audubon society. He urged me to stop and settle down and start a film compound with him and work together.

We discussed it favorably but I told him of our plans for filming in the mountains with Des and his wife, also that it would last only a month. We were in Springdale which is down in a canyon at the mouth of Zion park, one of the most beautiful in Utah, and very photogenic. The sights were completely different from the mountains where Des and all of us were going because of the difference in elevation.

Ours was a slow trip, 50 miles of steep uphill highway and, for the truck and trailer, a two hour trip. At Cedar City it was 5,000 ft. and where our camp would be, 10,000 feet.

Tourists were flocking around us when we settled in one of the camp grounds of the national forest. Soon the forest rangers showed up, a congenial bunch that enjoyed seeing the animals and talking. Des and Jen found a spot next to us. We lit a fire and wine was served to top the evening off. We spent a month filming grizzlies, lions, coyotes, beavers and more. Des shot film for both of us while I worked the animals for both of us.

A month had gone by as we toted up what the bill would be for the use of the animals. Maybe $1200 or $1300. It ended up to be $235. By the time the bills were paid, gas and groceries, and food for the animals there was $35 left in my pocket when we reached Springdale.

Bob Davison had leased a couple of chicken coops and they were going to be our new home. How were all these people going to make a living now? $35.... The trailer was parked behind the coops, the animals unloaded and made comfortable and then the cleaning started. The big truck could really haul a load and there was plenty to haul: chicken manure, old boards and coops, weeds and bushes, nests of snakes and ground squirrels, and then we had to decide what to do with it all.

Two days had gone by. I had $10 left and the last couple of hundred pounds of food in the freezer. At the post office there was a surprise! A letter for me from the MGM Documentary Dept. It had been following from Tucson. It said to phone collect as soon as possible. Wow! I hoped it was business. Getting to the lone pay phone, for this town had only a few motels, a general store and a couple hundred people, I put in a collect call for Irwin Rosten. He accepted the call and asked, could I do a job for them? Well, probably. Could I have a group of wolves get a deer? Of course, and how long did I have? A month. How much, he asked? I thought a minute and made the price...$6,000 with $2,500 up front for the pre-production. OK... You'll have your check tomorrow. I didn't have but one wolf and would have to find some more and would have to find a couple of deer. It was to be a full length documentary called the "Wolf Man" for MGM and would appear that winter.

By a miracle the check came the next day, and we were back in business. Wolves came from the LA Zoo and deer came from a game farm. We found a lake in the high mountains on private property behind Brianhead mountain close to where Des and I had filmed before, and with Bob's help, put in a compound fence around the area with 1800 ft. of 6 ft. high fencing. It was quite a job, cutting through the woods and adjusting the fence so it wouldn't be seen by the cameras. It was the nicest compound that I'd seen for filming.

The work on the chicken coops was going forward, a little concrete poured for pads for the animal's cages and then we framed up the walls for a kitchen in the middle of the whole building. It kept Pat satisfied while she was by herself to have something to do.

When everything was ready, Bob agreed to help me film if some could be done on our own and then split after taking the footage out for MGM and sending that off.

They were pleased with the film. It was only a short piece in the picture, after editing, but important to the show and they asked us to do one more small piece for the film: a wolf howling in the sunset. It shouldn't be hard for there was just the right spot for it on top of Brianhead mountain; however, that night an important call came. The jaguar from the Bill Burrud show had been returned to the woman in Lake Tahoe and now she was calling in desperation for she needed to get rid of it as well as the lion because it had chewed a neighbor and they both had to go. There was still time to do the shot for M.G.M. if the trip could be held down to two days.

Gloria Michaels was a woman who had exotic pets for years, was outgoing and popular for she and her husband once had a large eating place outside Reno but now she was down to working for others. She was a beautiful woman who had the drive and desire to start her own business again and get back the lost fortune. This was a trauma in her life that had to be overcome for she loved the animals but now had to go on to other things. We spent all day consoling and listening to her while the cats were being loaded for the trip. One of her friends dropped over to help. They had a cheeta which they inveigled me into taking along to board for a few weeks while they took a vacation in peace. I understood their need.

Each cat had a cage of its own in the back of the truck and the cheeta was to ride in the front seat with me. Gloria spent half the night taking me around Reno to show me everything and then to dinner. She just didn't want to part and get away from the animals. At two in the morning, the final break was made, and the truck and animals and I headed off into the night for SLC with Gloria crying as she headed for home. It took 'til the next afternoon to cross the desert and mountains to get to SLC with no sleep. There was chicken to pick up at the wholesalers, a thousand pounds, for the animals at the compound. LaMar McQuaid and his family stopped by to see me and we visited for an hour, talking about old times. It was a hot evening and late when all of us headed off for Springdale. It usually was a six hour trip from SLC but it was a hot night and I had been short of sleep and my eyes were getting heavier and heavier all the time. One hundred fifty miles south was all I could do and, when the top of Scipio pass appeared, there was no going any further. Parking the truck under a large juniper tree was the only thing left to do. Just sleep, and more sleep, with the cheeta crawling up and lying on top of me. The cheeta and I. Just try sleeping on the seat of a truck with a full grown cheeta sleeping and digging around on top of you. No wonder those people needed a vacation.

The sun streaming in my eyes brought me awake and, groggily, I sat up to the steering wheel, started the truck when the cheeta started digging at me. He had to be walked. Stumbling around outside at least got me awake and when he finished we got back in and headed down the road.

After 50 miles we came to the little town of Fillmore and a good breakfast. After walking leisurely outside, with a good feeling that life was doing its best for me, I climbed up on the side of the truck to talk to the animals and say good morning. There was an empty cage! Smoley hokes! The lion was gone! What happened to her? Talk about consternation; I couldn't even see where she had got out.

Climbing over the side and making a closer inspection of the cage revealed a section of wire that she'd pushed aside and it had let her squeeze out, then snapped back. Sid looked askance and just wanted attention for the two of us were good friends by now. The only logical time she could have got out was when we were all sleeping and that was 50 miles back.

Now, with the sun starting to beat down and melting my chicken, I knew it was too late to go back. Besides, the last shot had to be filmed the next day on the wolf show.

There was nothing to do but head for home and hope for the best. Stopping at the deputy sheriff's house to tell my story brought on the remark that he would keep an eye open for this critter and what else is new? I said that I'd call and be back but I didn't tell him my name. I couldn't blame him much, for the story was purposely vague about what took place. Even if the lion were tame and something happened, Dick Robinson would be responsible.

It was some story to tell while the animals were being unloaded for this would have to be speedy. Bob was ready to go, so, with the wolves in cages, the long trip to Brianhead began. It was 11,300 ft. high and my truck could go right up on top of the mountain on a small road. Ah, the last shot, hopefully. A piece of fencing was put along a point that jutted out about fifty feet and had a seventy-five foot drop off. It was so positioned that the wolves could be filmed against the sunset for it was really beautiful here.

Both the wolves were half tame so we just put them out to run around while the sun was just dropping to the horizon. When it came time to shoot, Bob shooed them out to the point where they started to run back and forth. One jumped off into space. My God! Seventy-five feet straight down onto a rock ledge. Now I'll have to skin the darn thing out, I though. Bob ran down around the edge and then climbed down and out on the ledge. I hollered down.

"Where is it?"

And just then the other one jumped. He looked up at my head and said.

"They're running down the mountain."

"You're kidding!" I muttered.

Getting a catch net and a gun out of the truck and running back, I pitched the catch net off to Bob and then ran around the far side heading down the mountain. A quarter mile away was a band of 1500 sheep and, when those wolves got hungry, if they weren't caught tonight, well, there goes a bundle. There were only 15 minutes 'til dark. The ski resort was only a mile away and, although it was summer, there were still people around. Now there were an African lion and two wolves missing. I ran harder.

The sheep herder opened the door of his wagon with a plate in his hand and a question. How about some mutton? No, thanks, there'll probably be enough tomorrow to go around, I thought. The situation was explained to him; if he saw the wolves would he shoot them? He assured me he would. Bob was coming around the side of the mountain and waved to me. He had followed them but they wouldn't let him get close enough to catch them. We had to go home and it was a thousand ft. to climb back to the top to the truck, put away the camera and gear, load the cages. What a day! What would happen now? This couldn't be happening to me. It had to be a TV soap opera. That's the only place this would or could happen. OK folks, tune in tomorrow to see the adventures of the amazing Dick Robinson.... Wow!

I called the patrol office the next day. They gave me the news about the lion:

1. Sunday. Invaded the Mormon Picnic of the Ladies Relief Society and stampeded the ladies.

2. Monday. Gone to caretaker's cottage at a dam. Lay down on the front porch in front of door. When people came out and stumbled over it, scared lion and people.

3. All days. Roaming along road, could provoke accident among tourists. Come get your damn cat.

I hired a cat hunter to catch her, shoot her or whatever necessary. He spent 2 days at $100 a day, but it was raining and made poor trailing, and then a tourist ran into her in the middle of the night, bent up the front fender of his car, and badly damaged the cat. Another tourist behind, shot her and the next day a piece appeared on the front page of the Salt Lake City paper.

Luckily my name was never revealed. Two days after the wolves escaped they were dispatched, one by the sheepherder and the other by a ski instructor when the animals approached his daughter at the ski resort where they lived at Brianhead. There were lots of rumors flying around over southern Utah and, luckily, none came down and hit me on the head.

Not getting the sunset shot concerned me for they said we should take a few more days but Bob wasn't around to help, so it was a lot to do by myself. I took another wolf, a wild one in a cage, used the same point, got the camera ready and running and turned it loose. This time there were no chances taken for this wolf was mean and, besides hurting me, he could hurt someone else. The gun was handy. Just as the sun was going down he was turned loose.

He casually went out on the point, lifted a leg on a rock, and ran back to the wire where the camera was. Shouting didn't do any good to get him out on the point. I left the camera running by itself, took the gun and tried to herd him out; he just growled and snarled at me. Then pushing by the wire he darted off across the top which was flat. At a hundred yards I bagged him. Well, that was it with wolves. It was necessary to raise them from pups, and have nice tame ones to work, in order to have them return to you.

The money from the wolf job went into building some permanent cages and finishing the kitchen in the large building. The main building was about 125 ft. long and 40 ft. wide with high ceilings and needed to have the roof fixed to get ready for winter. It was a job that I had to do by myself. Bob was doing other things.

31 / *Toklat*

Salt Lake City was 325 miles north, but it was the base of supplies for the animals. Bob had introduced me to Mel Hardman, who had a small movie company, and gradually Mel and I started working out a deal with Hugh Hogle on putting together and financing a movie company.

We worked out a deal so we would all be together in a corporation called MHP Studios. All my film, animals and equipment were put in for a third share. Willie was put in too, which was a terrible mistake, for while Hugh or Holly, as he was called, promised me I would never lose him, it didn't work out that way.

Holly's family had been in Salt Lake City for years, owned a great deal of property and some said they had a controlling interest in Goodbody & Co., a stock brokerage company. Holly put in $125,000 in the company for working capital for his share and we decided to do a grizzly bear film. The chicken coops were going to be used for an animal compound and the company signed a lease for them and bought Bob out of the deal that he and I had made. We decided that we would get started on the picture.

I picked up some work on the side to help keep us going. We agreed that we needed some help in the management department; so we hired Mike Ridges as an office manager. Eventually we gave Mike the title of President to give him more prestige in helping to raise money for our new projects.

DICK ROBINSON

Mel Hardman brought us a deal for some real help about this time from American National Enterprises, which was a distribution company that handled animal pictures, mostly hunting pictures. These were on the way out due to the big push in ecology, so we're going to help them make a picture on mountain lions. With Wild Kingdom these were called specie pictures, all about the life of a particular animal or animals.

A great deal of film had been done by Ernie Wilkensen, of Monte Vista, Colorado, who was a hunter, trapper, taxidermist, and cameraman. Ernie had several animals that were tame and handleable and he filmed the way Wild Kingdom did. He had accumulated 35,000 feet of all kinds of animal action. Russ Neihart, from American National, had purchased it and was going to work with Mel to help put it together. Our company would finish the picture with the music and the works.

When Mel got into the editing he found that there was a shortage of action, so additional footage was shot with my mountain lion, snowshoe rabbits, trout, and elk. We used a good deal of grizzly bear and mountain lion footage that I had brought into the company. It finally turned out great. The picture made American National a good deal of money, grossing $3.5 million over the winter. We offered them our grizzly bear picture to market the same way, and to have them help us finish it both idea-wise and financially.

American National used the TV saturation method to sell, which really promo'd the film and brought in droves of people. At a meeting with Russ we discussed the situation and he told us that they could sell anything they had on television with their method. They didn't need our product, they could come up with their own, and indicated that we should do the same thing. It was just as well that we did. Borrowing $125,000 from the senior Hogle and starting our own distribution company, "Sun International" as a Delaware corporation we proceeded to finish the picture and get ready for distribution.

Then disaster struck. A recession!

Early in June, I had made a private deal with a man who had a custom-built horse van with beautiful living quarters in the front and room for many horses in the back. It was 40 ft. long, had air-conditioning, huge water tanks and holding tanks, only nothing seemed to work. He had a practically new Ford tractor with sleeper and air-conditioning, so I had arranged to buy the whole thing for $17,000 which I thought was a bargain at the time. This was all on payments which I knew were going to be slow but all of us figured to be millionaires after this picture.

Alaska was where my mind was made up to go, for the bears fishing for salmon would be the most colorful action part of a picture. "Toklat", was what the picture would be called. A good name! The crew rebuilt the trailer, built two grizzly cages to go into where the stalls had been and a bunk room back of the living quarters. They replaced the water and holding tanks, built a new section on the top to haul hay and movie gear, and got new tires all around for the 10,000 mile trip.

There were several people working for me now, both in the compound and with the filming. One girl working for me was called Jackie and she was very attractive and so amply endowed it was embarrassing. She did animal handling. Men flocked to see her, but really she was good at her work with animals. The crew included her, another handler, Gordon McGoughlin, and Dale Hansen, a still photographer and movie cameraman who worked for the company. My instructions were, no mixing among the crew! It was a long trip to make, and we had to have some rules.

The journey north started from Salt Lake City in the middle of July. The trailer was rigged to carry 150 gallons of gas on top in storage barrels and 100 gallons in side tanks, so that we could take advantage of wholesale prices when we found them. It took a lot of gas at 2 and 3 miles a gallon! The first day we drove continuously through the night to make to the border by 5 o'clock so the veterinarian would still be on duty; and then we went on to Calgary. This made a total of 900 miles in 24 hours. Top speed on the truck and trailer was 55 mph, so it was slow going.

The living quarters were fitted out with an electric kitchen, fridge, large bed, bathroom, and small dining table with sofa. All three stayed in the trailer living area, but Dale would ride with me in the cab once in awhile to keep me company.

The trailer had a wide deck on top with a 3 foot solid wall around it, so all three would ride on it for hours, watching the scenery from some deck chairs. The road was gravelly and dusty for a thousand miles but we got used to it.

There was only one axle on the back of the trailer with duals on both sides, and that's where the trouble came. Having good tires with high tread was great on the highway but murder on the gravel. A rock would get in between the treads and pound until it broke the tire. After changing several flats I discovered that a smooth tire or one with off-road treads was better.

The trip was several thousand miles and we'd keep on the road until 12:30 or 1:00 in the morning. It would still be light until 1:00, and light would return again at 3:00 a.m. Jackie drove on pavement for a while one day but she scared me to death, for the tractor was just too big for her to handle and too hard shifting for a woman. It had no power steering. It was hard steering for me and, when the dust got worse, was nearly impossible.

The weather climbed to 90 degrees which was a heat wave in the north. It bothered the regular truckers but my being used to the heat and having air-conditioning made it allright. When we stopped, the other drivers remarked that even though we were slow the air-conditioning was worth it.

Things went well through White Horse, Y.T. (Yukon Territory), and we were nearly into Alaska when we got two flats on the trailer and were in trouble. Parking and unhitching the trailer at the side of the road, leaving Jackie and Gordon with it, Dale and I headed for Alaska to get the tires fixed. Without the trailer the tractor was rough riding, and the roads, even if paved, were rough in Alaska. We found a service station after 70 miles and we got the old tires changed, and headed back.

Close to our trailer we were stopped by a highway patrol car. Mounties were seen patroling regularly, but this one was different. They waved us to a stop, and two men in civilian clothes got out. Asking if we were owners of the trailer, which we said we were, they asked about it and we told them what we were about. Carrying bears

Never Kick A Bear in Your Bedroom Slippers

It seems robbery of anything on the highway was common, and these men were with the Y.T. government and were worried about the trailer. A helicopter had been sent out from White Horse to see what it was, and a patrol car had been assigned to watch. How nice of them! But how about Jackie and Gordon?

Evidently they had been having a tête-à-tête inside with the door locked, and wouldn't come out, but the two were all innocence when we got there. The new tires were put on, and we continued on to Alaska.

We went into Alaska about a hundred miles to the American customs and immigration at Tok, where customs were cleared without trouble, and then we had a rude shock. We were to pick up our permit for bears at the border. I was carrying a letter from the game department in Juneau but the permit was to be waiting for me at customs. The local game warden was a real ass and laid a fat ticket on me. He couldn't even wait to get things straightened out after I told him about our letter and showed it to him. Now all hell was breaking loose. Both the company and I were on the phone and the head office in Juneau couldn't find the assistant director of the game department with whom we had to deal, so the game warden confiscated the bears.

"Ok," I said, "take the whole outfit and we'll get to Anchorage and get back to the States. *You* be responsible for everything." I drove the truck and trailer into the warden's backyard, and the Alaska State Police came and started inventorying everything that was there piece by piece. Every bit of it was dusty and dirty, and the officer was complaining about getting his uniform dirty. We all got a laugh out of that. In the meantime the warden wanted to get us immediately into court. I went, talked to the judge, who was a woman, and explained the situation. The judge thought we ought to refrain from holding court until we got all the people concerned together, and I agreed.

The office in Salt Lake City was moving. The governor of Utah was in New York City, and was hunted down so he could help us intercede with the Alaskan governor. After several hours of calls, our office found the Chief Executive of Alaska on the north slope out of

Fairbanks. He called the judge by radio, then we were instructed to go to Anchorage and pick up permits. Talk about hard feelings! Later I heard the game warden was put in a far northerly post! Way north!

I drove to Anchorage, picked up permits and went back to Paxson where we partied and filmed for three days. There were 2 days of foggy weather, and one good day. Willie and Poo, the other bear, had a great time catching and playing with the salmon. Dale got lots of stills, and I filmed a couple of thousand feet of film. It turned out great! Dale and Gordon caught a bus for Anchorage and a plane home, and Jackie and I headed for the states with the truck. What a trip! Six days of steady driving but we made it to Edmonton with no more flats on our smooth tires, so, taking time to clean up, Jackie and I went out to a fancy dinner in Edmonton then headed for home.

32 / Warner Brothers, Sid Pollack, etc.

Doc, (the self-taught vet) and I had kept in touch over the years, and, after the compound was taken over by the company, it was decided that someone should be there to be in charge when the filming was going on and I wasn't around.

Earlier, Doc had sold his house in California, fixed up a trailer for hauling his animals, got an old panel truck to sleep in and to pull the trailer; then he got another trailer for an old '56 Cadillac he had and fixed it up to carry more animals, and headed off in convoy for Florida, where he established an animal compound as a tourist attraction. It lasted a year, and was falling apart when I heard from him.

A deal was made for him to be the supervisor of our compound and doctor our animals. In turn there would be a vet hospital built for his work, with areas for both him and his animals. I converted one end of the second coop into an office, examining rooms for animals, an isolation room, and then a string of sleeping rooms for people living there, plus one for Doc. Across from the sleeping rooms were animals in nice permanent cages, and a couple of cages for some of Doc's big cats.

In the other end of the building was room for Doc's other cages, and some new ones that we were building for his house cats and jungle cats that he was using for breeding experiments.

225

Doc loved to talk to people, telling them about his exploits in research, in cross-breeding cats and jungle cats, and about the personalities of his animals. He made a show with his big lion, Valerie, for when he took a tour around, he would demonstrate how tame she was, wrestling her, and ending up with French kisses. It was appalling to me, but people would come from far and wide to see this terrible show. It brought words between us about his behavior in front of people, and he stopped it finally but not without some hard feelings. He still liked to have the animals sleep with him, and kept several in his room at all times.

While I did make it clear that cleanliness was to prevail around certain areas, I forgot about his bedroom. When someone went in, since he invited many people in to see his animals, it was a case of clearing out their sinuses for the odor was pretty rank.

Doc started taking in some private cases on the side which brought him into conflict with some of the legitimate vets. He could talk their language so they thought he was for real, but when they found out differently they got rather put-out and people began complaining about some of the things that were being done to their pets. We had to stop the private practice to keep the compound from being shut down, for there were questions coming from the state people in Salt Lake City.

There were several eagles and hawks that had been brought in from some of my trips, and they needed to be trained, so Dave Currant was brought in from Wyoming to help. He worked on some of the "Wild Kingdom" shows in Jackson with his own eagle, and now he could help with the animals too. He brought his wife and new child and they moved into some of our rooms.

As the control of the compound moved gradually from me to the company, when the move was being made to Canada, Doc and Dave would now run the compound for the corporation. It was a big responsibility, for not only did they have to keep the place up for the tourists, but had to try to do some work for the company in the way of animal jobs. The company kept pouring money into the compound in hopes that it would make a profit, but, from my view, there was no way.

226

The compound sat back from the road about 400 to 500 feet, had a road by it to a dump about a half mile farther and a ball field was situated about a quarter mile back where our line bordered on it. Everything in the back was surrounded by the high mountains of Zion Park. There was a triangular lot in the front that was owned by an individual who lived close by and wanted to sell. We put up a large sign to attract tourists who were driving by to help make the compound a commercial success, but we had relatively few takers.

Everyone hemmed and hawed around at the company in Salt Lake City about buying the front lot. It was only $600, but no one would take the first step. The owner told me that he was going to sell it to someone else if we didn't buy it. Well, I put a $100 deposit on it. I told Mike about what I'd done and the resulting clamor was immense. Being accused of everything from "corporate opportunism" to much more convinced me I had done the wrong thing. I pulled back. Later the owner sold the lot.

A new rock shop was built right in front of the compound and effectively cut it off from view from the highway. It helped spell the demise of the compound as a tourist attraction.

After our trip to Alaska both Jackie and Gordon went their separate ways. Jackie went to work in the office in Salt Lake City and Gordon changed to distribution for it really suited his personality much more.

MPH had an office on what was called "film row." It was in a group of offices that had been used for major film distributors and had large storage vaults for film. These offices worked very well for us. Our company, MHP, was remodeling, putting in a nice sound recording studio, installing a color lab for for stills and a group of editing rooms in the basement, and we leased $100,000 worth of sound recording equipment.

There was a cute blonde out front at the reception counter in the office to take care of customers while we were doing film work and she would also book the sound studio. Usually I would come up once a week from Springdale for meat, and would drop in to see what was happening.

I went back to Mike's office one day and saw a very glum face.

He explained that several customers had come in complaining they had caught a social disease from the office girl.

"Tell her to go to the doctor!" I said.

"Well," he said, "how about the 10 or 12 customers?"

"My God! What do we have to do, furnish 'entertainment' besides doing good work? What else?"

He thought a minute, then replied, "Well, Vicki downstairs has been picked up for cattle rustling and taken to jail."

"What! That cute little thing who can't weigh more than 90 pounds soaking wet, rustling cows?"

Mike replied, "Yep! Picked her up this morning." Well, that did stump me. I guess it was better at Springdale with my little problems.

It seems Vicki, the girl downstairs, was with her boyfriend when he took a shot at a cow and he went out in the field to find it and perhaps butcher it while she drove around. The sheriff saw the pickup, stopped her and asked what she was doing. She told him she had had a fight with her boyfriend and was out driving around to settle down. OK, the sheriff said, but cool it and put the gun away. He let her go, but took her license number. She sneaked back, picked up her boyfriend and went home.

The next morning the farmer complained and the sheriff put two and two together. He found the truck through the license number, found blood stains in the back and both of them were charged. Later they turned her loose. What jury was going to convict this cute little chick?

The crew had rebuilt our place completely in Salt Lake City. It was beautiful! They had spent $25,000 working on it, but there was one problem. The lease was up, and no one would sign a new one 'til the bank, which held the lease, would fix the roof. It had a small leak. Mike and Mel told the bank, "Fix the roof and we'll sign a new lease."

"No," said the bank, "we've fixed it once, the rent's cheap, now you fix it." Mel and Charlie Stockdale, who had a film company next door, had had many words. Mel was infringing on his business, Charlie said, and, not ethically, he insisted.

Never Kick A Bear in Your Bedroom Slippers

One day Charlie was in the bank paying his lease payment and something was said about the lease next door, which had now gone over several months. Charlie simply said,

"I'll take it." He signed, and then paid Mel and Mike a visit. "I'll be a nice guy and give you three months to move." We moved. Charlie took over a great place. Some lesson! We ended up with an old church to rebuild into another sound studio and offices.

That fall MHP was contacted by Warner Brothers Studio to work on a Robert Redford picture. Warner needed a lot of animal work and asked if I would work in Hollywood with the grizzly. No! They needed grizzly work and Willie was really the only good one around, except for Lloyd Beebe's which was tied up by Disney. Didn't I think it could be done there? Yes, but I wanted no more of Hollywood. Evidently they talked to Redford and asked him the same question. No! He would only do it in Utah.

Later, I talked to John Coonan, a great production manager, and it was agreed that, for $15,000, I would do the animal work. I did the first pre-production work in October for just a week's shooting, since they were planning on using this material for fund raising. It was a short crew for a major movie, probably 40 in all, and we spent three days with Willie chasing Redford around and up and down a tree. When he was first being used I informed everyone to stay back; this was a grizzly bear which could be *mean* and *dangerous* and to let us keep him under control. Great! It worked for about a day.

The second day they could see what he was like for we were rather casual, and people would now stand up beside him and get pictures and pat him. The third day they were now ignoring all restraint, putting kids on his back, climbing on themselves and generally acting as if he were a dog. He was very tolerant of everyone.

Willie loved to chase Robert Redford around but finally, there was just one last tree scene. He was to chase Redford up a tree; first Bob would run, throw his gun up into the tree, then scramble up himself. But something always seemed to make it go wrong. Then they decided to do it in pieces. Bob and Sidney Pollack had been arguing all day and everyone was getting "antsie" and now they needed to get the grizzly standing up to the tree trying to get at

Redford in the crotch of the tree. Good, I put some cookies hidden in some bark, and he would try to stretch and reach at his full height to get them.

It worked great, but, like most photographers, the cameraman wanted a more exotic shot. Lying down under the bear's bottom was the second cameraman with a hand-held Arri 2C camera with matte box (a square shield around the front of the lens to keep the sun from shining on the lense) and he was going to get a shot along the back of the bear with Redford above him in the tree. I don't know how the shot turned out, but Willie sat down about this time and the square corner of the matte box struck him in the fanny bringing a woof of "hurt feelings" from him. It was even worse for the camera-man who was underneath. Willie refused to do it again.

Then they brought out their ace-a bear suit. Now a bear suit looks great for a quick flash shot, but always looks phony to me. They got Al, the prop man, all decked out in the suit and he took Willie's place at the bottom of the tree, clawing and raking his claws after Redford. All the animal people got a great laugh out of it, for it looked so artificial, but the crew was really egging on Al to greater action. With that we left for home.

Sid Pollack was a great guy to work around as a director. He would carry on a conversation with anyone, was easy to work with, could explain well what he wanted and could understand what you had to give. They hadn't brought a sound man, and when he volun-teered to run a Nagra tape recorder no one objected.

Redford was cautious around the animals, and I couldn't blame him. He was friendly but we had little in common, so it was all busi-ness with him.

We filmed in the mountains behind the little town of Kamas and plans were for the picture to start in February if all the financing went through.

I got a $5,000 check for the week's work and turned it over to MHP. At that time I was getting a thousand a month after working for 6 months at $500. It wasn't much with all the expenses I had personally.

Later on when I met Sid Pollack and asked him about the bear suit incident and how it turned out, he was rather cryptic.

"Like a man wearing a bear suit."

Our company started getting more pressure to repay the notes from the Hogles for they were beginning to feel the squeeze. The recession was having its effects on many different companies except the movie companies, who in bad times always seemed to do well. I took Mike to Los Angeles and introduced him to many of my contacts in the movie and TV business, and we started making overtures to the Wolper organization which was interested in "Toklat" and some distribution for some of their own films and other products. There were several meetings but nothing came of them.

Leon Ames, who had been the actor in "Toklat", had been talking to Terry Moore, the child actress, telling her about the young fellows in Salt Lake City that were into good clean G rated films. She was a Mormon and felt a kinship for this type of project. She packed her bag for a quick trip to Salt Lake City. She met with everyone, then set up some things in Hollywood for some financing.

In the meantime I stopped and saw Pat Frawley. I told him what was going on and he found he knew one of the participants. We all had a meeting at his house and he decided to help out. Time went along; there were meetings going on and one day we all met at the Schick offices to finalize the details. Frawley was going to put up $150,000 and another man was going to do the same. While sitting at the table deciding what to do, the other man said that it would take a few days to cash in some bonds for his $150,000 then Frawley stood up and said he had decided to take it all. This surprised everyone. Mike, Mel and I were there representing the company, and there seemed nothing to do but say yes. The other man left. Next Patrick said we ought to have the name Schick. We all said we didn't need it but if he thought it would do any good, well.... He said fine, that he'd just take $350,000 in stock for the name. It took a minute to sink in but then everyone screamed. He dropped the idea 'til a few years later.

Then he pushed on us a plan that he would buy 51% of the company for $150,000 and lend us $150,000 as an option for approximately 32%. It was a great deal...for him! One thing I knew from my past experience was that there would never be anything in it for any other stockholder, so immediately I advised the others of my 30 day notice to sell my stock, while I had the chance.

There went the million dollars that I'd been counting on....

My shares were finally purchased at the end of May for half what I had in them. The dealing had gone on for weeks. Mr. Frawley became the big boss. But I was still there.

33 / Jeremiah Johnson starring Robert Redford

On the 4th of February they had started the Robert Redford show; "Jeremiah Johnson," it was to be called. There was a big meeting at Heber City, Utah, in a motel, with Sid Pollack laying down the law about the budget. (Sid was the director). They had *only* 4 million, and anything over would come out of Sid's pocket. It eventually came in at 5½ million, I heard, but everyone was well pleased and I don't think it came out of Sid's pocket.

There was a hundred-man crew, and, while it was snowy and cold at times, everything was done without too much trouble. The major shooting at that time was done at Sundance around Bob's ski resort and his home on the hill. Trucks and trailers, buses, and snow machines were everyplace, and a large Cinemobile carried camera equipment and lights.

My work was intermittent and it took time to get the animals together. I got a nice big buck deer for a scene and waited for days to use it. When the big moment came to use the buck, we went into the cage, grabbed the horns, intending to steer it out, and one of the horns came off in my hand. Sid suggested we bolt it back on, but that was impossible. We took the other horn off and we now had a doe. It was the time of year that deer lose their horns.

They were going to have a hunting sequence with Redford actually shooting a deer; people were grumbling about this and we

233

had a huge crowd. Somebody brought a couple of young kids, 6 and 8 years old, and I questioned even having them around. It was explained that they had been told what was going to happen, but even that didn't set well with me. After much decision-making at the last minute, it was decided not to shoot it. We filmed the deer. It accidently fell in a hole and stumbled and looked like it was shot. In the final cut it turned out well.

All the elk that were to be used for the picture were in a temporary pen. They would fight on occasion and finally the female escaped, then another got in a fight with the bull and was killed. At last there was none but the bull left, but we did the scene successfully, much to everyone's relief. We had to make sure that all the elk had been tested for brucellosis, and other diseases, before they came in to the state, in case they escaped. It was a good idea, for one did leave.

Willie's big scene was to chase the old trapper into the cabin and then he (the trapper) was to jump out the back window and holler to Redford that he'd get another grizzly when Redford got done with this one. The camera was mounted on a dolly so that it could get the shot of the bear chasing the old man into the cabin, follow to the back of the cabin, and see him jump out the back window in one shot.

Willie had been trained to run down and into the cabin after the actor. One of the men working at the compound was dressed as Will Geer, and the whole thing worked well until we got ready to do it. Everybody wanted to see it, the *big scene,* and there were people standing on the roof of the cabin, in trees, behind trees, everyplace— probably 125 crew and friends.

Everything happened as planned except Willie would come to the cabin door and balk. There was too much activity and too many things to tempt him so he was put back and Poo, who was Willie's brother from another litter, was tried! Sid quickly moved the crew for another shot and said we would do it next week with a small crew as I suggested. Willie was trained a few more times and, with a crew of only 12 the next week, we shot the scene and it worked beautifully. There was another shot in the desert with Del Guzzi in sand up to his neck and that also turned out to be one of the biggest laughs in the show. "Sight" gag!

I had to furnish 4 vultures looking hungry to sit around Del when he was buried up to his head in the sand.

There were no regular North American buzzards around so I ordered some from India. Fortunately they came in to Las Vegas the morning we needed them. We were working in Snow Canyon out of St. George, Utah, and Snow Canyon is actually the most beautiful red sandstone and sand dune area I've ever seen, very unique scenery. My driver arrived with the birds 30 minutes before we needed them, so, working fast, I tied their wings, using a piece of black nylon to pinion their wings so they couldn't fly, then tied them down with nylon fish leader around their legs, so they had to stay in one spot.

This was a messy job, for they'd be throwing up everything in their stomachs and the smell was terrible. They'd break the nylon, and off they'd go, with 2 or 3 of the crew chasing them. They were long legged and as large as turkeys. At last there was one tied down with 3 loose, being chased from all directions by members of the crew. The scene was quickly shot and worked fine. At least the film crew had something to do that afternoon. Everyone was laughing at the crew running and chasing vultures. They ran through the sage brush, over sand hills and through the rocks, with all kinds of people laughing and chasing them. A vulture rodeo!

In a few days we moved to the Kolob, which was high in the mountains in what was called the red rock country, for what the crew called the "crazy woman" scene. I turned Poo loose for a scene and he just took off down the road and ignored everybody. Off he went into the mountains with me tracking behind. There was still some snow so I kept up slowly but after several miles I turned around and went back to the truck. We were about 30 miles from the compound in Springdale so we left for the night.

The next day one of the fellows took the truck and cage back and I got a plane. I followed his tracks for miles but never saw him. At a couple of hundred feet I could see he had been wandering around looking for something to eat and saw his trail going through a large wild turkey trap hidden in the trees baited with corn. It had a net 60 or 70 feet across and could be triggered by an explosive charge from a blind.

There were lots of birds around the first day that you could see from the plane but when I walked in the next day there was little sign of them. Following tracks all the next day was rough and I must have covered 20 miles. The next afternoon we came back to the same place we lost him after having looked up the road and back for miles. There he was! Three days of wandering around and now he was *hungry*. We put a ramp up to the back of the truck and he ran up into the cage which had some chicken in it. He never did run off after that. They get smart about food after they've gone hungry once.

The animals that I had brought into the company were growing old for most uses so, for *Kazan,* there were many young animals needed and we were buying. The company refused to buy so they came out of my pocket. A coyote or racoon would look like an adult at a year old, still be frisky and playful and you could get a lot of action out of it. Also they weren't inclined to bite or be so independent as they would be later.

The animals that were left in the compound were mostly cage animals and some very rough working animals. When you go on a shoot there are a great many responsibilities to be considered. First is safety for both animals and people around. Is there a tourist or animal handler apt to be endangered? What precautions can be taken to safeguard other people and yourself?

There would be weapons handy depending on the circumstances, basically in case of attack on the cameraman or handler.

On one trip to Death Valley, I visited a Bill Burrud show as an outsider, and there was a good case in point. Their photographer had been bit before by a jaguar. He wasn't careful around animals and it took only one slip to have trouble. Dave Currant was in charge of the compound. I passed on the advice not to do this job considering that the Burrud crew was hard and irresponsible, that the coyote they were going to use was not very controllable and would bite and the mountain lion was dangerous; but it's just human nature to rebel against someone who tells you not do do something if you're newly in charge. Dave went to Death Valley. Fortunately they had permission to use National Park ground and started filming. They turned the coyote loose and he promptly went over the hill, literally, and they had a chase that lasted for hours. The coyote was gone! Then when using a cougar and turning it loose to film, some people came along as they have a perfect right to in the park. The cat was loose, stalked a little boy and jumped him. Chewed his throat! His people took him to the hospital and later sued. This was a good case of asking for it. The same insurance company was involved for both Burrud and MHP and eventually paid something like $25,000. MHP lost money, time and a good animal plus insurance as did Burrud.

34

Canada–
beautiful country,
horrendous red tape.

Rod Allin came down from Jackson and started working with us. He had parted with WK temporarily (Rod had started to work for WK after I left) and decided to work on the Kazan project and others with me. He supervised the building of sets, designed a custom camera trailer, and bought camera equipment we would need. We built table top sets in the back of the compound under my supervision for use in desert scenes. These were actual pieces of desert real estate on a 4 x 8 foot piece of plywood, about 3 feet off the ground, that we could set the cameras beside and film sequences of action from small animals and reptiles. We put in creeks and water holes, for much action occurred around watering spots where animals would come.

Dens were fashioned for skunks and their babies, larger dens for desert foxes and their babies, and places where we could film insects. Both Rod and I enjoyed this kind of work.

We built a complete inside set for a cabin that could be used for our Kazan show, since we needed a place for the main character to bring in some rescued wolf pups to be raised. Then, in Canada, we could build the outside around this set, for it came apart in panels. We built a large den inside the building out of concrete, coloring, rocks and sand for the wolves in Kazan, for here I would have to come in and rescue the little ones. Rod hadn't done much set lighting before we found, with the new lighting gear we'd bought, he was most talented and did a good job.

We purchased an office trailer and a movieola editing machine so that we could do our own editing; and then we hired an editor, after much consulting, from Los Angeles. His wife worked for me doing the office work, but after a couple of months they moved on to Salt Lake City to do editing for MHP.

Small animals were now being filmed for the desert show. It was May and June when the small animals were young and playful and grew fast so now was the time for filming. The people in the company were asking, "Where is the film for Kazan?" There was none, for we were utilizing that time of year with animals on a desert show. They didn't understand that spring and summer comes in July and August in the high mountains and that we would have to move fast. We filmed some great desert footage that never has been duplicated, but no one liked it at MHP.

In July we moved the filming crew to the lake at Brianhead, where Bob Davidson and I had worked on the "Wolf Man", and at the same time I had crews hauling people, trucks, and trailers to Canada, setting up a camp on the Kananaskis River about 10 miles from the main highway. We were right on the edge of the Rocky Mountains, 45 miles west of Calgary, and only 30 miles on into the mountains was Banff. The country was beautiful but the red tape horrendous.

Fortunately we were on a National Government Forest Experimental Station and they were most cooperative, but across the river was provincial government and another set of permits was needed.

Pat Frawley had me take his son, Mike, who was 17 at that time, to work in the film crew to help Rod. He had helped with the cabin scene in Kazan with the little wolf pups and now he moved up to the mountain with Rod and his crew. Rod had an assistant cameraman, Beaver Nelson, whom we met in Alaska and who was going to help on this picture. Rod was nervous about having complete charge of filming certain animal scenes, but I had all the confidence in the world in him. He would teach and help Beaver any way he could, for the two of them worked closely together, and he helped others the same way.

Rod's filming was excellent, and one day, coming up in the evening bringing feed, I found everyone laughing. They'd been working on baby racoons for days and finally had a payoff. The racoons had gone out on the end of a log over the water and really clowned around. It turned out as some of the best footage ever seen.

Wolves were being worked now, big ones, and this was my responsibility. We had wolves downing deer, which was always hard, but it was part of nature. Mike was rather nervous about the big wolves, and got trapped at the fence by a group.

I heard him holler and dropped everything and ran, for it was my job to fight if necessary, and it was a fight. One wolf had him by the leg while the others were just sitting watching. Quickly I drove it off, and when a couple of the handlers got there we collared the group. Mike got a good bite, it was bloody and the leg was chewed, so one of the men took him to the hospital at Cedar City while we went on working. This filming was good, and was well done in the final version.

Mike spent a couple of days in the hospital. His mother flew up from Holmby Hills to be with him, and he later went home to recover. Later, Mike Ridges told me that Patrick had talked to him about suing me.

The animals in the film were mostly ours but we took advantage of what we found that could be used. There were wolf pups sliding down a snow bank on top of Brianhead Peak when a weasel stood up in the rocks and looked around. Rod filmed it, and so the piece eventually was called "Pop goes the Weasel", for they used the music and edited that sequence with the tune, and it was excellent. The scene consisted of the pups running up to the top of a snow bank and sliding down, and every time a break came in the music, the weasel would pop his head out. The pups loved it, for it was the middle of July and we'd gone to the last snow that was around at 11,300 feet.

One morning I found duck eggs in a nest by the pond, and a few days later there were baby ducks and mothers swimming on the pond. Getting into costume, as I was the actor in the picture, we got the cameras set, and let the wolves go.

They went with me as I waded out in the lake and showed them the ducks, and then they had a great time chasing and trying to catch them. Of course, they would go after the mother, and she would lead them up and down with the old wounded wing routine. She bounced and flopped on the water to draw their attention, then they would come and she would fly another 20 feet and start again. They finally got tired of swimming after her and chased along the bank. So they forgot all about the small ones and, when her ducklings were safe, the mother flew off to the next pond. It was great footage and well-used in the finished movie, but the ducks never showed up again.

Moving to Canada was a large operation for me. Everything had to have customs paid on it as it went through the border. There were 8 or 9 trucks and 15 trailers, 60 animals or so, and all our movie equipment. We would have to go back and forth to Utah to carry more loads, pick up trailers, and there were 12 or 14 people who had to clear immigration so they could work in Canada; and then Canadians had to be hired.

A camp was established on the old so-called Disney compound, where they had brought their equipment to make many of their animal movies for years.

A pipeline from the river had to be put in, a thousand feet of it with pumps to furnish all the water we needed. The power company wanted so much for the installation of power and the price was so high that we purchased a diesel and generator to furnish electricity. It ran day and night from tanks that held hundreds of gallons of fuel which could be transferred into smaller tanks for the generator and the trucks and equipment that used it.

We had a large kitchen trailer with a shower, washer, and dryer in the back; then we built a large dining room beside it. The camera trailer had a built-in bedroom for Rod, and two large apartment trailers were custom-built and brought up. Each had 2 complete apartments for the crew. Some of the Canadians brought their own large living trailers and we had many smaller ones. A couple of cabins on the grounds were turned over to the crew to use, roughing it.

DICK ROBINSON

We built a large garage to work on the vehicles with facilities for a mechanic and welder to work on the trucks and the sets. Panels for the cabin set were trucked in and the cabin built around them. The crew started to build filming compounds and the actual sets. Animal cages had to be constructed, and we had to move 70 large transfer cages full of animals from the States. To complete all this, we had to buy a backhoe to dig the plumbing system for all the trailers, and to lift cages and move things.

With all the construction work going on, we still had to film and find an editor in Vancouver to work on it. Gradually I ended up getting an office there, for that was where all the film facilities were. Mick Winters, a free lance writer, came to work and started doing all the writing and the research on several of the projects that I was endeavoring to finish.

Grizzly Adams was #1. It kept my mind occupied with the possibilities of a great show, for I felt at that time that he influenced my life from the "past." Mick and I had artists and architects make a plan for a village, while Mick worked on the story for the movie and figured the budget.

Shooting went well, but everyone at MHP thought there was nothing being done so they hired Bob Davison to come up and check on me. They paid him a great deal of money to run back and forth a couple of times and look at what we were doing, but he couldn't find any fault. We were on schedule. There were 2 years to cover in the show. The first with pups, and the second as they grew up, so it meant going through summer, fall, winter, and spring. We could shoot summer as spring and summer, and then fall and winter by using two sets of animals, which I was doing. But it took time for the seasons to come around.

My wife, Pat, and I were just barely getting along. When it got rough I'd leave and go to the coast or Los Angeles. She didn't feel well and just wanted to lie around.

One afternoon a fire started in the 1½ ton truck which was sitting next to our gas supplies. We had two full drums sitting on the back, waiting to be unloaded. The motor caught fire, and as soon as the hollering penetrated my head, I ran. The motor was burning, but I jumped in, started it, and drove through the smoke until it was out of the way of everything. As luck would have it the hood opened easily and a huge cloud of black smoke poured forth. We had one little extinguisher, which we couldn't get to in the cab, but the crew was so excited that three fellows grabbed a barrel, three-quarters full of water, lifted it up, and dumped it on the motor. The fire went out, but it was close.

The next day a pole was installed at the center of the buildings with 6 big fire extinguishers hanging on it, for gas and oil fires and also electrical fires. We weren't going to take chances after that for there were no fire departments to call.

The next week we had a chance to use them. I bought a little bulldozer in Calgary that had been rebuilt and looked like new. Beautiful! They came and delivered it on a large semi, and left after showing me how to run it. I was pushing some dirt on the far side of the village when the man from the butane company showed up. Leaving the machine idling, we all adjourned to the cook shack to talk. The cook served coffee and rolls when suddenly one of the men stuck his head in the door and hollered that my bulldozer was on fire.

Everybody ran, and I leaped up from the table in a fast get-away but fell flat on my face. My God! My feet were hooked together. Looking down, I discovered my shoe laces had snagged. It took me a couple of minutes to untie them before heading off.

Everybody had left, grabbed extinguishers from the pole, and were using them on the fire. It looked like the engine was on fire, and, as it was a diesel, I couldn't understand it. Taking the last extinguisher, I crawled under the cat where the fire was, turned on the foam, and got it out. We discovered that an electrical wire had crossed the fuel line. It had a bare spot and burned the copper fuel line, setting the oil on fire from the fuel tank. It was a minor episode but the ribbing was fierce. How could I foresee an accident like shoelaces tangling?

The equipment company took the responsibility for the cat, came and picked it up, repaired it, and brought it back the next week. It cost them a thousand to fix it, and they weren't happy.

The winter gradually got colder, and it started hitting 10 below.

Then the water line from the river froze. No showers nor bathroom water! We found the old out-house, cleaned it up, and put lights and an electric heater in with a new set of seats. The crew bragged to visitors that it was the only one like it around. We found out that water lines had to be 9 feet deep to keep them from freezing in Alberta. We had a well-digging company come in and start drilling in the spring, as soon as it got a little warm.

It was hard filming in the cold, but it had to be done. The worst was getting in and out from the camp to the highway. We had many 4-wheel drives, and finally a large 'dozer, the small one, and a log skidder with rubber tires and a small blade on the front to clear snow off the roads for it was 8 miles to the freeway. On one flat, for a mile, the wind would blow, and gradually the drifts reached 10 ft. high. The government didn't help, so we just had to do it ourselves.

We had done some scenics on the far side of the river, and, when the little cat came back repaired, I took it across the river and made a road on the hillside that came down to our shooting compound. When I finally got back that night, Rod was really upset. There was now a great road through the scene that we used for our opening scenic. It would be ruined! Luckily we got enough on it when the opening scenes were shot.

When the forest people saw it though, they grumbled about half-wit movie makers.

That fall we needed shots of Willie and a cub catching salmon and with me taking our year-old wolves and teaching them to fish. The scenario called for Willie, the bear, to catch a wolf, take it down, and then, seeing what was happening, I would grab a small switch, run and hit the bear with it and scare it off. At last, looking at the switch in my hand, I would realize what I'd done and run and climb a tree.

We contacted the fish and game department in British Columbia for help. I wanted a shallow creek or river with a run of red salmon, sockeyes, such as we had filmed before in Alaska, and these people were most cooperative. They gave us permits for grizzly bears, wolves, a young mountain lion, and racoons but there was one no-no. If we brought 2 racoons, we left with 2 racoons. They had

244

no racoons in this part of the country, and they didn't intend to have any.

They met us at the Adams River with a patrol car, red lights flashing, and guided us to a private camping place in a gravel pit and then showed us where to find the salmon. They were great. We had brought the "cat" in on a large flatbed with one of my diesel trucks in case we needed it, and the large travel outfit for living. The crew was Rod, Beaver and the production manager, plus 3 animal handlers and myself. I took the 'dozer and cleaned up a road to get a place to work, which was conveniently close.

The fall leaves were just coming on the trees, and the red swarm of salmon was incredible.

The next day we filmed the wolves catching salmon, then underwater shots with the salmon and the mountain lion and racoons around the fish. The next day we took the grizzly cub down and filmed, then Willie.

Now the big scene! Everything was set, Willie grabbed a wolf pup, (they were nearly as large as German sheperds) on a sand bar and was dunking him up and down. I was screaming and hollering and walking toward him waving my arms. Rod was behind me filming. Garland, one of the animal handlers, ran across the river and asked if I needed help. No! I told him to get the hell back. Now I was in a position to do exactly as planned. I had a small branch and charged Willie, who had the dog down, but just as I reached the bear, both of the other handlers got there to help me. I blew up! I started hitting Paul, my brother-in-law, with the switch. It didn't hurt, but gave him an awful scare for he'd never seen me so mad before. I was doing such a good job of acting they thought it was for real. Boy, was I mad!! We loaded everything and went back to the gravel pit.

The next morning a racoon had disappeared. That did it! Someone had been careless and not left the cage door tight. We loaded everything and headed for Alberta and home but left the 3 handlers to find the racoon. They had to bed down in a couple of large crates with food for a week. Everything was taken home, and several days later I came back. No racoon. Garland had gone back to the States for he was homesick, and this had upset him. We took the other two home.

That racoon was tame, everybody saw him at various times, and he even decided to live with some people for a couple weeks. For months he was seen up and down the river, and we ran an ad with a reward, but never got anything but a letter from the game department, saying that we were no longer welcome in British Columbia. They just didn't want racoons to get started on that river!

Everything worked out well, except the big scene. We were able to use only the first part. After that, there was a clear rule. Never help me while filming, except when I shout *HELP!*

As fall and winter set in we had most of the filming done, but money was getting critical. There were 20 people on the payroll that had to be fed and kept occupied, which required a steady supply of money. Mick was working on a jaguar show that we called "Jhora". This was an action adventure picture that was a story about the life of a jaguar from the time he was young and was captured in the jungles, sold to an animal company in Canada, taken to the U.S. for filming, and then escaped. I was negotiating with MHP.

People hadn't been paid for a month, and everybody was really hanging on when the contracts were signed a week before Christmas and I brought money home.

There was plenty to celebrate that Christmas. We started filming using one of the girls who was working for me, and we put one section of the show together in the next couple of months. The crew needed to go to Arizona and Florida to shoot the rest, but we were still having to shoot pick-up shots on "Kazan." Rod had to go home for it was hard to be away from his family for so long and he was anxious to return after several months. But this kind of film was one you don't rush; a couple of cameramen friends came from LA to help finish the work.

Many trips were made running back and forth to Los Angeles. An editor in Vancouver had been doing the work on the film under my direction but I found that he was working on his boat most of the time, and that convinced me that someone with more professionalism should do the work.

Many of the animals that were being used in the "Brother" picture were on loan to me from the company for they were animals that I originally sold to the company for stock, and now after leaving the company, they could be used, but would have to be returned to the compound in Springdale. Willie, was the one I was really upset over, for he was like one of my family.

When I had come into the company, it was with the understanding that Willie, particularly, would never leave my control, and that I would never lose him. Now I was faced with that loss. We sadly took back the animals after the show was finished: Willie, Lobo the wolf, and several others, including Mabel the black bear. Everytime I talked about it with Frawley it brought on negotiations for a heavy penalty on my part.

It was like trying to get somebody to give back your child and then having them try to make the most advantageous deal they could. He would play with me from time to time in these negotiations, as he loved to make deals. It was a game to him, for he had the money and the time to play. I had learned much about his methods of manipulating, and could see the final results. I had to learn to accept that fact of life: that some people like Frawley use you for a time when you are valuable to them, and, when they feel that it is done, you're gone!

Mike Ridges had to make everyday decisions as president, but he consulted with Frawley on anything that was of importance, especially where I was concerned. We had all kinds of letters and negotiations going on over the various films that I was working on, and finally after "Brother" was so successful, they wanted to run it in some big cities where the price was higher per day so a deal was struck to get Willie back by changing the contract. It cost me probably $150,000 in lost residuals for giving this up, and then, to make it even harder, I was to do some free filming for him. It was to show two bears fighting, and even after that he wasn't altogether satisfied.

This piece was to be done for the "Toklat" picture, and, when I had originally shot that particular scene, it was summer and the grass was green, and Pat couldn't understand why I didn't rush right out and do it; for even though it was winter and the snow was thick in Utah and Canada, he sat in Holmby Hills, where there wasn't too much difference in weather, and he couldn't appreciate that I lived a thousand miles away in the mountains.

Always, when you negotiated a contract with Frawley that had dragged on for months, there was one little thing to be thrown in, for free, when it was time to sign. After "Toklat" was finished and out, he decided to change the picture and put in a drinking message. I had played the drunken brother of Leon Ames, and was killed by the grizzly in the picture. Frawley had John Mahon film a scene in a cemetery where the preacher at the burial gave a short lecture on the sins of drink. (There's nothing like a reformed one—I'm told.) It cost a good deal to do this, and later the story about it brought gales of laughter from everyone. It was so blatant that even the actor broke up laughing at the untimeliness of the message when they were filming at the graveside.

Neil Wise told me later that he did put the scene in a few prints that were showing around Los Angeles, in case Frawley checked, but didn't bother any place else.

When finishing the "Brother" picture to the "sole satisfaction" of the owner, I learned that here's a phrase that will never go into another contract of mine—I was to change the end of the picture to Frawley's satisfaction. I had planned on dying...a sad ending for me, but in Frawley's version, I was living and happy. He insisted that, after being mauled and injured by the grizzly then being saved by the wolves I had befriended, that I go home to my cabin, kneel before my bed, and say the rosary as some old-line Catholics do. I refused. He thought I was being stubborn. He never had heard of Vatican II or didn't listen; besides I am an Episcopalian.

Later we got talking about having Loretta Young do a picture with me, and this brought on more difficulties. Here was a woman, a star, a friend of his, retired, who did completely different things in TV and movies than I, and was in a class of her own. He continued to harp on it, and arranged to set up a meeting with the two of us one night.

When I arrived, I was exhausted from driving, for I had been on the road for a full day coming down from Vancouver. There were several people around drinking; although Frawley didn't touch a drop, there was always liquor around for those who wanted it.

The talk was interesting, and Loretta Young came in and we were introduced. She was a great lady, one of the most intelligent women I had ever talked to, could talk about anything, and of course we soon sat down away from the others, and discussed a picture.

She said her attitude was this: she had done everything she had ever wanted to do, had all the money she could ever use, and, unless we could show her something that was so unique and different and challenging that she couldn't refuse, she just wasn't interested. I concurred. What could we do in the way of an animal show that would do justice to her? Nothing to my knowledge.

Frawley had a big 110 foot yacht in which he had invested a great deal of money and he had been trying to unload this on the company to use in a picture, so he could write off the operation of it; now he had the idea of using it with Loretta in a show, some kind of sea adventure-animal film. He came along and insisted that we all go down to Marina del Ray and spend some time on the yacht. It was late. I was beat; but away we went.

Everyone was aft in a salon talking when I finally excused myself and went below decks and climbed into a bunk for some sleep. Later Loretta came down, woke me up, and sat and talked about a character by the name of Edgar Cayce. It was interesting, she was interesting, but I was dead. She must have talked a couple of hours about the times that she had been back to Virginia Beach and researched the case histories this man had left behind.

The party broke up, most of us leaving for the mansion, where Loretta gave me 5 books on Cayce, and I headed for a motel and dreamland. What a night! What an opportunity to meet someone like her. Later, these same books would greatly influence my life.

Next day I met with Frawley again, and got in a discussion about Mel Hardman. Mel had kept his stock, along with Holly Hogle, and he worked in the production department of Sun, running some of the activities. Mel was outspoken against Frawley pushing the alcohol thing at times, and an article came out in the paper about some things Mel had said. Frawley got furious and fired him. He was really mad that afternoon, and told me something that stuck with me from then on.

"Doesn't that little f..... know how rich and powerful I am?

Mel didn't know. That stayed with me for years, and certainly influenced some of my decisions later.

My Pat had been getting ready for the baby, so I had stayed closer to her.

She went to the hospital when she thought the baby was due, but it was a false alarm. She stayed for a few days, waiting. Having joined the Canadian government health care plan, which cost us a dollar for the first 3 months and then $32 a quarter for the two of us, was going to help.

The doctor, who had been helping Pat, started getting together with us socially, along with his wife, and every week they regaled us with great stories about their sojourn in the Northwest Territories, Dawson Creek, and Yukon Territories, where they had been a doctor-nurse combination working for the government.

A month after we'd finally got everything moved and settled, I had a pain in my chest, which moved to the left part of my chest, and then my left arm became numb. I started worrying. Then my breath started to come shorter. Now I really worried.

Finally I went to the doctor. He gave me a short physical and told me there was nothing wrong. Take it easy. Somehow that didn't seem to help. The next day on a trip to Calgary with my production manager, I had a *real* attack. It was bad! My breath nearly stopped, and the pain was terrific. He rushed me to town, picked up a police escort, and by this time I couldn't care less.

They rushed me into emergency, where we were met by a doctor, I was given a quick shot, put on a bed, had a heart machine hooked on, and then everyone disappeared.

It ran through my mind that if I was dying, they surely weren't paying much attention to me. I had a picture, like on television, where they would have a whole crew working on me and that it would be a real fight. Nothing! My pain eased. Someone took the paper off the machine and rolled it up. Still nothing! Finally the doctor came in and said,

"OK, get up! We need this bed for sick people."

I looked at him.

"What'd you mean?"

"You're not sick! Here's a couple of tranquilizers to take now. I'll write a prescription for some more. When you get a pain, take one. The girls will give you the bill on the way out."

I climbed weakly out of bed, paid my bill, and went home. The telephone calls had been going back and forth, and everyone was concerned. I felt humiliated. Not even sick.

The next day I made another visit to my doctor, and he admonished me,

"Dick, I told you that there wasn't anything the matter. You're healthy as a horse, but you are going through a let-down. Having gone through a lot of stress and, being keyed-up from moving, you're letting down now, and it brings on a case of nerves."

He gave me a bottle of 100 pills, and in the next few weeks the pain all disappeared. Funny what nerves can do. I'd rather be chewed up by a bear, and get it over. The pills lasted several years.

I was in Los Angeles when Pat had the baby. I sent her a check for $350 to pay on the hospital bill when they let her out, so she stopped at the office to give it to them. The bookkeeper refused to take it. Pat insisted! The head nurse was called. They insisted the bill was $5 and that was it.

"No!" she said. "My husband said to pay this!"

It took awhile, but they explained that for a hospital visit, on health care, it was $5 for a week or a month, and everything else was paid, even special shots. She left mumbling. We found out later that indeed all was paid, including the doctor and several subsequent visits, and that she would now be eligible for $18 a month from the government for just having the child. We thought it was great.

There had been a photographer working for me from Los Angeles, who introduced me to John Mahon, a former professor at the UCLA film school who would be interested in doing post production on "Kazan." He had never done a feature like this, but obviously had the qualifications to do the editing, put the sound and music on, and finish the picture.

DICK ROBINSON

Taking him up to Frawley's mansion one night and introducing him, provided Frawley with a feeling of confidence; Frawley had to approve everything that went on as post production was the job of the company.

My job was to do everything in the way of story, direction, acting, and filming. It was agreed that John would do the post production. An editor was hired, the film sent in from Canada along with the story board, and with my help the story was laid out so these people could understand what was happening. They had never edited or worked on animal pictures, but quickly learned.

Going back and forth to Los Angeles every 10 days or so, to see what was going on, kept me busy, along with working on the jaguar film. There was only $150,000 to film a whole feature, and now part of that was being used to hang around and wait for some shots that had to be done on "Kazan." These were shots that Frawley personally wanted to put in. He had a thing about putting in messages about drinking and smoking, which were upsetting to most of us, and especially to the people putting the picture together. Certainly they didn't help the pictures, and they were very distracting.

It was costing me $25,000 a month to operate, so money didn't last long. John Mahon finally came up one day, shot a few shots in the snow, and left. Just cut-a-way shots of my face. Frustrating!

Many of the people that worked for me would listen to me talk about what happened on the trips I made to Hollywood, what the problems were and about all the difficulties that arose; but it was one thing to hear about them and another to participate. If possible I wanted to take one of my people along to see just what went on, so he could pass on an understanding of the problems I had.

Peter Van Uum, was editing and running part of my operation in Vancouver, so he came along with me on one trip.

The first thing we did on arriving was to go to Frawley's mansion in Holmby Hills. Peter waited in the car. Usually, the cook or the housekeeper would take me directly into the small dining area off the kitchen without announcing me, for Pat and I were good enough friends that it created no problems. This morning it was ten o'clock, when he was usually down for breakfast and, when she took me into

252

the dining room, he just blew and started raving and ranting about her doing this! I got mad, left the house and drove off with Peter.

I mulled over what had happened out loud. Nothing was unusual; Pat was in his bathrobe but then he was usually like this at that time of the morning. What had happened? I was so mad at the explosion that I was ready to quit and forget about him. What crude and rude manners! I was furious.

Peter was a Dutchman, methodical and fairly even tempered. He said,

"Dick, why not wait, let everything cool and come back in an hour?" I was still so hostile that I needed to blow off steam. We drove around for awhile, stopped for coffee and then headed back to Frawley's house.

We drove up the winding road to the front courtyard. I parked and left Peter in the car, went to the front door and rang the bell. Patrick answered the door, dressed in a business suit and welcomed me,

"Dick, it's great to see you; how've you been pard?"

"Oh, great....how about you?"

"Good, good! Who's your friend?"

"It's Peter Van Uum, my manager in Vancouver."

"Well, have him come in." I waved for Peter to come in.

"Let's have some coffee in the den and chat."

The three of us held a discussion of whatever we had come for and left. There was no reference to the happening of an hour earlier and I could only thank Peter for persuading me to come back again. It has left me with a question mark to this day. Whatever came over the man? But it was indicative of his personality.

Later we did business with some of our suppliers, picked up repairs, visited the office and finally went to the little motel where I usually stayed. We went to bed and next morning there was a great surprise! A sneak thief had come and taken our pocket books and pants. I didn't lose much money, but I lost my credit cards and the usual things in a pocket along with Peter's things.

He had forgot to put the catch on the door and the night chain. Luckily, the office cashed a check for me and we got home, but nothing that was taken was ever found. The good part was that, while the thief took these things, there was an aluminum camera case with a $5,000 camera just sitting there untouched. Close!

It was a relief and Peter learned a lot. When he got home he had plenty to tell the rest of the crew about what went on. Certainly these trips were eventful at times.

35 / *Peterkins and the Smeetens*

Back at camp we had many visitors, some tourists, local people or officials of one kind or another. We had many animals, mostly tame, and people were inclined to put fingers or hands in cages and try to pet them, sometimes with disastrous results. Someone had to supervise and keep an eye out for those that slipped in. It was always left for a member of the animal staff to be responsible during the day and, if not, then anyone else who was around.

One day lying around in some buckskins we were fitting and trying out for Grizzly Adams, Pat brought an old couple by and introduced them: Miles and Bea Smeeten. They had a game farm she told me, with some moose and geese they were raising. Moose were interesting for we had none and they were nice to have around, like elk. It was snowy and cold but we spent some time going around and seeing all our animals. The Smeetens were retired, he a Brigader, tall, dignified, very old, and both were the same sort of charming people, still active, but looking like they had only a little time left.

They told me they were having trouble holding in their moose with 8 foot fences, for the snow was drifting deep. The moose were long legged beasts and they would just walk out over the top of the fence on a snow drift. When the Smeetens left, it was with an invitation for us to come visit and it all happened sooner than we expected.

DICK ROBINSON

The next night about 8 o'clock we received a call. Peterkins, the bull moose, had left. They had tracked it for miles and would we bring a few men and help them get it back. We would.

Practically all of us lived at our own village so we rounded up 6 or 7 people, passed out new snowmobile suits and hats that had just come in, got 3 trucks and a couple of snowmobiles loaded, and took off. It was 40 miles to their place in the country, over rolling hills, covered with much tall brush, a cultivated field here and there and snow everywhere. We'd never been there before so we had Miles Smeeten meet us a few miles from the ranch in his Land Rover and guide us in to the farm house where they had last seen the animal.

Everyone spread out in the woods to look. It was dark but with a full moon so visibility was quite good. I climbed over a ridge by myself and spent a half hour cruising around. There was a foot of snow so it was slow going. Finally I heard a faint voice calling, "Peterkins, here Peterkins." Bea Smeeten had a bucket of food walking through the snow. We looked for a couple more hours together. The snowmobiles circled around looking for tracks but they discovered nothing of interest.

Later, we rounded up the crew, had coffee and cakes at the ranch house and sent them home for most had been working all day and it was now past midnight. Pat and I stopped at the Smeeten's home for a spot of tea and promised we'd be back in the morning and start again. When we got outside the house I looked at the thermometer, 10° below.

They had told us inside, while enjoying the tea, the story of how they got there. Miles was a British tank corp commander, had retired and bought a sailing ketch, and, together with his wife, had started sailing round the world. Going round the Horn in South America they had run into a storm, Bea had been washed overboard and disappeared; then, by a miracle she was washed back. She broke her shoulder. The ship was dismasted but made it back to Rio. Gradually it was refitted, then sailed the Pacific. They settled on Vancouver Island for a time while Miles wrote a couple books on that adventure. Then they moved to Alberta where they had found land that was suitable for them. They wanted a small lake for geese and some forest area.

They built a new house, fenced a quarter section to raise some moose and write a book about raising them. They had two moose, Peterkins and a female, Patruska, who were each about 3 years old.

The next morning the crew was back again and searched over miles. It was mostly small hills and much brush, tall brush with a few small pine trees. Most was in small farms, of three to four hundred acres. By this time of winter, the fences were mostly covered with blown snow and the moose with their long legs could go right over. Also, there were many wild moose and deer drifting around. No luck! There just wasn't any way of identifying tracks that well.

Snow machines covered miles of snow and several people walked through the woods. In the afternoon everyone went home to do their chores and the Smeetens and I went back to their house for tea. Miles and I had a long talk. I suggested a helicopter, which would cost several hundred dollars but would find Peterkins quickly. After all, the moose was worth $1500 at least.

Second best, I told him that a plane should be able to do the trick but he wouldn't do either. It seemed a shame that a good tame moose should go to waste. Miles was writing a book about raising a moose and what it was like having them around and this certainly wouldn't do, losing it for a matter of a little money. I thought about it to myself, then I put it to him.

"Well, Miles, if I spend the money finding him and let you use him for breeding, can I have the moose?"

He quickly agreed. Also I would fix and raise the 8 foot fence to 16 feet, where the wind was blowing snow the worst, and clean out the snow that was there with the 'dozer. Great! he said.

The next morning I took one of the young chaps who worked for me, having been a trapper and hunter, got a plane from an airport 30 miles away, and started out.

First we flew low over the house to tell them we were hunting and then off in the direction he was last seen. We flew at a couple hundred feet up and down in a grid pattern and started to check out everything we saw in moose. He was big, 3 years old, and had a nice set of horns. Every couple miles we found moose, cows, young ones, bands of deer and finally a big bull. Now we went down to a hundred feet and inspected it. No, a big old one. Nice for some hunter though. Back and forth. Wow! I zipped over one that just stopped and stared. It sure looked like the description. Now we went down close again several times and figured we'd found it. Pulling up, we now had to find out how to get to it.

We found a farm close, traced back the roads to the game farm where Bea was standing outside in front waving. I wrote a note, stuck it in my jacket pocket, flew low over the house and threw it out. Damn, I was too good. Everything landed on the roof and they couldn't see it. We cut the engine and I hollered as we glided over them, but she didn't wave an acknowledgement so we brought the plane around again in another circle and went down to fifty feet in a glide. I put my arm out and made an O with my fingers. Hopefully she got the idea.

After landing and getting our truck, I called home and told them to bring a portable plywood crate big enough for the moose, to bring a small trailer, the crew, and to meet me at the Smeetens. It had to be at least ten miles to where the moose was from the house. Bea was waiting when everyone returned and she was stocked with a few loaves of bread, oats and her metal feed bucket, for it was something she could bang on that would bring Peterkins to her.

As everyone assembled, the trucks loaded, maps drawn to guide drivers to the farm, the convoy emerged from the game farm looking like it was ready to face any enemy. One truck had reached the farmer who stood outside staring with amazement that he should be chosen as the recipient of this raid. We explained our mission. The old farmer, a bachelor who was retired, assured us that we could do anything necessary to perform our mission. Only just come in and have tea and cookies first.

It was agreed that Bea would head for the woods, find Peterkins, and have him come in. Then perhaps he could be chummed into the barn or the trailer. Off she went into the woods, banging and calling, "Peteeerrkins!"

A half hour later some figures appeared in the trees and gradually Bea emerged with a huge moose ambling along behind. He was big!

Peterkins was interested in strangers so we all moved well back and she led him right into the barn. Great! She came out all smiles and we closed the door behind her.

The crate and trailer were backed up to the barn door and we opened them. Darned if he didn't come right in to get some bread that had been placed in the front. Quickly the door was closed and now he was trapped but he did the unexpected. The roof of the crate hadn't been put on yet and he just stood on his hind legs and tried to crawl out over the top. Bea quickly crawled up on the tongue of the trailer while someone sat a box there. She climbed up on top of it and started to talk to him. She literally took her life in her hands, pushing his horns and legs back into the crate and, while I thought it was an extremely foolish thing to do, I had to admire her for it.

We slid the plywood into place covering the top, which darkened it inside and would keep him in. We bolted down the top and the trailer and truck pulled out into the driveway of the house. He was thumping around inside with his horns and not even some bread would keep him quiet.

The old fellow invited everyone in for tea and cookies for he couldn't believe all the excitement and he wanted to be part of it and talk about what had happened. His house was absolutely spotless. What a housekeeper! He was starved for company. I thanked him for everything and headed off with Peterkins banging and rattling around in the crate. Some of the crew stayed on for some of the stories the farmer had to tell about that part of the country.

The ten miles went swiftly, back to the Smeetens. The gate was opened and the truck stopped inside on the drive. When the door of the crate was opened Peterkins looked back from inside, then started to move slowly backwards, gently dropping his back hooves to the road bed and then moving out slowly, carefully extricating his horns. He slowly meandered off into the brush, quite unconcerned about the whole business. You could see from his attitude that he'd do it again if something wasn't done to help keep him enclosed.

A couple of the crew headed straight back to our camp, loaded the little bulldozer there and brought it back that afternoon. I worked for hours that evening and night with the lights on, plowing out the snow next to the fence where it was the highest to keep the moose in that night. The machine just barely made track through for half a mile but it was enough to knock down the high drifts. Much of it was 5 and 6 feet deep.

The fence was made of steel poles which had wire netting 8 ft. high fastened to it. It was our job to add 6 ft. on top of these steel posts and string more wire in case the snow got that high. We brought a portable arc welder and steel posts from the camp and added on to a half mile of fence and strung wire. It was a lot of work for days and Pat would come along and talk to Bea while I worked. Peterkins would stand back and survey the work, along with Patruska, then wander off for brush to nibble on.

The Smeetons had a new house with a barn-type roof, double car garage in the downstairs, which opened into a workshop area. There were stairs that led to the next floor where they lived and when we arrived there were alcoves, hanging beds and swings to talk and sleep in, and, best of all, was a firemans' pipe to get to the downstairs. Bea would put her leg and arms around it and zoom to the bottom, while everyone else would walk down. It made her unique. She always had some biscuits of one kind or another that she had made to go with tea. In fact I learned that's what "tea" meant.

Now that Peterkins was my property there were certain obligations that went along with ownership. One telephone call brought me out to fix a playblock for him. Bea wanted me to string cable between two spruce trees behind the house with a sliding ring and block for Peterkins to have something to butt and play with when he was unoccupied.

Driving out one day in my spare time with the equipment that was needed, I had an experience with the moose that would be needed in the future to know how to handle him for filming. In fact this is the big secret of successful filming: know your subject and what to expect from it.

I strung a light ¼″ steel cable between two trees. I fastened one end with a clamp to hold it there, put a ring with a block attached onto the cable, and fastened the other end to the other side. Peterkins was standing there watching, and then started to interfere. Bea was watching from the window and came out. She said,

"Now Dick, if you'll take my pick handle and lean it up against the tree and tell Peterkins about it, he'll leave you alone."

This dutifully I did, but Peterkins would walk up, lower his horns, and move in and try to touch me. This was a little scary, so I would threaten him. He would just roll his eyes. Bea called out,

"Dick, take the handle like I do and threaten him."

I picked up the handle, held it up and did like she did, shaking it at him. No results.

Now the moose has two huge, wide sets of horns that he pushes against other moose, with lots of points that catch, and he can ram hard or just push. Down the middle is a clear path to a spot on his skull where there is no protection, but this is a place that is ordinarily never hit by another animal. Bea would tap him lightly with this pick handle at that spot.

Finally I'd had it with his fooling around, and he wasn't showing me any respect, so I hit him very forcefully between the horns. Bam! Poor Peterkins rolled his eyes, staggered around a little and went off to lean up against a tree. Bea came storming out and said,

"Now, Dick, *I* never hit him that hard!"

Well, Peterkins and I came to an agreement after that, and I remember one day when we were filming a couple of wolves with him in the field. He would walk over, put his horn down in front of the camera that I was filming with. He would slowly put it right up to the lens, stopping a quarter of an inch away, and would roll his eye to see what was happening.

My stopping and peering around the camera at him brought a delayed reaction. He would slowly pull away and amble off when the pick handle came in view.

Some people pick up a rolled up newspaper and hit an animal, which is all right for some, but usually if they learn their lesson when young, that something in your hand can hurt them, they will carry this forward for their lifetime. My bear, Willie, listens to me with even a little limb.

The best way to teach animals about something small is to use a little limb one day, and a steel bar the same size the next day. If you're out working a big grizzly and he misbehaves, you can always find something to get your hand on to threaten him, then he will listen, most of the time. TLC with discipline.

Peterkins had a bad habit of playing with peoples' radio antennae. There was a quarter-mile drive to the front of the house from the outside fence and people always drove in. He would play around the car till he found the antenna, rub it with his horns 'til the antenna would break off. It became a nuisance to have to replace them.

I brought the Smeetens a small elk that wasn't tame enough for me, and helped with the compound they were building for some small desert foxes they were going to raise.

Peterkins had sired some small moose. He was standing by the fence one day in hunting season, and some hunters came along and shot him, just for fun. They just left him lying there. Some people in this world!

Pat had our baby on the 4th of February. I was in Los Angeles working on "Brother of the Wind", as it was called now. The baby was a little girl, Shauna, she called it. She had been in and out of the hospital a couple of times on false expectations, so we decided that I may as well go about my work.

Now it was back and forth on the jaguar picture, and trying to get moved to Arizona to work on it. Part had been filmed at the Calgary airport, with shots of the jaguar coming home, and what happened when it got here. Very nice so far. Pickup shots of "Brother" were finished and at last people and trucks with animals started to roll south to the ranch in Arizona as our work was done. Half a dozen trucks left along with 8 or 10 people. Mick, the writer, went along to write on the advance script of "Grizzly Adams" and the last of the script of "Jhora."

Leon Bijou, the head photographer, Mick, Garland, Beaver and the production manager went along to run things and these people were all Americans and had some feelings about the country we were going to but not the Canadians. Everyone of them was apprehensive about the snakes; what would happen to them if they were bitten? How safe was it to go to bed at night?

There were few snakes in Canada, so this was something new to most of them. Of course some of the Americans took advantage of this situation with a little horseplay since some of the girls were nervous about snakes in the extreme.

The same people welcomed the crew that had been here before. The camp was set up under the palms, a shower and bathroom were built and septic tank installed, water and electricity were brought over from the house; but there was still extra electricity needed so we brought a generator in from California. Another couple came in that had been working for me, Wolfgang Obst and his wife Sharon, and they built sets for snakes and reptiles. They had been filming in the Utah valley on beaver houses with the mother and babies inside.

All the Canadians could talk about was the rattlesnakes, "Yes," I'd tell them, "there are lots of them around, for we'll be camped next to a stream, and they come for water, along with lots of other reptiles and animals....but remember, they're as much afraid of you as you are of them. Besides they don't like to be stepped on. It hurts."

"How about tarantulas?" they'd ask.

"Don't worry, they won't bite."

It was hard for them to believe that there were more animals around here than in Canada. It was a pleasant surprise when everyone was finally settled. There were snakes all around, but they got like us. If one met a rattlesnake around the trailer, he walked around it. It was warm and only one of the Canadians couldn't stand it, left after a week, more from homesickness than anything else.

Mick loved it. The people who ran the place had a lovely pool which they opened to all of us, for they liked the company. Their grown children lived in one of the houses close by, and a couple of other families lived there. Mick's girl friend came down for a visit and they spent much time around the pool working, for that was just his style. Lie around the pool and write, now that's living.

Beaver, who was just finishing the last of his filming for me, was going with Dorothy, who was playing in the picture and who was also one of my animal handlers. Beaver was leaving to go back to

Boise and start out for himself.

There was the normal share of bickering and arguing for a group this size, and it was my job to straighten things out. There was lots of partying at night around the pool, which helped morale, for I was gone most of the time and left the filming up to Leon and the crew. At this point, hustling the money to keep the company going was my big concern.

As it got hotter and hotter, the work hours decreased 'til, finally, everything had to be moved to the high mountains at Brianhead, Utah.

Wolfgang and his wife were doing the filming for me now. Leon had gone back to LA and Beaver had left. Wolfgang was just generally working on mountain flowers, bears, and shooting a beaver show for I had found some investors in Calgary to put up the money on a little cheap show. Even at that the money came in so slowly that we could hardly operate. Small coyote cubs that had been saved from a trapped female were filmed around a band of sheep, and all kinds of other animals, for a possible sheep and coyote show. All kinds of good action was obtained and much in the way of flowers and scenics with the animals for it was a beautiful year for flowers. An actor was found who was a sheepherder and Garland worked with him in building a story on the coyote pup.

In the middle of the summer we returned to Canada and the crew continued filming on the beaver show.

Going back and forth between Vancouver and Los Angeles, where they were finishing up "Brother of the Wind", kept me busy, and it felt like I was getting further and further from that part of picture-making that really mattered to me, that of directing and working the animals. Also this could be seen in the product that was coming out. For years I had been building up the experience of learning how to make animal pictures and here it was being turned over to other people while my job was raising money now to keep this large group of people working and in pay.

Seems like it wasn't working the way it had been planned. Wolfgang and his wife were filming for me on the beaver picture and, while they were extremely efficient people with what they knew the show slowly bogged down, money became short and we finished our filming with only half a show. Our filming on the jaguar film had been brought to a halt for lack of money too. The company had looked at the work and refused to go over the budget of $150,000. We were now scraping for every dollar we could get to stay alive.

36 / A few bad maple leaves

Our permits ran out at our location on the experimental farm, so after six months of extensions, we had to move. Our choice for a temporary location was the Rafter Six Dude Ranch, about 6 miles away, which consisted of a big lodge, bunkhouse, and about 8 cabins that were fixed up for guests. It was winter when we moved in, cold, but a delightful time of year. Nothing was being filmed at this time, and we were just waiting to move across the valley to a new location we were leasing (slowly) from the government of Alberta.

Alvin Guinn and his wife had built up the Rafter Six ranch to be one of the best in Canada. It was well-known, and, as Alvin and his wife had come to retirement age, they had decided to sell it and use the money to live on for the rest of their lives. They sold, but to the wrong people. On a small down payment, the new owners moved in, took over, made no more payments and ran the whole operation down. Now the courts were acting on getting the place back for the Guinns. Everything we had was moved in pending a final disposition on who got the place. It would take maybe a few months, maybe a year.

The Guinn's had a son, Rick, who was twenty at that time, who went to work for me. He could do about anything, make costumes, built cabins, fences, or whatever was needed.

Never Kick A Bear in Your Bedroom Slippers

The lodge was a large log structure, a big dining room for 60 to 80 guests, an expansive commercial kitchen, living quarters upstairs, which Pat and I lived in, and a dining area in the back for the crew. There were meals for everyone, a cook with a cook's helper to prepare everything, and the crew could relax in front of a huge fireplace in the evenings. Families were scattered around in cabins, and the bunkhouse had singles in it.

The lodge had a hill behind it that was flat, and this was where our zoo was placed: ninety animals, all our trucking and construction equipment, with a new garage that was being built, and a heated area in a small dance hall for the animals that needed warmth, (like the chimp.)

A lease on several hundred beautiful acres across the valley was going methodically through the department of Lands and Forests. We planned to put in a film town for "Grizzly Adams", get a film studio set up, build a natural zoo, a shooting compound for animals, and a shooting location for a series we had drawn up, called "Plimley". It was an ideal location, and would mean much for the movie industry in that part of the country.

"Grizzly Adams" was, of course, mostly on our minds, and we worked toward that end, making costumes and props, training the animals, and getting film experience on how the costumes would work and wear.

Finally the leases came through, two of them, to use certain areas. We thought about how to use them. There were fences needed, roads to be built, areas for animals and for our village. Across the road from where we were going to build was the set-up of Mickey Bailey, who had animals, and was making small TV shows. He had government backing and loans for his project, and was going to build a large animal habitat area for the public to view. He wasn't competition for us, nor we to him. Ours were the feature-length films and soon-to-be TV series. We both got much newspaper coverage, aired our views about the government, which was slow, and about the red tape and bureaucracy, which were astounding. He was an American, with a wife and a couple of kids, and they had signed up as Canadian immigrants. His wife was a good amateur artist, and became very friendly with my wife, Pat. The Baileys had great plans that were published in the Calgary paper, and promised a new zoo that would be a great tourist attraction. Mickey did a television show for one of the stations, which classified him as a TV Personality, but my bag was movies. Yet, sooner or later, we would be in competition, since his land was just across from mine.

We used the small bulldozer to clear a road to the spot where we decided to put in our camp. Pushing over small trees to clear the roads meant cleaning up and burning, and the area for the camp covered a couple of acres that had to be cleaned up. It was a big job, and I did much of it, for it was something I enjoyed. Trailers were moved in, then lumber from the sawmill that we'd had running for our use at the camp on the Kanasanskis, and then a sewer system was installed for the trailers. The office trailer arrived then kitchen trailer, bunkhouse trailers, several small moveable shacks to store material in, and one for the sawmill crew to live in.

A couple of weeks later a letter came in the mail saying that the agreement with the government had been violated, that there was to be *nothing touched*. They were slapping a $500 fine on me for putting in the roads and making the camp site. A lease, but nothing could be touched!

Later, at a party at the ranch, the real problem presented itself: a forestry official wanted a pay off! He approached my production manager and me in a corner of the room and suggested that, if we gave him a very lucrative job he would stop it. I was very impressed! After Hollywood payoffs, I had no intention of paying off again. I really couldn't believe my ears at the conversation, and just shrugged it off as a person who was drinking and bragging. But later, he approached me again, sober, and repeated the offer.

At the same time, there was a move from several other people in the government at Edmonton for the same things. Three of them approached me and indicated they would protect me, and help me with the government for the things I needed, for only $300 a month. It would be paid to one of them every month as a retainer, for supposedly finding locations when they were needed. We signed an agreement that they worked out, but it left no doubt in my mind that the $300 was going to be split three ways. There was to be no contact with any person in the government from my people. Coupled with the offer from the forestry official, it all rubbed me the wrong way.

Travel occupied much of my time. We made a cheap movie for a tax write-off in December, just in time for the December 31st deadline, then sold my desert show to a group of investors in Vancouver in the first part of January. It gave us enough to move a film crew south to Blanding, Utah, for work on the coyote show, on which some preliminary work had been started and edited the summer before.

Our story was about a little coyote pup that had lost his mother, wandered into a sheep camp, and was trained to become a sheepdog for the herder. When the owner of the sheep was going to come to camp, and would probably order the coyote destroyed, the herder had it carried by a friend to Navajo land and turned loose to run around on the reservation. Now we were going to do the section with the Indians.

A long convoy of us left Canada, crossed Montana, Idaho, and got into southern Utah—right into the teeth of a howling blizzard, and we were still 40 miles from our destination. It was mountainous, dark had settled in, and the snow was blowing cross ways to the road. No one stopped, visibility got worse, and my nerves took a dive for the bottom—a dozen people in jeopardy. We crawled up and down hills.

Here we had come a thousand miles for good weather—what next? We were twenty miles away, and it started to lighten—the snow was coming straight down now. Nothing had yet occurred in the way of an accident—what luck! In another ten miles it started to rain. Now it was only miles to a warm bed and comfort. We all pulled into the motel where were going to stay, went across the street for coffee at a cafe and compared stories.

Pat had come along with the baby, and we had taken over the motel for housing, and of course we had the cafe across the street for meals. A couple of blocks away we had a house where we kept the majority of the animals and a couple of people. We had all kinds of activity going on with different animals, but mostly we used the work of the coyotes.

We filmed a medicine man doing a sand painting, which was done to get rid of the coyote from around the Indians' camp and sheepherd. The sand painting is really a religious ceremony conducted by a group of Indians, with a medicine man leading the group, and everyone works together on the construction of one of these paintings, for it is done for a specific purpose, and, when done, the whole thing is scooped up in a cloth and thrown to the wind. We filmed this and recorded it all afternoon from beginning to end. It was something that was done so seldom that it was almost unknown. to the outside world.

The next day this same group of Indians did another ceremony to ease the effects of the one they had done the previous day. It was something that even we didn't do justice to in the movie, for it took a great deal of agonizing over what material to use and how much.

These were strong ceremonies, with much sound to raise the vibrational level and voice communications to reach the spirits that would heal or resolve a situation.

I was feeling more uncomfortable with Pat all the time, and would stay away rather than have harsh words with her. The baby was around, but I couldn't get close to her. She would start screaming when I got close, which was an unusual thing for me; most kids like me.

There was much traveling to be done, for it was a certainty that either Sun or American National would use this film for a new picture. I was taking the film back and forth between the two parties, and the biggest problem was the people involved in the negotiating between myself and Sun. We spent the afternoon in Frawley's private theatre looking at the show one afternoon with Neil Wise and one of the other people. Neil had replaced Mike as president by this time for Mike had a falling out with Frawley and what Pat needed was someone to sign his name as president but under Pat's supervision. Neil lounged around watching the film and said it was nothing they could use.

How short-sighted these people were. From my position it was a

25 / Dick with Rick Guinn riding "Grunter," the buffalo.

26 / Dick and "Willie" heading home after a days shooting in Alaska.

27 / "Misty" the wolf on a Mike Douglas show. Mike, Dick, Bea Arthur, Jack Douglas and wife, Reiko (ankles on right).

28 / Dick and "Kodie" doing a scene for *Grizzly Adams.*

29 / Dick was mauled by "Kodie", the bear.

30 / Dick and "Willie" in Arizona. An obviously actionful moment in *Grizzly Adams*.

31 / Garland Wilde, Dick and Carol discuss action for *Grizzly Adams*.

32 / Dick and "Willie", the bear that is never more kicked.

case of turning down everything and anything that I would do. For several months to a year I could see what the problem was, at least in my mind. When "Brother" was done and released, the success of this movie was instantaneous, and it soon became apparent that I would become a rich man over my percentage, and Sun would also make a fortune. Most of the executives of the company were at the $25,000 to $35,000 level, and to see me make close to $400,000 in one year just didn't agree with them. It seemed to me that they would go to all ends to frustrate anything that I would do.

They forgot that, at the same time, the company made $2,800,000 and that wasn't the total of the profit from the picture. Later, Mike told me of some of the ways they had shorted me on residuals. It was just human nature, and I could understand their feelings. To them I was just the man with the animals that shot the film, and they did all the work on making the money, only we couldn't do anything without each other.

One day I was complaining about the trimming that they were giving me. Pat Frawley and I were walking behind the house in the gardens and he put his arm around my shoulders and said,

"Dick, have you ever made this much money in your life?"

I replied, "No."

"Then what's a couple hundred thousand more?" he asked me.

This was one of those times when there wasn't anything that would come to mind to say to counteract this remark; yet I was thinking of words like honesty, integrity and agreements. Somehow there seemed to be so much more coming that it wouldn't make any difference. What a mistake!

I was doing much of my traveling by car as there was no air service from Blanding, so I used one of the girls to help with the driving. Carol had been working for me for a year, had come from Calgary, and, while young, was an entertaining and perceptive person to relate to and be with. As we started to travel together, she became the daughter that I had never raised, and could be shown the things that I enjoyed most and got something out of. Everything was new to her, and she was always enthused. After three months in Blanding, we were going to have to move back to Canada, for the talks had been going on over "Grizzly Adams" with both Sun and American and, seemingly, would soon come to fruition. Also we had finished most of the coyote show.

It was hard to leave Utah; everyone there was so cooperative and helpful that to go back to bureaucracy and red tape was rather dismal. It was a big job to get everything ready, so the first day Carol and I left with the cameras and movie gear in a small 20 foot travel trailer. When we got to the border we checked out on the American side and drove to the Canadian side.

A young officious customs officer started on us. I filled out the papers for him, and then we went to a building for inspection of the trailer. We opened the trailer and started laying out all the camera equipment. There was a mountain of it, and all had been listed by the crew for me to pass on to the customs inspector. We dragged everything out, and started through camera cases and boxes. Stacks of them. Aha! He found a small box with some spare parts that weren't listed.

Now he started searching with a real vengeance. We had no keys for a couple of side compartments on the trailer, and we had to break out the sides so he could look in. Hours went by! Now he found about 30 paperback books that were read by the crew on the book shelves. Not declared!

He called the mounties to see if we were wanted, and they checked my ID, of course. Ah, an Alaskan driver's license. They checked, nothing! They told me to get another license, one for Alberta, and left.

The officer was listing all the books in a column on a sheet with the different prices, some $1.25, some $1.95 and what they were worth now. All the fines, customs and everything came to $94. Naturally I was fuming, and, if the rest of the crew had the same trouble, it would be ridiculous. The man knew that I was the head of the company, and was getting great joy in this process. If this was what the Canadians were all about, with everything else that was going on in the way of demanding payoffs, well, compared with the attitude of the people in Utah, I was working in the wrong place.

At midnight the crew changed. A new man came on who knew

me, and asked what was happening. It was all carefully explained to him, and just then my broker walked in. He got furious. He told the officer I had a special letter from the minister of National Revenue, and, as a film producer, I didn't have to pay duty on camera equipment. What good was it going to do to make me mad? It was silly trying to charge duty on used books. Of course, Carol and I were both furious by this time. We were now on our sixth hour.

Finally they turned us loose. I drove the truck and trailer around the customs house and back to the American side. What was going on, asked the American customs officer? I told him. They laughed, and sent me to a service station where I made a deal to store the trailer with all its gear for a few days while I returned to Canada. I would have the other vehicles turn around and go to another location in Utah where we'd do our filming on "Grizzly Adams."

Leaving the trailer we headed back for the ranch in Canada. At the Canadian side now they just waved us through and we headed out into the starlite night with the moon waning over the horizon. Carol was laughing by now about the whole ridiculous situation but I was still grumpy. She teased and tickled me and got me to see the absurdity of the whole situation when, just at that minute, the car sputtered and burped to a stop. What now for crying out loud? Checked. Out of gas.... I meant to gas up at the border and was so mad I forgot and now we had gone through one town ten miles back, while it was thirty miles back to the border where certainly there was gas.

We locked the truck and hand-in-hand, started down the road. It was a beautiful starlit night and, as we were walking, she told me not to feel bad, that God really was looking over me and to quit worrying. It was dark, no traffic, 1:30 in the morning, and here we were, walking with our arms around each other and laughing at our experience.

All of a sudden a small sedan popped over the hill behind us, and screeched to a stop. Did we want a ride? You bet! We got in and introduced ourselves. Well, it just so happened, the man told us, that he was the principal of the school in the town we'd just gone through, and had the only key to gas at night in town. Great! After getting gas for us in a can that he carried in his trunk, he ran us back to the truck and saw that we got started. A very nice individual! We got 5 gallons and had 60 miles to Lethbridge, where we could stop.

Happily we went down the highway, found a motel on the edge of Lethbridge, where we could stay 'til morning. The tank was empty again!

Getting up, I glanced casually out the window, and there was a mountie marching up and down the parking lot in full uniform. My God! What now! Really, it was so funny, with the two of us looking out the window, wondering what to do. He would go by the car, glance at the insignia on the side with the grizzly on it, march to the end of the lot, turn, and march back and look again. Well, Carol laughed, if they were going to drag us off, let them come and get us. Finally, after sleeping another hour, getting a shower and straightening up, I headed out to see what was going on. Now, there were two mounties. I marched up and accosted them.

What's going on? Oh. Well, sir, ahem, we're just out of school in Regina, and, you might say, walking the dogs. Oh! Interesting. I laughed, and went back in and told Carol. We hadn't seen the dog running around. We went to breakfast in good humor.

When we got to the ranch I passed the word. We were going to stay in the States and film "Grizzly Adams," and everything in Canada would be sold or taken back. The prices were 30% higher in Canada, duty was high and there was too much red tape and unnecessary harrassment. Carol and I took a pickup truck at the ranch and headed for Vancouver. She had some animals to bring back, and I would fly from there to the States.

My production manager was told to find a place for us for 3 months in the vicinity of Kamas, Utah, where I had worked on the "Jeremiah Johnson" show, and on the movie "Toklat" for the company. It was beautiful forest and mountainous country and, while it didn't have the breathtaking elevation of the Canadian Rockies, it had everything else and a whole raft of co-operative people both in government and out. In a few days he had found a place in Oakley, a small farmhouse with a few acres for a headquarters.

37 / *Grizzly Adams*

In Los Angeles, I was involved in conferences on selling my interest in "Brother of the Wind", for I was badly in need of money, and also to make a contract for "Grizzly Adams." It was something that needed to be done in the summer. It was back-and-forth type of dealing. I'd paid back all that I'd borrowed from MHP. "Brother" had made me $375,000, and most of that had been paid back for what I borrowed from Sun. The film was a tremendous success, still they had me in a corner financially by refusing to advance me any more, knowing full well that even if I had money coming they didn't have to account and pay me for several months. They used this to their advantage.

Good thinking on their part to squeeze me out, if that's the way you do business. Frawley might have been a friend, but not when it came to money.

Pat, my wife, left the first week in June for England and took the baby for the relatives to see. She was deathly afraid of flying and took everything in sight to steady her. She was going to be back in three weeks, but ended up coming back in six.

Carol and I spent all the time we could together with all kinds of excuses for she thought she could hide it from the crew. Actually they were well aware of what was happening. She lived in the small trailer that we had taken to Canada to haul our camera equipment and then returned it to the States.

DICK ROBINSON

She liked to argue about anything that could be argued about, and with just about anyone, only she didn't know when to stop. This brought on hard feelings with a couple of the people who couldn't put a damper on her. She had a dog that was with her everyplace that it was allowed to go, a German Shepherd whose name was Krin. It was a well-trained guard dog for her, and she would sic it on some of the fellows for fun, and they would have to climb something in a hurry. She had a light heart by nature, got the most out of everything that was happening and would seldom get down in spirit. Her one rule was, when you go to bed at night, you leave all your grumpiness behind. It was something well worth learning, especially for me.

There was a big confrontation when Pat got home. She immediately heard what was going on, and went to Carol. I heard about it shortly after it happened from Carol. Both were upset at the confrontation, and Pat and I shortly got a divorce. Most people don't know that Utah is a quickie divorce state, and that it can be done in one afternoon at the judge's discretion. Pat moved into Kamas with the baby, stayed a month, and then headed back to Canada.

Finally, the last of July, we got the contract signed for "Grizzly Adams" with MHP and got started. I'd also signed a contract for the coyote picture with American National Enterprises. This was to be finished in a couple of weeks after the first of August. Meanwhile we would be preparing the props to start the filming on "Grizzly Adams," so we had time to finish filming the coyote show.

A crew from CVD Studios in Denver, a subsidiary of American National, would come to finish the filming. CVD was headed up by Charles Sellier, Jr., who hadn't been able to make a go of it and had been taken over by ANE. Everything went fine finishing the show, even though there was quite a list of things to be done.

What ANE had decided was to use me for the star of the show, so I had to do all the exciting things for television advertising, then get a person in the show, as handler who related to the animals. Basically it was now a show about a young coyote whose mother was poisoned by hunters, and how it survived to become a sheepdog for a herder and then found a mate and had pups. It was my job to see that it became afraid of man instead of thinking of him as a friend,

284

so that it would be able to survive.

We used a helicopter flying over and shooting the coyote with light shot to make it afraid of planes and helicopters. I actually used light bird shot that wouldn't really hurt. I used Carol and Rick Guinn to turn the coyotes loose when I swooped in and started shooting from the helicopter. The coyotes got scared, ran back to the two of them for protection, and everybody thought a war was going on around them. Carol and Rick were lying in a hollow hidden from the cameras, with the coyotes standing by them. Standing it no longer, they bolted for the trees with me right behind in the helicopter shooting at them with the shotgun. It did well. They were glad to see the handlers come to rescue them.

I had a grizzly chase me up a tree, and the coyote came to me and bit the bear in the tail; the bear then turned on it and started chasing the coyote, thus saving my life. I taught the coyote to stay away from poisoned carcasses, especially sheep.

It wasn't that good a show in my mind, but everyone liked it. Chuck Sellier guided the outcome of the show as Executive Producer, and it didn't please me at all. He'd had little experience with this type of show, and I believe it was only the second full-length feature that he had ever worked on.

People started to come back and forth between MHP (or Sun as I'll call them) and the camp at Oakley to confer on things. Mary Frawley Thompson, Mr. Frawley's sister, came with Curtis Kent, (whom I'd known for several years in conjunction with my friendship with Frawley) to see how we were doing. Mary was helping out with some writing and book reviews and was doing some research on Grizzly Adams.

Pat had these people come, for he knew I had little communication with any of the other executives. All were rather negative toward me due to my attitude, which was caused in turn by their attitudes.

Everyone knew that Frawley and I were friends, and most thought that I was bucking for the job of president of the corporation, which was the farthest thing from my mind. But I did want to run things for the benefit of the pictures that we were doing, for none of them had any taste in animal pictures, or the know-how to do them. These animal pictures were their bread and butter. While their "Trap on Cougar Mountain" was losing a barrel, "Brother of the Wind" was making it big.

Carol was out in the field playing with some small mountain lions when Mary and Curtis sat down and watched them for some time. Mary came to me later and suggested that we needed a woman in the show, and why not Carol?

"No," I said, "the show's been written, and there never was room for a woman."

Frawley had slipped a small section into "Brother" which had my daughter writing a letter to me. I didn't approve of it, and it brought questions about why it was done from the newspaper reviewers. I told Mary no. She called Patrick that night and suggested it to him. Carol and I also talked that night about it and we agreed that it wouldn't serve any good purpose.

Everyone knew that Carol was my girl, and they would just say that she wanted to be in the picture and, as her boyfriend, I would put her in. As she pointed out, she knew nothing about acting, and wasn't interested.

We were now filming cabin scenes where I had saved the Indian and was doctoring him. Several of us were sitting on a log eating lunch when Mary took up the torch again about Carol the next day. We all said "NO!"

Patrick called and told me about the conversation he'd had with Mary the previous night, and insisted that he would like to have a woman in the show. I was doing everything possible to satisfy Patrick, for this movie was going to be a success and I wanted to do a good job and still try and have things go smoothly. Why, I even agreed to cut out my pipe smoking to every third scene. In "Brother" I had smoked in every scene so he couldn't take any of it out.

It was finally agreed that Carol be brought to his mansion in Holmby Hills to see what she looked like. We got two dresses from the costume house in Salt Lake City and headed for Los Angeles.

When we arrived, Patrick was in the swimming pool, and he insisted that she come in for a swim. She told him that she had no suit. Well, he said, I have several daughters and some your size, so why not go in the dressing room, find a suit, and come in. She did.

He immediately started talking about alcoholism and all its effects, and asked what she thought about the whole subject of drinking. Carol had never had much to drink 'til we had started to go out, and then only an occasional mixed drink. They carried on quite a conversation, and we left with an invitation to go to dinner the next night with Mary, Curtis, Jerri (Patrick's wife), and Patrick.

We left, returned to our motel, changed our clothes and headed out to find some excitement. We had a great meal and then found a little night club so we could hear some good music. Carol ordered a mixed drink, a fancy one, that the waitress brought in with a flourish, sat on the table, and touched a light to it. It had a beautiful flame and it certainly was impressive. Now, she asked the waitress, "How do I put it out so I can drink it?" The waitress took a paper napkin, dabbed at the fire, sloshed it around getting drink all over the paper, which also started to burn. She dropped the napkin and she spilled part of the drink, which started to burn on the table. We ended up with a splendid pyrotechnical display. Several of the help arrived with fire extinguishers before the whole thing got out of hand. The waitress was new they said, and this was her first time out with flaming drinks. It did liven up the evening, and we enjoyed ourselves thoroughly.

This reminded me of a time once when we had come down from Canada with a large diesel pulling the big living trailer. We stopped in a little town in Montana, which we usually patronized, for the distance from each way worked out to be just right for a rest stop. The name of the town was Wolf Creek and it was high in the mountains; a small logging town with one really good bar and restaurant.

We went in and jumped on a bar stool; it was late in the evening, and there was quite a crowd around. The bartender asked me what I wanted, and then Carol. Very hesitantly she said a Singapore Sling. Now, in a logging town most of the inhabitants don't bother with the fancy drinks, and the bartender said,

"I don't know how. Tell me what to do and how to make it."

Well, Carol didn't know either, she had just heard of the drink, but the group at the bar weren't going to let this pass. Everyone started to tell the bartender what to do. A shot or two of this, a shot or two of this, with a little dash of that, and a maraschino cherry on top. It filled a huge glass, looked lovely, and when Carol tasted it, well, great! She swigged it down like she would a coke.

"Ok, that was great, now give me another!" Well? Ok....and he started to build another. Everybody was really getting interested now. There were all kinds of comments going around about these crazy flatlanders.

There had to be at least five or six shots of various kinds in the drink, but, with all the sweeteners, she didn't really notice it. When she started on the second, all eyes were on her, waiting for the results which weren't long in coming. By the time she reached the bottom, the first drink was starting to work, for she started to get noisy, and, as luck would have it, wanted to leave and head for the trailer. She waved to all the good people, thanked them for the delightful evening, and headed out the door with romance on her mind.

A short time later it hit! And she was in just the right place for the tornado that descended on her. I got up in the morning at an early hour, saw that she was still safe in bed, fired up the diesel and headed down the road for Utah. At noon, when I stopped for lunch, I opened the door to the apartment and went in. There were a few groans from her, and she continued to suffer the rest of the day. Her hangover was intense!

We spent the next afternoon with Patrick and his friends, having dinner on a wharf where he knew the owners of a fancy eating place and an aquarium next door. He liked Carol for the part in the picture, whatever it would be, for it was going to be my responsibility to work her in, and they would pay an additional $4,000 for adding a room on to the cabin set and revamping things for her. The biggest objection which he made known was the fact that he thought she ought to wear falsies, because her breasts weren't too large. She got highly indignant at this, refused, and nothing more was said.

We then went to Marina del Ray where Frawley kept his yacht. It was a huge minesweeper converted to a beautiful white seagoing vessel. Mary played the piano in the forward salon, then Patrick toured Carol around the ship and had one of the crew get drinks for us. We all sat around on the fan tail for an hour watching the boats going in and out of the harbor. Carol told me later she would enjoy this kind of a life.

The Los Angeles zoo had a couple of bear cubs that were surplus, so I bought a small Ford Courier truck and the two cubs from the zoo, and we loaded them on the truck and sent it home. I finished my business and took a plane back to continue the work on "Grizzly Adams."

We didn't film every day, for there were sets to be built and change as the picture progressed. To take up some of the slack, we would take odd pieces to shoot. One day, when we knew that one of the company people would be there, we arranged for him to see some action shots being filmed. A montage called for me to be jumped by a mountain lion, so we picked a spot on Bald Mountain Pass that had an ideal cliff from which to throw the cat down on me.

Everyone gathered to watch. We set up three cameras, one regular speed, and two high speed to catch all the action in slow motion. I had tried to prepare for every possible contingency that I could imagine to safeguard this shot. The cat would come down about seven feet at a pretty good clip, knock me to the ground and run off and escape.

OK, we got ready, got the cameras running, and threw the cat. Great shot. It landed right on me, knocking me down, but I hit my face on the cap lock of the muzzleloader that I was carrying. It dazed me for a few seconds; I slowly got up, and then the blood started to flow. Boy, did that hurt! We finished getting pictures; the cat had casually walked off and was picked up by the handlers and put back in the cage.

Ed O'Brien, the man from the company, was impressed, but not me. It hurt! and if anything more serious than this happened I could be out of the show. I made up my mind that if any really unsafe shots were required, it would be at the last of the film. They next day Dr. Hogle worked on my face and I was X-rayed at the hospital. Nothing was broken, but the swelling would take a week to go down, and the cuts would have to be healed over a little before any more work could be done.

We had built up a crew for "Grizzly Adams" over a couple of months in order to get ready. A film crew had come from Boston on a contract with me, to edit and film in July. After a hard day filming no one wanted to edit, so we did little of that, and at that point the story was unclear. We'd done a script, had it revised and approved by Sun, and now with Carol added in, there would be more changes. We shot along as I perceived the story to be flowing, and, as every day was different in weather, it had to be changed to fit everything that was happening. I thought it went well.

The first big scene we shot was up in the mountains. I was to be bathing when a grizzly came along, chased me through the pond, and ran me up a tree. We used three cameras. I was bathing in my long shirt when the grizzly came alone, he chased me around, got a bite at my rump, and got me up the tree. The rushes were sent in and Frawley looked at them. He didn't like the color of my beard. Now I was following the real Grizzly Adams, and he looked just like me or vice versa. Frawley thought I should look younger. Well, that ruined that work, and a couple of thousand feet of film. We then started to color my beard and hair every morning.

The actors were now stabilized for the show. I would be Grizzly Adams, Don Shanks would play the Indian, Gárland Wilde would be the circus man, and Carol would be his sister. We generally followed the script, except with the inclusion of Carol, and made changes that would improve the story, especially with odd pieces of animal action that occurred during the filming and that we could pick up when happening.

One sequence was playing with the baby animals in front of the cabin. Carol, Garland, and I were all around the front of the cabin when the mountain lion started playing with Carol and me. Carol was peeling potatoes, and rolling one for the mountain lion to play with which started the whole thing. The cat jumped on me and then Carol, I threw it on Garland, and then the bobcat got in the act and started to play with everyone and wrestling with the mountain lion. "Killer", we called the baby bobcat, for he wasn't afraid of anything and would attack on sight.

Never Kick A Bear in Your Bedroom Slippers

Both Garland and Carol could really work well with the animals, for they were both animal handlers and loved them. During "Brother" we had filmed some of these animal sequences that just happened, and they brought a freshness that was unexcelled. This was something that the editors had to cope with, but with my help it could be accomplished.

On most of my shows there were animals killed in hunting scenes, and this was no exception. If I had animals that we were going to get rid of anyway and were going to hurt someone, then they were the ones to be used. I shot a buffalo, a grizzly, and Carol shot a deer. We saved and used the skins, and anything else we could. Grizzly Adams was one of the most prolific hunters there was. He did it for the people in the mines, the Indians, and generally to make a living. He didn't waste, but used what was there to all the advantage he could. I never liked to fool people in a movie, and this one would be made as realistically as possible. I don't believe in fluffing for kids and lying about what life is really like, so I tell them how it is.

We went to Arizona to do the buffalo hunt for the film, took my own buffalo that we'd been raising to eat, and filmed the state buffalo herd in the background. Using a large .50 caliber rifle, I put mine over in one shot. We filmed around it with the wagon and bear and then picked it up, took it to the state's dressing station where we skinned, and dressed it out. The next weekend we had a barbecue. The meat was cut, wrapped in foil with sauce and seasoning, buried in coals for half a day, and served to the community. It was great! The remainder was frozen, and we ate it for a year.

One night we had all been to the local show house in Kamas, and on arriving home we were waved down on approaching the house by a man with a flashlight. We found our neighbor, a fellow about 23, waiting for us.

"What's the problem?" I asked.

"You've got some wolf pups running around," he replied. Sure enough. There were images of pups running around in the field. We were keeping some in a cage in the yard, and they were loose, but how? We investigated, and could see that the cage had been torn loose. That was a mystery...

We got a glimpse of one close, so Rick and the neighbor walked through the back door of the house for some flashlights. Everything seemed funny to me. I was following when I heard a yell.

"There's a bear in here!" I heard bear noises and hollering, and then there was a stampede out the door. They didn't even get a light on.

"Which bear?" I asked.

"Don't know," came the answer.

Now, we had some bears you wouldn't want to be close to, and, of course, tame ones, so we had to find out what had happened and who it was.

We finally got another flashlight, and I went into the kitchen. It was a shambles, cabinets cleaned out, everything pulled out and messed up, flour over everything, garbage lying around, and furniture thrown here and there. I got across the kitchen to the light switch and saw the extent of the damage, and then peered into the front room. It was "Bud", a half-tame half-grown grizzly who was busy tearing the davenport apart after finishing off the bedroom and kitchen. What a mess! Rick got a chain but Bud wasn't in a mood to leave. A struggle ensued, and afterward we led him back to the cage he'd been in.

Someone had left the bolts unpinned, and Bud had opened the door. We surmised he'd gone around to the front and torn up the cages, scaring the wolves so badly they had climbed out, and now we had to catch them before they left the country. Everyone was looking through the brush and pastures trying to find them.

Carol turned loose one of the dogs and it ferreted out one wolf, after an hour we found another, put them back in the pen and put a cover on. It was 2 in the morning before we got to bed. Next morning we found that the last wolf had come back to the cries and howls of those in the pen.

I had bears loose on many occasions, especially Willie. He could unfasten nuts and bolts, pull pins, and just walk out. He was always interested in what we were doing and would walk up, stand behind you and watch. He enjoyed just walking around and sight seeing.

One crazy bear needed to be disposed of, but Carol wouldn't let me do anything until one early morning it had got loose, went over to the deer pens and tried to get a deer. Now deer really panic when the bears come around their pens, so we lost three. Carol was furious and accused the bear of deliberately doing it, and in this case she was wrong. He was just nosing around. Finally I did get rid of it, but used the shot in one of the movies. It was hard getting rid of animals but occasionally I could sell one. Most of the time I had to put them to sleep myself. We'd get one of the men to skin it and we would eat the meat if good. Of course, we did get tired of bear meat sometimes.

At the end of September, the crew that I had contracted for were let go, and the cameraman that had been doing the documentary filming took over, plus one of the assistants. The people at Sun were generally non-committal about the film, liked it, but couldn't understand quite how it was all to go together. I insisted that it would be fine. We picked up a few shots later, but we had a good show.

Carol began to enjoy doing the acting, took more interest in it, and managed to do much of the still photography on the show. She was extremely good with this. We'd given her a motor-driven Hasselblad so she could shoot fast, taught her how to get the aperture opening from the cameramen, and a little about composition. She had a natural eye for composing pictures and for knowing just when to shoot, for timing was the most important thing about shooting animal pictures. I would keep telling her to stay with it, and we got some books for her to read and plenty of film to use, but she never did take that much interest in it.

We had one section of the story for her where she had to go out and shoot a deer for feed for the animals. We were all gone on the buffalo hunt in the picture, and she was left to take care of all the animals. Dutifully she walked through the woods, being filmed, and finally found the deer and shot it. She got down and cut its throat, ready to cry and not caring what happened. Rick skinned out the deer and she dragged it back to the cabin, saying for the movie, "If the animals didn't have to eat, I'd starve first but....", and this was her attitude. She had a great love for animals. The mice over-ran the farmhouse where we lived, for she wouldn't let us trap the mice, couldn't poison them, and they got so tame they'd come out and thumb their noses at us.

All the goods we had brought down from Canada to southern Utah now had to be taken back to the border of Canada and re-entered to the U.S., have duty paid, or be checked back to Canada on a permanent basis. This kept us busy with convoys, going back and forth to the border for several weeks. Money was hard to come by, and I had to borrow from Sun to keep me going. Frawley had decided that we would have to do some more exciting scenes for the picture to make it work, and I dutifully agreed to do what I could. If this was going to be like "Brother", it was going to take time to finish it, but would be worth it.

Against my wishes the people at Sun decided to have John Mahon "finish" the picture, as before on "Brother." This didn't set well with me, for I was convinced that he wouldn't do a job for me, and, after having a couple of cursory meetings with him, I was convinced. He wouidn't talk about how to finish the picture and what it needed. I had no say in it, so it just had to happen.

38/ Goodbye Carol

The compound in Springdale was becoming a rock around the neck of MHP, and in November I talked to Neil Wise about buying all the animals and cages and moving them to Oakley. There was nothing that I needed particularly, but it would be good to keep them out of the hands of any other party that would be able to use them in competition with me. We drew up a list of the animals and assets that were there, a contract on paying for them, and decided when to close the place down. Doc would have to go his own way but they would give him adequate notice.

I had been down to the compound and discovered a man had moved in with Doc, with his family and was going to take over the lease on the compound. He drove a big Cadillac and tried to impress me with his importance, and told me that he was a retired attorney from New Orleans. He and Doc were going to start a research organization for running the compound, at Doc's behest.

It looked phony to me and I informed the MHP people about it, and later, when the people in the compound found out that I was going to buy it, I received a telephone call from this individual, with a message that he wanted a job. I thought to myself that if he was retired as an attorney he certainly didn't need a job, and I had all the people that I needed to handle the animals. I didn't bother to call back, and later it was a big point in all the confusion that followed.

295

On a weekend we loaded a large semi-truck with cages, took the animal trailer, and headed for Springdale along with 6 of my crew to help with the loading. Some of the people in the compound watched as we approached and as the crew and I walked in through the back door of the compound we were met halfway down the aisle by a Mr. LaBlanc. A short way behind was his father who was in the act of loading a shotgun. He hollered for the crew to stop, holding up the loaded shotgun, but I just walked by and into the office of the compound which was the recreation room.

Before I left I turned and told the crew to leave 'til we got this straightened out. I was to have the animals picked up by the next couple days to make my contract good and this man had no intention of letting me. We talked for an hour, not getting anywhere. He asserted that he knew the law, that we were breaking it by taking the animals and that they wouldn't let us take them and would instead charge for taking care of them. He wanted money naturally. I told him to stuff it in his ear and left. That he was really mad at me for not answering his telephone call several weeks before, was what generally came out of the conversation.

My intention was to keep the property tied up and away from anyone getting into competition, which was being done now. We groused back and forth for months. The compound was gradually sinking, for they didn't have Sun to prop it up with a steady influx of cash. Bob Davison had been in on the deal with Doc and LaBlanc and he ended up with the compound in the long run. A call eventually came from Doc asking me to come and take the animals. No good. Sun had to absorb that deal. Turned out that Mr. LaBlanc was a plumber from California. Doc left for Florida again with his animals to continue his research.

Carol had come down to Los Angeles with me during the winter, around the end of November or the first part of December. We had lunch with John Mahon and Mary, then we went out to Ray Folsom's to look around. He had a couple of racoons beyond the bottle feeding stage though still small, but really wild. They had come from South America, where the seasons were backward from ours, and Carol fell in love with them.

Never Kick A Bear in Your Bedroom Slippers

She chained this one into the corner of the trailer so it couldn't get in trouble, but to me, keeping a racoon with you was living in a racoon cage. I had outgrown it, but not Carol. She was intent on taming this monster. Days I could stay out of the way and not be involved, but nights were different. We were still keeping up the charade of not sleeping together, so we had to be the last to bed and the first ones up in the morning.

When we got to bed, Carol would unleash the racoon, turn on a long play record of Rod McKuen's with whom she was in love, and crawl into bed. First loving; then animal training with me trying to sleep. Unfortunately, most of the time as soon as the lights went out, the racoon would become friendly, come over and grab Krin, who was trying to sleep in the bed beside us and give her a loving bite. Krin, who had had a hard day wanted sleep just when the racoon was waking up so an enormous fight would erupt with the dog chasing the racoon around the trailer, barking and snarling 'til it usually ended up on top of us. We'd pull the blankets over us and try to ignore it, but, so much for love.

She'd finally get up, put on her welding gloves, turn on the night light, catch the racoon, chain it up and try to pet it into submission. I'll never forget the sight of this very naked woman with heavy welding gloves up to her elbows, breaking up a fight and trying to hold this racoon and pet it.

Carol had a standing ground rule. When you crossed the edge of the bed you became instantly happy, no matter what the problems, otherwise you got tickled and teased 'til you couldn't resist. It became a habit. It was hard for me for I had never known of this before and it ran against my nature, for I was rather sober-sided and tended to be rather quiet at times as I did my thinking.

Carol could argue and fight with people all day and she loved it, but she had to be happy at night. She could take either side and fight to the end. Unfortunately, she didn't know when to stop. With my production manager it brought real problems, for he didn't approve of her arguing with him and I would hear about it. But I learned more from Carol that any other woman I had ever known.

She liked her freedom and really resented the fact that living out

DICK ROBINSON

in the country didn't bring her contacts with people her own age. Finally, we hired a friend of hers, Kathy, from Canada to help us. She was a sight for sore eyes to Carol for they did many things together. Now Carol still kept in touch with her old boyfriends and one came by to visit the girls for a few days and that really brought on a fit of jealousy in me for it was something I wasn't used to. It was hard to choke down.

I would get rather tired of listening to Rod every night and bought a Perry Como album with some different love songs but she wouldn't play it. It was hard with Rod croaking at night when I was cranky and had a hard day but then I'm sure it was good for my self-discipline.

Patrick had been working on a show that was his pet project, "Instinct for Survival", which had some of his heavy messages on alcholism and smoking built into the show. He spent a great deal of money on this, only to watch it go down that January. I would tell him that first of all you have to have an entertaining show to be successful, then a message can be slipped in if it works along with the theme of the movie; but he never took the time to build one right.

Later, I got all the blame for this losing so much money. He rarely put the blame where it belonged.

Neil Wise, who was president of Sun and MHP that summer, had been contacted by Stu Raffill to make a picture called the "Snow Tiger". It had been done and I heard that it was a good picture but that Patrick had changed it, and later it also bombed. Patrick wouldn't let me in to see the picture for I called them as I saw them, and if it was a bummer, I said so. My judgment was very good on this kind of movie for it takes a certain kind of picture to make it with our type of 4-wall distribution. African and jungle pictures are the kiss-of-death, or anything that resembles them, as "Snow Tigers" did, and "Instinct for Survival", which was an African picture. It takes a North American animal show to grab them, with the right perspective and theory behind it.

The first part of December I had to borrow money from Frawley again. As usual it would cost me. I got a $25,000 loan that would come out of my residuals and I had to throw in several sequences for nothing at his behest. I agreed to try and do some wolf, grizzly and deer sequences to spice up the picture. There was nothing we could do for the picture now except snow work and it was so bad we could hardly make it with snowshoes much less with animals and machines. Day after day I would use the bulldozer to plow the road. Snow drifts piled up over my head but then it would snow again. Eventually a one way road was pushed through. We leased a large Thiokol snow tractor and built a trailer to keep people warm and sleds to carry the cages.

The compound fence was shoveled out which was 1600 feet of hand shoveling along the edge so the animals couldn't just walk out over the snow. After days we got some wolves and grizzlies in and set in cages close by. There was nothing that could be done. When let out they would bog down in the snow to their stomachs and with the bears it was impossible. Bears need the hard crust to walk on and with the action we would need they would end up milling around. Beside, if I was to be working, there would be room needed to have animals chasing around and fighting. I didn't want to be hurt in this. One sequence consisted of the following:

Dick Robinson on snowshoes early in the morning: Dick goes on through the snow leaving tracks. As the day progresses, the wolf pack comes upon the tracks, sniffs, and follows the tracks. We pick up Dick again going on showshoes. A herd of deer follow the tracks behind Dick or in front of him. In any event, when the wolves come upon the scent of the deer, they follow the deer's tracks instead of Dick's tracks. Late in the day the wolves drop the tracking of the deer and return to the original tracks of Dick Robinson and start tracking him again. That night Dick stops and lights a fire. Late in the night the wolves surround the campfire. Just as the fire is burning down and the wolves are about to attack, the friendly grizzly bear drives the wolves away and watches over Dick.

We also discussed the possibility of Dick crossing the stream and thus losing the trailing wolf pack. We also discussed the possibility of an unfriendly grizzly also following Dick's tracks as well as the wolves. Later, the unfriendly grizzly attacks Dick as the fire is burning out but the friendly grizzly drives off the unfriendly grizzly and saves Dick's life.

The above was written and dictated at Frawley's house with Curtis Kent, Frawley and myself discussing the scenes that Frawley would like to have added into the picture. There was nothing to do but acquiesce in trying to produce these.

In "Brother" there had been several scenes with no pay and it had cost me a good deal of the money from the budget of "Jhora" to do these. Later when Frawley made changes and additions to "Brother" these were also added into the budget and were paid for partially out of my pocket. Now it was to start again.

Mike Ridges was now on a consultant basis with Sun and one bright day while I was bulldozing snow at the end of the road, one of my snowmobiles showed up with him on board. It was 3 miles of rough plowed out snow to make it this far but he was enjoying the trip. He walked up and talked and I showed him the situation that was facing us. He laughed and said, "Better you than me." Later that day the weather closed down again and snowed.

In the middle of January, Carol and I left for Los Angeles to see the showing of what John Mahon had done on "Grizzly Adams". We had had no communication about the picture. He wouldn't talk at all about the actual construction of it. It looked like a hatchet job was being done. We all got together in the offices of Sun and then moved into the theatre, where everyone concerned saw what had happened. One of John Wayne's sons was there, sitting next to Carol. Patrick and most of the officers were there, along with John Mahon.

It was embarrassing. There were a few places that were acceptable, but most looked like something that a kid would do in a high school film class. It had been edited down to 3 hours of film, and strung together. There was some sound on some, but after watching it for awhile it got boring and in 3 hours, well, it was a washout. We went home feeling that John Mahon had got even with me for my opposition, and been well-paid for doing it. John had been given a part of my percentage as a bonus in "Brother" which amounted to something like $20,000; this time there was to be none.

The first part of February I visited Los Angeles again to get some more money to run on. Patrick wanted me to give him everything I had in the way of equipment and animals on a tax deal for a write off for him and then he would return it at the end of a year for a dollar. This went back and forth and he became more insistent with each call. There were four or five calls during the afternoon of the second day at the offices of Sun and he became more insistent. He had been telling me that I needed to trim the size of my crew and operation in order to stay alive, and I agreed. I got a check for $10,000 and caught a flight home. I told him I'd think about it.

Patrick gave me a book on what to do with your life, inscribed the front fly leaf with a nice inscription before I left, and on the plane home that night I read a chapter. It asked, "Are you doing what you like to do?" To which I replied a mental, "NO!" It went on to what to do about it. I didn't want to be one of Frawley's 'yes men' as most of those around him were. I was always the one who spoke up and would say what was on my mind. I didn't want to do some of the crap that he insisted be in his pictures. If there was going to be any message in an ecology picture, it wouldn't be about drinking or smoking.

He had offered me a deal on this trip that was unique. He said he would let me make a picture for myself my way, but that I would have to then make a picture for him his way.

When I got home I talked to Carol about what was going on, and as there was nothing to be done in the way of filming with the weather the way it was, I decided to go to Tucson and talk to a good friend, Dr. Peter Bartel, about what I should do. Carol and I loaded the big trailer, put in our horses, my trail bike, a cage with Mister, the jaguar, and headed for Tucson.

We stayed at the Bartels a couple of delightful days. They lived in a comfortable house on the outskirts of town, were dedicated animal lovers, both of animals that came from the wild to be fed, and theirs in pens beside the house.

Both Peter and his wife had come from Germany after the war, had three children, and had been very friendly with Pat and me when we had been there before.

This man was a professor at the university, and was one who could give me some help in making a decision. He and his wife felt as I did. Stay independent and use my own values to live by and not someone else's. Depend on myself.

We left and headed south to spend a couple of days at a dude ranch, where we could ride and rest. Carol was cranky for some reason, but we enjoyed the scenery, took the jaguar out on the front lawn so some of the dudes could get pictures, made a visit to Nogales on the trail bike for Mexican food and got a couple of days riding in the desert on our horses. It was a welcome relief from the snow in Utah, for it had been at its worst that winter, and gave me time to think.

We were gone for a week when we pulled into the yard at Oakley. There were telephone calls from the office in Los Angeles all over the place. Where had I gone? What was going on? Mostly from Curtis Kent, Frawley's aide. I replied. Curtis insisted that I had gone down to film on a jaguar picture for their competitor, American National. No, I hadn't. We went down for a vacation. Then why did I take a jaguar and a movie camera? To take some pictures if I got around to it and some test shots for the sequel.

When I had signed the contract with MHP for "Grizzly Adams" in the summer, I had also signed another contract for a sequel, using Grizzly and a jaguar. Evelyn had come up to see me that fall and was filmed with one of the jaguars and me. I had put on a winter costume and had been filmed with the jaguar as test shots. Later, John Mahon had seen some of the film that had been put in with the regular GA film, and had edited it into the show. No reason, he just put it in. ·

One of the unfortunate things was that the coyote film that I had done for American National had been test marketed in Virginia and had done quite well. Frawley's picture had fallen on its face. They were getting paranoid to a larger degree all the time.

The coyote picture, "Birth of a Legend," now finished by American National Enterprises (ANE), needed more help with the commercials, more small pieces that could be used to draw people into the theatres, and asked if I would shoot some of the things they needed.

Of course I would, for it was in my best interest, so, with a photographer, I took a small mountain lion and a badger, and went up the road and filmed them playing around under a tree for a few minutes. They liked it, and said they could use some more, but needed green grass. It was nothing but snow where we were that winter, so we waited for a couple of weeks and headed 350 miles south for St. George, Utah's Palm Springs.

We loaded a trailer-load of animals, cameras, and people, and headed south. The trailer was one of my big ones, 30 feet long and filled with cages, and we used a ¾ ton flatbed with 4-wheel drive in case we ran into snow in the high mountains where we were going. We had called ahead and talked to some people that lived a few miles from there and they said that the green grass was coming up and that the snow was melting. Good news!

It was hard driving down, for the wind was always high, and we had to buck into it for hours. George Griner, the cameraman, was driving, and early that morning we made it into the location for our filming. Rick Guinn and Paul, my ex-brother-in-law, were riding in the truck and Carol and I were driving a big 4-wheel drive suburban wagon.

We filmed the large grizzly, Kodiak (Kodie), playing in the creek, and then with the two of us playing in the creek and just sitting around. We filmed the elk walking around with my arm around it, me wrestling with the wolves on an island in the little creek, playing with the mountain lion and badger, and just standing around talking to the animals. We had found that people just like to see you communicating with the animals and appreciating them.

There were no problems, and enough good pictures and film to help boost the commercials. These were all animals that I could relate to, and I could bring through on film my love for them. It was good, and we headed for home.

Now it was downhill through the mountains to a valley where there was a small town with summer homes. We started down the long grades to the valley, with me leading in the station wagon and, after going a quarter mile past a corner, I leisurely glanced in my rear-view mirror just in time to see the truck and trailer overturning and being blown sideways in the road. A tremendous gust of wind had swept down the small gulch on the side hill, got under the trailer and turned everything over.

I stopped, turned around, and rushed back to the wreck. I jumped out and raced to the truck to see if anything had happened to the men in the truck. It was smashed flat. The cab was smashed down, everything in the back of the truck had been smashed, the windshield was smashed out, and here came the fellows out through the hole it left. Not a scratch on any of them! Everyone was shaken and talking about how lucky they were.

All of us inspected the large trailer and found that nothing had happened to any of the animals. The cages inside had just rolled over and the permanent cages in the trailer had let the animals roll with them. The trailer was blocking the road, so we quickly went several miles down the road, called for a wrecker to clear everything, and to move it to safety.

We got on the phone with home and got trucks on the way so the first thing in the morning we could pick up all the animals and equipment from the trailer. We got out the movie cameras and filmed around the wreckage for future film use. Carol took stills and had me pose by the wreck.

When the wrecker arrived, we turned the trailer over and towed it to the town a couple of miles away. We had the truck towed to St. George, 30 miles away, to the Ford agency where we had leased our equipment. Everybody headed for home, and over the next few days we rescued all the animals and got all the equipment into St. George.

It was a pretty expensive commercial.

Back at the mountain again we had done some additional filming one afternoon for Grizzly Adams. A crew made it in with all the equipment, the large Thiokol snow machine with its trailer, and my bulldozer to help tow pens, and got some shots. I used some cub bears and myself in costume, and then turned a couple of wolves loose. It started to snow, and there were some great mood shots that could be used in winter cutaways and transitions. It was hard to work wallowing around in deep snow but we did, and then sent the film south to Sun.

I now started going to Canada to retrieve some of the machinery that had been left up there, selling some of the equipment as I could. At the end of February or into March there was one trip on which I sold a couple of the bunk trailers to the same individual who had tried the shake-down. He had bought some land, and bought my equipment for a song. He was the only one around that seemed to have money for something like this.

With this money we were going to make another attempt to do some shooting at the "Grizzly Adams" cabin.

It had started to warm up considerably but the snow was still deep, so the bulldozer was again brought into play. We worked up the road to as close to the cabin as possible. It was over three miles from the main road, and during the winter, drifts of 6 and 8 feet high had piled up on both sides of the single track that had been plowed out.

Now we had to take the fresh snow from the last month and pile it up to clear out the roadbed. All of it was through the forest, across small streams and around steep side hills. We worked hard for days. We brought the Thiokol with the camp trailer to within a couple of hundred yards of the cabin, where we turned it around, disconnected the trailer for the use of the tractor alone, and to use the trailer for heat and food. The cage with the grizzly bear was skidded in behind the Thiokol.

The crew worked the first day at the cabin with Sunshine, my female grizzly, which was a good bear, but hadn't been used much. I worked in and out of the cabin in my Grizzly Adams costume with the bear, cavorting with her in the snow at the side of the corral and just generally having fun.

I had one second cameraman, George Griner, working steadily for me, but for the second day we had Bruce Graydon flying in from Denver to help.

Close to the cabin was a cave that the bear was supposed to sleep in for the winter. It was my job to take a shovel, dig down into the cave, wake the bear up, and get her to come out and enjoy the spring, for I was getting lonesome.

The first job was for me to shovel out the bear. There were paths shovelled all around the cabin, to the privy, to the spring, and one coming in from the front. I walked around the corner of the cabin, climbed the snowbank, for it was still nearly 3 feet thick, walked to the place where the cave was and started digging through the new snow to get to the bear. I shoveled out a huge opening, put the shovel down into the snow, and climbed into the cave. This was all being filmed. The last you saw of me was going into the cave and disappearing.

Our next job was to put Sunshine into the cave, and let her come out with the camera running, to make it look like she's been in there all the time, and I was to follow her out.

I stayed in the cave, they brought Sunshine on a chain, threw it down into the hole with me, and I was going to pull her in. I pulled. Nothing, she refused to come. The whole idea was to get her in without disturbing the snow.

After a hard struggle I pulled her in, and they started the cameras. She headed for the outside again and I followed her, so it looked like she had been asleep and had come out mad. She was. I followed her and she slipped the chain. Paul, my ex-brother-in-law, caught her and dragged her back. She was getting even madder.

Paul cut me a short club and threw it to me. Now Sunshine was chewing at the chain. I wanted to tie her to the cabin, but she pulled free. We hooked another chain to her, and I took the club with me and laid it on a barrel and started to move her.

When she balked, I wound up, took a huge breath and gave her the hardest kick in the ass I ever gave. Then she caught me by the leg and started biting! Grabbing the club, I really started on her so she threw me on the ground in the path. The path was down through the snow, and there was no place to escape or get out of the way. I toughed it out and kept on thumping her 'til she ran off.

Everyone rushed in to see how bad it was. Carol got a towel and wrapped it around my leg. I had on big thick furry boots that came off easily, but the bear had chewed my leg above the boot. This was my second lesson, my confirmation, *Never Kick A Bear.*

Everyone started putting away all the equipment, one of the men helped me into the Thiokol, and Carol jumped in. We headed down the hill, but after a couple of hundred yards I asked the driver to turn around and take me back. He asked, "Why?" I told him, "I haven't finished the scene."

Back we went, I limped back to where the bear attacked me, and told the cameraman to get set up again, and let's finish the scene. From my view point, it was going to take me a couple of hours to get to the hospital, so what was a few more minutes, and why waste a scene and not finish it. I started where I left off, limped to a snow bank in the path in front of the cabin and, grimacing in pain for the camera, slowly lifted my pant leg to show off the wound; and everyone started to laugh. I had on a green dress sock that no good mountain man ever would have worn. I took it off, threw it in the cabin door, and started from scratch again. This time the whole thing went off well.

They loaded me in the snow machine again. It was 3 miles to the road, where we got another vehicle, another 3 miles to the house, where Carol called Holly Hogle at his office to say that I was coming in. Holly had me go to a hospital, where he would meet me. Carol loaded me into a station wagon and we headed for the hospital.

When we got there everyone was waiting for us, and they hustled me into the emergency room where they looked at my leg. Now it was really hurting! They started giving me shots. They installed me on the operating table on my stomach, with my pant leg up. It must have been funny, seeing this buckskin-clad mountain man, with a big knife hanging over the edge of the table. There was a steady parade of doctors and nurses to see the man chewed up by the grizzly. I can remember seeing a steady parade of pretty legs going by, and listening to Holly telling about what he was stitching up now.

Sunshine bit almost through my leg, severed a good deal of muscle, and generally made a mess of me. They finished up, loaded me with pain killer, provided crutches, and told me to stay off my feet for 10 days. I hoped they weren't serious, as it was hard for me to keep down.

As soon as Carol got me home into bed in the house, we had a telephone installed in the bedroom, and I thought I was ready to do business. Fat chance! They were giving me 10mg. of valium every four hours. The next couple of days I would wake up, get on my crutches, make one tour around the shop and animal cages, go back to the house and pass out again from the tranquilizers.

After 3 days I talked to the doctor and told him I had to finish the scene in the mountains. Grizzly Adams was really a healer. He would heal his wounds by soaking the injured parts in a river or creek. I had to do the same thing for this scene. We did it in the snow, soaking my leg in the river and riding back home on my mule. It worked and looked good. Everything was fine except my big toe still hurt from kicking that bear. Would it ever stop?

I talked to Sun and told them what happened, but they didn't even send me any condolences. Instead they dropped a lawsuit on me. They sued me for a million in damages, wanted their production money back—$255,000, and damages—$70,000 and, get this, they wanted to keep everything that was done. They said I hadn't finished the picture as per my contract.

I hated dragging around on crutches, but it was altogether necessary. While driving along in the little Pinto wagon that we used for town trips a few days later, Carol was haranguing me about what was happening. She had to drive me around because my right leg wouldn't work and now she was acting like my mother and lecturing me.

A little was all right, but she would just go on and on. Yack, yack, yack.... We came to a light by Trolley Square in Salt Lake City, a shopping mall, where I jumped out and told her to go on home. I was mad! I stomped down the street on my crutches to the sidewalk and she jumped out, abandoned the car, and ran after me. Cars were honking in traffic, but she just left the car sitting in the middle of the intersection.

She was hollering, I was hollering as we went down the sidewalk. I was boiling mad! She said she wasn't going to leave me.

For the first time I was ready to belt this mouthy little lady. I just couldn't turn her off. She finally said she'd quit talking if I'd come back. She did slow down but when we got in bed that night I still had a mad on and she really had a lot of work to do on me to get me back to normal.

Never Kick A Bear in Your Bedroom Slippers

Neil Wise called and wanted a favor. A producer on the Mike Douglas show had seen "Brother of the Wind" on a flight between LA and NYC and asked if I was available to do a guest appearance. They were having Jack Douglas, the author, on a show with his Japanese wife and it was to be all about wolves. Jack had no tame ones; I did, and would I go back to Philadelphia and do a show?

There were many calls going back and forth and finally it was arranged that Carol and I would go, take a wolf, Misty, leave the next week and do an appearance. This was something I enjoyed doing if there was a reason but in this case I couldn't even talk about "Grizzly Adams." There was film on being chewed by the grizzly, but I couldn't use that either, so it ended up being a waste of time, accomplishing nothing except having the trip.

They put us up downtown, a couple of blocks from the studio, in Philadelphia. The wolf stayed in the Bell Captain's storage room and we took in the sights. Carol was always talking about Canada, how nice it was up there and what a great country it is until it got to be a little too much. She didn't take much interest in Constitution Square, didn't like some of the people we met and the next day after the show we split. She took the wolf home and I left for Montreal and Toronto to try and do some business. I enjoyed the trip, they asked me back for more shows but there was nothing to see except myself and that didn't need merchandising right now.

Most of the crew was gone now, things were bad moneywise and Sun knew it. Carol was cranky; all she could talk about was being an airline hostess and flying around the world having fun. Finally, I told her to go home and leave me. Do her thing. She'd been home for Christmas and left me again in the spring for a trip home. I loved her dearly but could see that there were other things that she should be doing, especially after having to hear about it all the time. I told her to leave. She refused.

"At your age you'll never find someone else, and I'm to blame for the whole thing."

"No," I said, "you're not to blame. It was just a matter of time 'til Pat and I split up. You might have hastened it a little but that's all."

"Well, I'm not going to leave you now, and, I won't let you fire me. You can't make me leave." She was walking along with me while I was carrying an armful of hay for the horses. She was jawing along at me again while I was thinking that really I must be going through my male menopause for I was thinking that the end of the world was coming for me. At 50 I was over the top and maybe there would never be anything more. Maybe this would be my last romantic interlude but I was sure that there would still be another one, some time or place, that would finally be just right for me when Carol left.

It was time for Carol to progress on to new things for, with her good mind, there was much room for expansion and new experiences and it was time. Still, she refused, and stayed on.

Her one racoon had got away, and now we got two more babies from Ray Folsom. They were small and she and Kathy were bottle-feeding them day and night. We scratched up money for a little filming and used the baby racoons and "Bud," the grizzly. We had a pair of adult coons; "Coonie", the male, who was completely docile, loved the little ones and would take care of them, and the other, a female named "Happy" that I had used on the "Brother" show. When young, Happy would run and jump up in my arms for attention but now she would snarl most of the time.

I was thinking that, like Carol, it was time for her to go out on her own, so, when we were having our last snowfall of the spring, we loaded the bears, Bud, and Mabel, the black bear, and headed up the road for the cabin.

The grass was green and the poplar trees were just leafing out, the Columbine was blooming and looked beautiful with all their violet colors and everything coated with snow which was coming down steadily. We discovered a good flat piece of level ground among the trees, stopped and unloaded, set up the camera and turned the bears loose. They raced around chasing each other, having sparring matches and then rolling and playing in the snow.

With this background of good natured horseplay I decided to turn "Happy" loose for the last time. We would film her playing and being chased by the bears and she would wander away over the horizon never to be seen again.

Rick opened the door of her cage, she came out slowly, sniffed around and started walking and surveying the territory. She was chased by one of the bears, ran over to my camera and stood up with her arms around the tripod leg. Most of the animals know it's safe there. She looked around frantically, looked at me and then jumped over to me, put her arms around my leg and looked with pleading eyes at me. "Sorry, Happy, but it's time you took your nasty temper some place else, and besides, I'm not going to let you have anymore people to bite." She started crawling up my leg talking to me. "Sorry, Happy." I gave my leg a big fling, throwing her free and just then a bear came running by and started after her.

She made a couple more turns around, headed straight into her cage and then pulled the door closed after her. I told Rick to get her out. He took the cage and shook it in the air, but she was clinging to the inside for dear life. Everyone relented. We decided to take her home. Her cranky disposition didn't change however.

I got working with the little babies a week later and found a small creek that was just right for filming. The water was rushing down but it was spring and wouldn't last long, for the snow high above fed it for a short time and then it trickled for the rest of the summer. The grass was getting long and green and the leaves were really coming out. We laid a log across the creek in just the right place; I placed the mother at one end of the log and placed the babies in the middle just over the center of the creek.

They didn't move too much, the mother came over and inspected them and walked to the end of the log. One little baby fell off and got washed down the creek, rolling and paddling for dear life, gasped a few times, finally stopped at a little island and slowly crawled out. The shrieks from the women were extreme.

"Dick, Dick, they're going to drown! They're going to drown!"

I was trying to film, wave the girls off with an arm and keep them from getting in the picture. Just then the other one fell off and was swept down. I followed on that one and filmed it crawling out. They were grabbed by the girls as soon as they got out, then toweled off and cried over. That big, mean man doing this to you. The filming was great, the girls mad; the racoon mother had come over and rescued her little babies and everything ended happily.

The racoons were doing very well and I said when they would get bigger we would do it again. The girls consented to it if I would wait for a few weeks. Slowly, everything got friendly again.

Kathy was going to stay for the summer and help with the animals for she was going to vet school, needed some work that would help her with animals, and some money. She also was good company for Carol for the two were always talking about what they would do after they left.

There was just Paul, Rick Guinn and Kathy working now. Paul was about 19, always coming and going, but he was so quiet with me that we hardly ever talked. Carol and I were still playing the game of not living together and we were always running into Paul. We felt as if we were being watched and it made Carol nervous although it probably wasn't true.

We now got a little money from equipment sales and kept filming on another show as well as getting animal footage that could be used for the "Grizzly Adams" show. My lawyer friend had answered the lawsuit and I was still trying to get things patched up to finish the film.

Right after the 1st of June, many of the top people at American National Enterprises defected and moved to Sun. Ray Jensen, who had gone back and forth with Sun, Chuck Sellier, who had been head of CVD and had moved to SLC with American, and several others. Chuck had watched my operation closely when we had been working on the coyote picture through one close to him and, as head of distribution for Sun now, Chuck would be in charge of production.

I talked to Ray the day he left and I was asked to work for very little to finish "Grizzly Adams" but I refused. "Grizzly Adams" was my picture and I wanted it done my way, but now they had no product and, having gone through the same fight with "Brother," I remained adamant that it be done my way with their help.

Self-serving letters were written back and forth by most of the Sun executives at Frawley's orders. One officer who had an office next to the other would write a letter to the second party for the record.

This would be passed around and copies sent to Mr. Frawley. They needed this kind of material for the lawsuit against me.

Curtis sent me a letter he wanted me to sign just to keep me from doing anything with grizzly bears but with no benefit for me in any way. Sellier was now orchestrating a complete take-over of the "Grizzly Adams" show. At the middle of the month, when I was at the Los Angeles office, I met with Frawley and Curtis Kent and discussed the problem. They took me in a room and put this proposal in front of me: cut my residuals in half, be the actor and animal handler (with credits for that only) and sign a new 112 page slave contract. If this was done they would continue the picture. They knew it was going to be a success following the same pattern as "Brother." I thought about it for a minute, then said,

"I've got a bad contract, but I've seen the new one you want me to sign and it's worse. I'll stick to the old one."

Just then Chuck Sellier popped into the room, turned to me and asked,

"Will you take the deal?"

I said, "No."

There it was. As simple as that. All over money and credits. I was going to make too much.

The die was cast. They started on their path. Production schedules were set, stories and scripts were prepared and crews assembled. Many of my old crew would join Chuck along with some of the people he had used before.

Frawley came to the compound the third week in June with Ray Jensen, looked at thousands of feet of animal footage that I had been taking and left. Mary and Mike Frawley had been there during the first week in June looking and compiling a list of my material. During the first week of July, Mary and Curtis were back again looking and talking, more to find out what I was doing than anything else.

The first part of July a letter was sent to them, registered, noticing them that I wanted to buy back my rights and that they had no right doing anything with "Grizzly Adams." They didn't bother to reply. My contracts simply stated that they had no right to make their picture without giving me a chance (nine months) to buy back everything that had been done and all the rights. We went to court and asked for a restraining order and then found out that they had given the right to make it to their subsidiary (Sun). They all had the same officers but were different corporations, for Sun was owned by MHP with whom the initial contract had been signed. I didn't have the money to continue court fights.

They were simply going to over-run me, I didn't have any experience with the courts, or the know-how to fight.

Sellier had another version written of the picture, so as to skirt my story, but still using all the ingredients.

Chuck had been working for American National (ANE) putting some TV packages together for syndication. They would package 8 or 10 films made by different producers but in the same category, animal films for example, into one big package with their name on them, do some re-editing if needed and let a syndication company handle them.

Chuck would now put his name on as many of these as possible. Some kind of a producer title. Later he claimed in his newspaper articles that he had produced twenty odd shows, G-rated full-length movies but this is how it was done. Ray Jensen had been head of distribution at Sun for a time and then had gone back to American National and was now going back to Sun. All had been prearranged to make these transfers.

Various excuses were used but Frawley offered good money and American National was getting into financial difficulties. Sun was in bad shape but they had been down before when "Brother" had come along and saved it. Now they were going to do the same thing with "Grizzly Adams." I had done the picture for them. It could be improved with more footage but that already was in the can. All they had to do now was put it together with my help. It would cost $100,000 or so. Chuck figured his budget to do an all new one would be $125,000 using the ideas he had gained by looking at mine. It was to have the best animal footage out of "Brother" and "Toklat". The idea...shoot 56 minutes of new footage and use 38 minutes of old. Using many of my old crew they started filming the last of July on their version of "Grizzly Adams". Later, during August, they took me to court to squash me. They needed a man to lie for them and found one. I was accused of moving all my assets to Canada to escape the lawsuit, but I only had 4 people working for me and 45 pieces of equipment so it was just an excuse.

I had been in Canada selling the last of the equipment up there to have some money. Now there was $2500 to be scraped together to defend myself against them, for they were trying to tie up all I had and keep me from doing business on the strength of their lawsuit.

Carol and I maintained a non-aggression pact for she was discouraged now and could talk about nothing but to get away and go back to Canada, join an airline and fly. It was a good idea. I loved her but it like keeping a butterfly clamped tight, cupped in your hands. Sooner or later you would crush the wings.

It was hard to part with the things that had been carefully planned for, the trucks, custom built trailers, all the equipment that was made for special uses and things that fit together with others. These had been planned for years with careful thought given to each for its use. Frawley had always reminded me that I should be small; well, I was getting there and not going broke.

I was hanging on and still shooting. No prestige now. Just work and the courts. After all I got started with a camera and a few animals so why not now work the same way again. It was hard going down. Meanwhile Sun was on its way up again with my ideas.

Carol and I had come to that time all of us face now and then, that of parting. We loved but in our own ways. She had a life to look forward to; mine was stalled. In September we loaded up a van with her racoon, dog, stereo, her Rod McKuen records, rocking chair she had got for Christmas and all her small things. Somewhere I rounded up a thousand dollars for her and she headed home. She called that night from Montana crying, but I told her to hang in. It was the hardest thing I had ever done. She made it home and we both moped around. There were all kinds of phone calls but it was the end....

After fighting the restraining order, it was partially lifted so I could use some of my equipment in the normal course of business but everything dragged....

39/
What sunset?

My toe was throbbing again. I left my camera and leaned against the sideboards of the little Courier. The camera was sitting up on the wooden bed of the truck which was backed up to the bank of this raging river at the very height of the flood season. There was a great view of the river rushing straight toward the camera, from the illusion of it, coming between two lines of trees out of the distance with the snow-capped mountains in the background. The river was brown with sand and dirt that had been dug out of the passing banks that were being eroded as the water raged through.

Rick was mounted on Grunter, the buffalo, decked out in his buckskins with the baby (doll) in its wrapping of canvas lying in his arms as he guided the buffalo into the raging river. Denise stood beside the truck with the old couple on whose land we were filming, also one fellow who was helping us with the animals and a couple of friends who were standing next to the truck.

Rick was going to do the big scene. He had to save the baby and get it to the family which was going to care for it and that meant crossing this raging river. He was to fall or get swept off the buffalo, swim with the baby and make it across with the buffalo following.

There had been a couple of entrance shots that had been complete fiascoes, then finally a good one. The buffalo bit had broken so the bridle had been discarded and now he was riding with nothing but

316

the big rope halter that was just snubbed around the nose of this giant beast.

If he got in trouble there was no one to help for he would be swept down the river and would have to fend for himself. He understood.

This was just he and I.

Everything that was going to come out on the film would be my responsibility. With one camera, it would all have to be done expertly and coordinated so it would play. Only one chance.

I saw the buffalo approaching through the leaves; I moved quickly to the camera which was ready and, started filming when the buffalo became visible as it was coming down the bank and entering the water. The camera was running smoothly, the lens was turned to the wide angle to get everything in to set the scene: the raging river, the trees and the mountains in the background, the buffalo in the distance entering the river.

The scene was set!

Slowly I turned the zoom on the lens, and the scene moved toward me until just a section of the river with the rider and the buffalo were in the frame. Rick guided the buffalo down the river, the water running above the stirrups. It was rough walking on the slippery rocks for the big creature, and Rick was holding his toes in just enough on the stirrups to hang on but ready to leave.

The muscles on his arms bulged from pulling the heavy rope reins to the left, for he needed to make a left turn to get across; but now Grunter was just taking the course of least resistance and coming down the river. The buffalo started to lose his footing. My lens widened out for more view and just then he rolled over in the raging waters; Rick jumped free into the water and swam for it. He disappeared behind the struggling buffalo. We all tensed and held our breath. This was not in the script but it's how great shots are filmed sometimes. The camera kept humming and through the eyepiece I saw him re-appear. Thank God!

Now Grunter was trying to get to him for Rick had stayed on the upriver side and was now wading through the shallows to return to the original bank. They didn't make it across. Grunter with the saddle hanging from underneath his stomach heaved himself part-way up the bank. Rick carefully placed the "baby" under a bush, pulled his large Bowie knife and cut the saddle free, for Grunter had been waiting for his freedom and, with that, he moved up further to the green grass of the bank and started to graze.

Rick pulled off his boots and drained the water. I turned the camera off. Great shots, all well coordinated with just the right zooms, catching all the action and all of it could be used.

The river water was freezing and now everyone rushed to Rick with blankets to dry off and to get warm.

I slowly climbed from the truck and congratulated Rick. It was great! Something that I'll probably never see again. I felt isolated on the truck but if something happened it was up to me to capture it on film.

All my training from the past years culminated in this one piece of filming. All that training from a diversified group of individuals who had pointed me in the direction that I traveled. I looked around and thought maybe I could go off into the sunset and gracefully disappear but, right now I couldn't find the sunset, so I would have to stay and fight the battle that "they" (some spirits in the sky) were directing. My course for the future was now up to them....but I would fight the fight and sooner or later win the war....with "their" help....

And I wished they would hurry up and do something about this toe!

DATE DUE

DATE DUE			
OCT 1 9 199	10/63		
JAN 28 1996	1/2		

Pet African lion of this ty

Collisio

Lion

Touri.

SCIPIO, Millard Coun
tourist involved in a hi
accident near here today
have trouble convincin
insurance company abou
details.

Richard Coid, a tourist
Lakewood, Calif., actually
lided with an African lion

The pet lion was forg
by its owner in the s
area Tuesday, accordin
Millard County Sheriff C
Stewart.

The owner stopped
to rest, drove off withou
lion, then called from
the road to notify us."
Stewart said.

"She's tame," the o
said. He added that if s
one got a rope around
neck, she might follow
out a fight.

Nobody tried that at ne
Yuba Dam picnic grounds
other night when the
invited herself to a ch
outing.

Nothing drastic happene
"The lion looked at the
nickers, they looked at it,
then the thing walked aw
Stewart said.

Darwin Anderson and J
Judd, employes of he Bu
of Land Management

ford, star of the recently released poli
tical film The Candidate, is now the star
of Jeremiah Johnson, a new Warner
Bros. film. The actor is seen here alongside a mountain grizzly who figures com-

man actor
mountain wilderness
comes tragically invo
with Indians of the Cr